DATE DUE

New Television, Old Politics

The Transition to Digital TV in the United States and Britain

This book examines the economic, political, and technological forces that are shaping the future of broadcasting by comparing the transition from analog to digital TV in the United States and Britain. Digital TV involves a major reordering of the broadcast sector and requires governments to rethink the legal apparatus for the communications industry. Through an in-depth examination of the digital TV transition in these two nations, the book uncovers the political and economic determinants of the emerging governance regime for digital communications and discusses the implications for the development of the information society in the United States and Europe. The findings challenge much of the conventional understanding about the deregulation and globalization of communications. Contrary to what many predicted, the transition to digital TV has been a vehicle for reinforcing government control over broadcasting and, as a result, it has reinforced preexisting differences in the organization and regulation of communication in advanced industrialized nations.

Hernan Galperin is an Assistant Professor at the Annenberg School for Communication, University of Southern California. He holds a B.A. in Social Sciences from the University of Buenos Aires, Argentina, and a Ph.D. from Stanford University. Dr. Galperin's research and teaching focus on the international governance and impact of new communication and information technologies. His research has been published in article collections and scholarly journals such as the *Federal Communications Law Journal, Telecommunications Policy, Journal of Communication*, and *Media, Culture, & Society.* He is a frequent participant in numerous academic and industry conferences, including the Telecommunications Policy Research Conference (TPRC), the International Communication Association (ICA), and the American Political Science Association (APSA). Dr. Galperin is a former Fellow of the Stanhope Centre for Communications Policy Research in London.

Politics and relations among individuals in societies across the world are being transformed by new technologies for targeting individuals and sophisticated methods for shaping personalized messages. The new technologies challenge boundaries of many kinds – between news, information, entertainment, and advertising; between media, with the arrival of the World Wide Web; and even between nations. *Communication, Society and Politics* probes the political and social impacts of these new communication systems in national, comparative, and global perspective.

To my parents and Dawn

New Television, Old Politics

THE TRANSITION TO DIGITAL TV IN THE UNITED STATES AND BRITAIN

Hernan Galperin
University of Southern California

CAMBRIDGE
UNIVERSITY PRESS

CAMBRIDGE UNIVERSITY PRESS
Cambridge, New York, Melbourne, Madrid, Cape Town, Singapore, São Paulo

Cambridge University Press
The Edinburgh Building, Cambridge CB2 2RU, UK

Published in the United States of America by Cambridge University Press, New York

www.cambridge.org
Information on this title: www.cambridge.org/9780521823999

First published 2004

A catalogue record for this publication is available from the British Library

Library of Congress Cataloguing in Publication data

Galperin, Hernan.
  New television, old politics : the transition to digital TV in the United States and Britain /
Hernan Galperin.
     p.   cm. – (Communication, society, and politics)
  Includes bibliographical references and index.
  ISBN 0-521-82399-4
  1. Television broadcasting – United States.   2. Digital television – Economic aspects –
United States.   3. Television broadcasting – Great Britain.   4. Digital television –
Economic aspects – Great Britain.   I. Title.   II. Series.
  HE8700.8.G35   2004
  384.55–dc22   2003060532

ISBN-13 978-0-521-82399-9 hardback
ISBN-10 0-521-82399-4 hardback

Transferred to digital printing 2006

Contents

CONTENTS

Figures and Tables

FIGURE

TABLES

Preface and Acknowledgments

When this project began in the fall of 1998, some colleagues warned me that it might have short legs. By the time of completion, the problems and debates about how best to undertake the transition from analog to digital television might be a thing of the past. Only a handful of academics and media historians would find interest in the intricacies of past battles about digital broadcasting standards, spectrum property rights, switchover strategies, and so forth. To my fortune, today, five years and a book later, these issues remain more relevant than ever. Moreover, the findings of this investigation reveal much about the future of communications in postindustrial societies. Television sits at the intersection of old and new media, and, for all the attention gathered by new information and communication technologies, it is still a dominant political and cultural force in modern life. As new technologies challenge the existing media industry arrangements, questions that have not been asked since the formative years of television in the early twentieth century resurface. The transition thus offers a unique opportunity to study how old politics and new technologies are shaping modern communications networks, for it is precisely in disruptive times that the political-economic foundations of our institutions can be best examined.

My first and foremost gratitude is due to the dozens of civil servants, policymakers, academics, industry analysts, and company executives interviewed for this project between 1998 and 2002. Without their generous cooperation and support, this book would not have been possible. Although only a few are identified throughout the manuscript, my deepest gratitude goes to all of them. Jonathan Levy of the FCC Office of Plans and Policy, Adam Watson-Brown of the European Commission's Information Society Directorate, and David Levy of the BBC Policy and Planning deserve special mention for their help in data collection and their valuable suggestions at different stages in this book's five-year gestation period. Several people at different institutions that served as home base for research and writing also deserve to be acknowledged, including the staff and friends at the Department of Communication at Stanford University where this project originated, Jacques Arlandis and his colleagues and staff at the Institut de l'Audiovisuel et des Telecommunications en Europe (IDATE) in Montpellier, and Monroe Price and those at the Stanhope Centre for Communications Policy Research in London. The librarians at the Independent Television Commission, the FCC, OFTEL, and the British Film Institute also deserve a mention for their help and hospitality over long research hours.

I am indebted to the staff and my colleagues at the Annenberg School for Communication at the University of Southern California. They provided the intellectual, operational, and, most important of all, social support needed to bring this project to completion. Peter Monge, Patti Riley, Jon Aronson, Titus Levi, Marita Sturken, Sarah Banet-Weiser, and Abigail Kaun deserve special mention. I benefited greatly from the comments and criticism from friends and colleagues who read all or parts of the book at different stages of development. Among them are Byron Reeves, Theodore Glasser, Gregory Rosston, Silvio Waisbord, Joseph Straubhaar, Chris Marsden, Martin Cave, Ellen Goodman, Jim Burger, Monroe Price, William Dutton, and Jeffrey Hart. I am also indebted to the participants at meetings and conferences where I shared and discussed my ideas and research before they took book form, in particular the Telecommunications Policy Research Conference and the International Communication Association meetings. A special mention goes to my former adviser, friend, and now colleague François Bar, who from the very first day offered invaluable advice and encouragement for this project. The book also benefited much from the skillful editing and comments of Seeta Peña Gangadharan. All of the above should of course be duly absolved from any errors contained in the book, but commended for its strengths. At last, I wish to acknowledge the support and encouragement from my parents Jorge and Silvia, and my wife Dawn Omura de Galperin, who more than anyone else is responsible for keeping me focused on the project when needed, and away from it when not.

Acronyms and Abbreviations

ABC	American Broadcasting Company
ACATS	Advisory Committee on Advanced Television Service
AEA	American Electronics Association
API	application program interface
ARPA	Advanced Research Projects Agency
ATSC	Advanced Television Systems Committee
ATTC	Advanced Television Testing Center
ATV	advanced television
BBC	British Broadcasting Corporation
BDB	British Digital Broadcasting plc
BiB	British interactive Broadcasting Ltd.
BREMA	British Radio and Electronic Equipment Manufacturers Association
BSB	British Satellite Broadcasting Ltd.
BSkyB	British Sky Broadcasting plc
BT	British Telecom plc
CAS	conditional access system
CBO	Congressional Budget Office
CBS	Columbia Broadcasting System
CCIR	International Radio Consultative Committee
CEA	Consumer Electronics Association
CICATS	Computer Industry Coalition on Advanced Television Services
COFDM	coded orthogonal frequency division multiplex
CTIA	Cellular Telecommunications and Internet Association
DCMS	Department for Culture, Media, and Sport
DLF	digital license fee
DNH	Department of National Heritage

DTG	Digital Television Group
DTI	Department of Trade and Industry
DTN	Digital Television Network Ltd.
DTT	digital terrestrial television
DVB	Digital Video Broadcasting
EC	European Commission
EP	European Parliament
EPG	electronic programming guide
EU	European Union
FCC	Federal Communications Commission
HDTV	high-definition television
IBA	Independent Broadcasting Authority
ITA	Independent Television Authority
ITAP	Information Technology Advisory Panel
ITC	Independent Television Commission
IITF	Information Infrastructure Task Force
ITU	International Telecommunications Union
ITV	Independent Television
ITVA	Independent Television Association
MAC	multiplexed analog components
MHP	multimedia home platform
MPAA	Motion Picture Association of America
MSTV	Association for Maximum Service Television
NAB	National Association of Broadcasters
NBC	National Broadcasting Company
NCTA	National Cable and Telecommunications Association
NII	national information infrastructure
NTIA	National Telecommunications and Information Administration
NTL	NTL Incorporated
NTSC	National Television Systems Committee
OBRA	Omnibus Budget Reconciliation Act
OECD	Organization for Economic Cooperation and Development
OFCOM	Office of Communications
OFT	Office of Fair Trading
OFTEL	Office of Telecommunications
ONP	open network provision
OTA	Office of Technology Assessment
PCS	personal communication services

PBS   Public Broadcasting Service
RCA   Radio Corporation of America
SDTV   standard-definition television
SSSL   Sky Subscribers Services Limited
UHF   ultra high frequency
UN&M   United News and Media plc
VHF   very high frequency

PART I

A Political Economy of Digital TV

ONE

Introduction

This book is about change in the television industry. It documents the transition from a world of spectrum scarcity, dumb terminals, and one-way services, to a world of on-demand programming, intelligent terminals, and abundant channels – namely, a transition from analog to digital TV. Heralded as the most important innovation in the history of the industry, digital TV involves the reconfiguration of a sector that, beyond its economic significance, is central to the mechanisms of democratic politics and the evolution of popular culture. This is certainly not the first time that the television industry faces reorganization on a massive scale. But for the most part past technological innovations have spurred evolutionary, not revolutionary change. An old black-and-white TV set would probably be able to pick up several color TV signals. Analog cable and satellite TV largely brought more (today, much more) of the same: branded packages of programming called channels. The transition to digital TV is different. It requires a complete retooling of the existing video production and distribution infrastructure, from studio cameras to transmission towers. It requires new mechanisms to compensate content creators and distributors in a world where conventional ads can be skipped and perfect copies made and distributed with the click of a button. And it requires new tools for viewers to navigate the maze of programming and new services available, much like Internet browsers help us find our way through the World Wide Web.

In a sense, the transition to digital TV is about a revolution long overdue. Compared with related sectors, the pace of technological change in the broadcasting industry during the past three decades has been much slower. Digital technologies have revolutionized the telecommunications industry, the information services industry, and to a large extent the film industry. But until recently, the use of analog equipment in the transmission and reception of video programming has precluded broadcasters from taking full advantage of fundamental innovations in information processing and distribution. By the same token, analog standards have sheltered the industry from the turmoil that has swept other industry sectors. The transition to digital TV removes this protection. Today, the same forces that over the past years have turned the telecommunications and the information services industries on their head threaten to do the same with an industry that until now had seen relatively little (or, at least, smooth) change. As a longtime industry analyst put it, "after a half-century of glacial creep, television technology has begun to change at the same dizzying pace as the wares of Silicon Valley" (Owen, 1999: 3).

The forces that challenge the broadcasting industry, however, are not only technological. The transition to digital TV is part of a larger process of change in the way information is produced, aggregated, and distributed in contemporary societies. This involves fundamental changes in the economics of the communications industry that has created new competitive advantages, eroded others, and altered the balance of power between different market actors. It also involves new ways of thinking about the implications of information infrastructure for economic growth, for cultural development, and for political participation. Along with the transition, fundamental questions have surfaced about the funding of broadcasting services, the protection of copyright, and the obligations of broadcasters vis-à-vis the electoral process, to mention a few examples, which have led policymakers to rethink the existing rules of the game for television. I suggest that the transition to digital TV is much more than a tale of technological innovation. It is a story about large-scale changes in the normative models as well as the institutions that shape television as an economic and social force – and, ultimately, about the politics of the information society.

This book examines the transition to digital TV in the United States and the United Kingdom. The main argument is that the transition has unfolded differently in ways that reflect each nation's political institutions and their legacies in the organization of the broadcasting sector. As a result, where one would expect to find convergence as domestic industries adapt to new technologies and common international pressures, we instead find that the transition has amplified differences between the American and the British broadcasting systems. Such comparative perspective offers a number of advantages. First, it allows us to evaluate the implications of the transition in countries with different arrangements for television. Despite a wave of privatization and the growth of commercial operators in the past decades, public broadcasters continue to be a major force in the European media landscape. Questions about the future of public broadcasters, their rights and obligations, and the proper balance between commercial and social goals were the subject of much debate both in the European Union (EU) and at the member state level. By contrast in the United States, where broadcasting has traditionally been organized around local commercial stations, the concerns centered on whether and how to promote "free" (i.e., advertising-supported) local TV in a context of near universal penetration of cable and satellite. In other words, the same innovation presented unique challenges and opportunities for market actors in different nations, resulting in distinct interest coalitions and policy strategies in support of alternative implementations. Digital TV thus offers a particularly rich case to investigate the interplay of domestic, regional, and international forces in shaping the way nations adapt to changes in information and communication technologies.

Second, a comparative perspective allows us to understand why some countries have been more successful than others in moving the transition forward. Take, for example, the introduction of digital terrestrial television (DTT) services. In Britain, within two years of the launch of DTT in the fall of 1998, more than 1 million households were receiving the new service. In the United States, however, despite billions in investments by existing broadcasters and strong government support, DTT was caught in a classic "chicken-and-egg" dilemma. Because the installed base of TV sets capable of receiving DTT signals was negligible, broadcasters lacked incentives to produce (or purchase) and distribute more digital programming. Lack of content gave the American public few incentives to invest in upgrading their receivers, which in turn made these receivers less affordable (because of small manufacturing volumes). As a result, after two years on the air, DTT services were received by less than 100,000 U.S. households. Scholars and industry observers pondered about the delays in the U.S. implementation of DTT. How is it possible that the world's technology pacesetter has fallen behind Britain and other European nations in the digital TV race? Typically, the answers focused on a number of factors affecting the decisions of firms and users to adopt the new technology, among them the presence of highly innovative firms, the availability of capital to finance infrastructure upgrading, the

5

penetration of alternative platforms (e.g., the Internet), the availability of attractive programming, and the switching costs involved.[1]

In this study I suggest that these market factors are inseparable from the digital TV policies adopted by governments in the United States and Britain. Governments and digital TV have been inseparable from the beginning. The first high-definition television (HDTV) system (a precursor of digital TV) was developed in the early 1980s by Japanese public broadcaster NHK at an estimated cost of U.S.$500 million. Shortly after, several European nations began pouring capital into an ill-fated R&D program to develop a competing system. Although the United States failed to develop a similar initiative, it would later impose a mandatory timetable for the introduction of DTT services and the shutdown of analog TV. Despite much discussion about industry deregulation, the fact is that governments continue to play a key role in allocating resources and shaping market dynamics in the broadcasting industry. For better or worse, they still decide (or at least regulate at length) who can broadcast what, to whom, at what prices, and using which technology, particularly in the terrestrial (also known as "over-the-air") sector. This investigation thus centers on what policymakers in the United States and Britain have done to promote, manage, or, more generally, regulate the transition to digital TV. In doing so, I side with the institutional economists in understanding markets as embedded in political and social institutions that create them and shape their outcomes.[2] I therefore compare American and British digital TV policies not for their own sake but rather for what they tell us about the particular form and the distinct pace that the transition has taken in each nation – and ultimately, for what they reveal about the way television is changing in the industrialized world.

The analysis should also prove valuable for the broader question of how globalization forces have affected the ability of individual nations to manage the evolution of domestic telecommunications and media markets. In fact, it challenges much of the conventional wisdom about the rapid decline in national sovereignty (e.g., Strange, 1996). The case of digital TV reveals that despite the ever increasing internationalization of markets, the development of digital networks on a global scale, and the expanding jurisdiction of intergovernmental bodies, nations

---

[1] See, for example, Institut de l'Audiovisual et des Telecommunications en Europe (2000).

[2] In particular the early work of Polanyi (1944), followed more recently by Willliamson (1985) and North (1990), among many others.

retain key instruments to direct the evolution of their media sector, whether in terms of market structure, technology, or content. While globalization forces have certainly undermined the effectiveness of certain policy instruments, national authorities have not passively accepted these changes. They have attempted to compensate losses in some areas (e.g., control over market entry) by enhancing control in others (e.g., competition policy), by creating new ways to exercise control, and by cooperating in supranational regulation. Although these attempts have not always been successful, they demonstrate that state authority over media has been more resilient than many have predicted, or preached.

Our findings also challenge a common interpretation of the regulatory reforms undertaken by governments in the United States and Western Europe in the broadcasting sector over the past decades. Throughout this study, I conceive the web of norms and rules that bear on the structure of television markets and on the expected behavior of policy actors and market agents as constituting a "broadcast regime." Generally speaking, a regime for industry governance tends to perpetuate itself as long as the underlying technological base of the industry holds constant and the regulatory agenda remains unchanged (Krasner, 1989; Zysman, 1994). On the other hand, technological innovations and/or changes in the regulatory agenda generate pressure for regime reforms (Pool, 1983). It is often accepted that the combination of rapid technological change in information and communication technologies and the emergence of a free-market agenda for the industry have resulted in significant deregulation of television on both sides of the Atlantic. Deregulation has taken place via the privatization of public stations, the opening of market entry, the relaxation of ownership restrictions, and an overall reduction in the level of state control over firm behavior. Based on the evidence presented in this study, I nonetheless suggest that this is an oversimplified interpretation that fails to account for changes in the manner by which governments regulate television. Consider the following examples: the UK Broadcasting Act of 1996 did relax ownership restrictions in the British media industry, yet, at the same time, the act established complex new rules for the licensing of DTT services and rejected the use of license auctions in favor of a traditional "beauty contest" to select the new licensees. The U.S. Telecom Act of 1996 similarly relaxed ownership limitations for broadcasters, yet, at the same time, it directed the Federal Communications Commission (FCC) to allocate at no cost a large slice of the available broadcast spectrum to the existing licensees and to make rules about when and how those frequencies should be used.

Are these isolated examples of government opportunism? Hardly so. As documented in the following chapters, there is little evidence to support the argument that the broadcasting industry has been by and large deregulated. Throughout the transition, governments in the United States and Britain have picked technology winners, have made rules in favor or against certain market actors, have allocated key resources, and have redesigned bureaucracies to renew their regulatory powers. The deregulatory argument is correct in that national broadcast regimes have experienced fundamental changes over the past two decades. Yet, this study reveals that governments have reorganized their control of the industry without significantly reducing the level of control over firm behavior. This reorganization has involved a gradual transition from a regime based on the idea of broadcasters (both public and private) as trustees of a public resource (the radio spectrum) – and thus under contractual obligation to serve the public interest as defined by the government – toward a regime based on competition law and access principles borrowed from telecom regulation. By blurring the distinctions between broadcasting and telecom services, the transition to digital TV gave critical momentum to these regime changes. However, the role of government in the new broadcast regime seems no less intrusive than in its analog precedent.

A DISRUPTIVE TECHNOLOGY

Ithiel de Sola Pool rightly asserted that "each new advance in the technology of communications disturbs a status quo" (1983: 7). The improvements associated with digital TV have challenged some of the basic technological parameters upon which the analog broadcasting regime rested. Digital TV originally emerged as a solution to the problem of bandwidth conservation in the transmission of HDTV. By translating HDTV signals into the binary language of computers, engineers managed to deliver HDTV over narrower frequency channels. Yet, it soon became clear that the same principles could be used to transmit any kind of video signal (not necessarily HDTV) through different delivery platforms. At its most basic, digital TV consists of sampling and encoding video signals as a stream of zeros and ones and transmitting this data stream through a transport platform (e.g., terrestrial transmitters, satellite, cable, the telephone network) to a receiving device (a digital TV set or a set-top box terminal) where the original video signal is reassembled. Data manipulation techniques (e.g., MPEG) allow the compression of

8

the digitized video signal to a point where it can be transmitted more efficiently (i.e., utilizing less bandwidth) than analog TV. Therefore, one of the key improvements of digital TV lies in the capacity to squeeze more channels within existing pipes.[3]

By allowing many more channels to be transmitted over the airwaves, digital TV has questioned one of the founding principles of the analog TV regime: radio spectrum scarcity. Government regulation of terrestrial television was generally premised on the notion that the natural limitations of the electromagnetic spectrum required close government scrutiny of broadcasting in order to ensure that this scarce public resource was used to the benefit of all (Mulgan, 1991). In Europe, the solution was to bring operators under the government's wings. In the United States, what emerged was a model based on the concept of commercial broadcasters as public trustees. By eroding transmission bottlenecks, digital TV has renewed old questions about the legitimate role of the state in the regulation of terrestrial broadcasting. Spectrum scarcity, one of the pillars of the analog TV regime, can no longer be taken for granted. The political engineering of broadcasting as a system in which only a handful of stations operate under the tutelage and vigilance of the government is thus laid bare.

Another improvement associated with digital TV is the increased interoperability with equipment and applications used in the telecommunications and information service industries. Digitization of broadcast networks facilitates the provision of services other than one-way video programming such as video-on-demand, as well as a number of information and transaction services. Digital TV therefore accelerates the convergence of the telecom, the computer, and the media industries because common technologies are used in the processing and transmission of data regardless of their nature (a news program, a telephone call, a Web page, etc.). As the boundaries between these industries become blurry, several regulatory problems arise (EC, 1997). New broadcasting services such as interactive TV often escape traditional regulatory categorization and, as such, create overlapping jurisdictions and turf wars between regulators (Galperin and Bar, 2002). Another problem is regulatory asymmetry: similar services provided by telecom and broadcast

[3] The exact efficiency ratio of digital versus analog TV depends on a number of factors such as the configuration of the network, the quality of the video signals, and the transport support (see Owen, 1999). The aggregation of multiple digital signals on a single frequency channel is called multiplexing. The digital equivalent of an analog frequency channel is therefore often referred to as a multiplex.

operators sometimes fall under different legal regimes, which often results in controversy when broadcasters that have been given rights to use the airwaves at no cost enter markets in which wireless operators have made large payments for spectrum licenses. By facilitating broadcasters' entry into nontraditional services, digital TV raises fundamental questions about the regulatory boundaries between media, telecom, and information services and, as a result, about the adequacy of a regime built on the distinction between one-way content delivery and point-to-point transmission services (Blackman, 1998).

An important difference between analog and digital TV lies in the role played by the receiving device or customer terminal. Analog broadcasting networks were engineered in such a way that little intelligence was placed at the network's edges. By contrast, in digital TV the customer terminal (whether an integrated digital TV set or a stand-alone set-top box converter) generally consists of an intelligent device that allows viewers to browse channels and services, store information, and interact with the programming. The digital TV terminal therefore represents a potential residential hub to a number of information, entertainment, and transaction services. Control in the television value chain previously belonged to a select group with property rights over transmission capacity – a handful of terrestrial broadcasters, monopoly cable operators, and the few (often a single) satellite TV licensee(s). As digital TV opens up spectrum capacity, these property rights become less critical. Some of this control has now shifted toward those presiding over the intelligent terminals that sit at the edges of digital broadcasting networks.

There are three basic components of a digital TV terminal: the application program interface (API), the conditional access system (CAS), and a navigation tool called electronic programming guide (EPG). The API is the software layer between the operating system and the different applications running on the terminal. Digital TV applications need to interact with the API in the same way a word processor has to interact with a PC's operating system. Issues of availability, control, and interoperability between different APIs are therefore critical for the new generation of broadcasting services, much like they have been in the computer industry (Pepper and Levy, 1999). The CAS is a means for controlling access to the channels and services offered by the broadcast network operator. Access control is necessary for implementing contracts between the operator, its subscribers, and content suppliers, particularly in pay TV. The CAS presents a classic example of gateway facility as programmers and other service providers wishing to access a certain viewer base are dependent on interacting with the security functions of the digital TV terminal for tracking usage and providing access keys to authorized customers.

The architecture of CAS thus raises important policy questions (Cave, 1997; Cowie and Marsden, 1999). If a dominant network operator (e.g., a satellite TV firm) deploys digital TV terminals embedded with proprietary CAS technology, it may utilize the CAS to discriminate against third-party programmers in order to favor its content affiliates. Regulators can mitigate such competition concerns by mandating the use of a standard security interface in the terminal to which different CAS modules can be attached. Yet mandated interoperability lowers the incentives for any particular service operator to subsidize customer terminals. Broadcast regulators have thus faced a trade-off well known in the telecom industry: how to create incentives for dominant operators to speed up the roll-out of new services while at the same time safeguarding competition in downstream markets. As we shall see, this has been a matter of much controversy in the British case.

The EPG is a navigation tool designed to assist viewers in choosing video programming and other services. In a world of limited channels, the EPG is a convenient way for locating and selecting services. In a 500-plus-channel universe, however, the EPG becomes a critical means of directing eyeballs and generating revenues (Mansell, 1999). Operating an EPG service is costly. Therefore, it is likely that only one EPG will become available in each digital platform. From a regulatory perspective the concern is about the potential use of the EPG by vertically integrated operators to escort viewers toward affiliated programmers and interactive TV service operators to the detriment of third parties (Graham, 1997). The issues are not unlike those related to other directory services: choices in the overall layout of the EPG, the interface functions, and the presentation of services can have significant impact on program ratings and usage patterns. Subtle differences become important as audiences are increasingly fragmented across an ever growing number of channels and services. The question is the extent to which and the instruments with which policymakers should regulate EPGs to prevent anticompetitive behavior and advance other government goals such as the defense of specific programmers (e.g., public service broadcasters).

In sum, digital TV offers a number of technical advantages over analog TV: increased spectrum efficiency, increased interoperability with telecommunications and computer industry hardware and applications, and increased flexibility for the provision of services other than traditional video programming. For analog TV operators, this represented an opportunity to expand the range of services, lower transmission costs on a per channel basis, and tap into new revenue streams. Yet the challenges were manifold. The migration to digital TV is a complex undertaking that requires large investments in coordinated fashion between different market agents, notably broadcasters, equipment manufacturers, content providers, and viewers. As we shall see, this has not been easily achieved, particularly in markets where the industry is highly fragmented. Digital TV also offered a number of opportunities and challenges for governments. By eroding transmission bottlenecks as well as industry demarcations, it represented a unique opportunity to introduce reforms in a politically sensitive sector and advance other goals such as universal availability of information society services and improved radio spectrum management. On the other hand, because the technology alters fundamental industry parameters such as relative prices, the location of bottlenecks, and market boundaries, the transition has forced regime adaptation. The blurring of lines between broadcasting and telecom created problems of jurisdiction and regulatory asymmetry. More efficient broadcast spectrum utilization raised questions about existing licensing regimes. The new network architecture of distributed intelligence created competition problems novel to the sector. As the transition was set in motion, national broadcast regimes faced scrutiny not seen since the formative period of broadcasting in the 1920s.

As it became clear that digital TV required considerable adjustments to the legal framework of the industry, the political battle to delineate the regulatory contours of digital TV escalated. Examining the transition thus provides a particularly rich case study of the politics of broadcast regulation: with the broadcast regime up for grabs, the agendas and strategies of policy actors become more visible, and their interactions reveal the types of coalitions likely to sustain the emerging regime. Although the battle unfolded on a number of fronts, this study concentrates attention on the issues related to terrestrial television. The reasons behind this research focus are threefold. First, despite the changes in the marketplace brought by the widespread adoption of cable and satellite TV, traditional terrestrial broadcasters are still a dominant commercial and political force in national media markets. Second, terrestrial operators depend on access to the radio spectrum, but so do mobile telephony operators, the military, public safety agencies, and radio amateurs, to mention just a few other users; as a result, the policy choices made with respect to the introduction of DTT and the shutdown of analog stations have broader implications for government policies in other areas than those made for the transition in cable or satellite. Finally, some of these terrestrial operators are funded by the state, which allows us to examine the challenges faced by public service broadcasters within the new regime.

THE THREE RESEARCH QUESTIONS

WHY DIGITAL TV?

While governments were attempting to introduce market reforms across the economy, they also found a renewed interest in industrial policymaking and government-led reorganization of the broadcasting sector. As we shall see, policymakers have generally been more enthusiastic about digital TV than market actors themselves, and this enthusiasm has transpired in a number of ways. In some cases, governments provided generous incentives for research in advanced transmission and display technologies, from which digital TV technology emerged. In others, they granted incumbent broadcasters additional space on the crowded airwaves to transmit both analog and digital signals throughout the migration period. Yet in others, authorities imposed a mandatory transition schedule on broadcasters (and, hence, on viewers). Again, there is hardly any evidence of industry deregulation in the development of digital TV. Quite the contrary, the transition has been a period of much regulatory activity. The question is thus: why have policymakers in the United States and Britain (and in fact in most other industrialized nations) aggressively promoted the transition despite a broad ideological agreement across the political spectrum about the need to reduce government control of economic activity and only lukewarm enthusiasm among industry players about digital TV? In other words, what made digital TV such an attractive policy initiative?

I suggest that the answer to this paradox lies in three interrelated forces that created incentives for government activism in digital TV. First, during the late 1980s the transition was perceived as a unique opportunity to revitalize the domestic consumer electronics industry and promote related high-tech sectors. To many policymakers, the Japanese lead in HDTV was particularly troublesome. The United States, the EU, and Japan were already at odds on a number of high-tech trade issues (D'Andrea Tyson, 1992). Worldwide adoption of the Japanese HDTV system would further the decline of American and European consumer electronics manufacturers, leading to job losses and widening the trade deficit. HDTV rapidly turned from a relatively obscure technological issue into a national policy priority, a question of life or death for domestic electronics makers (Beltz, 1991). Governments were called into action to help companies combat the latest commercial onslaught from Japan and claim a stake of what was estimated to be a fast-growing market. Most of the government initiatives that emerged in response to these calls either failed to materialize (in the United States) or were abandoned along the road after heavy losses (in the EU). While these policy failures certainly demanded a revision of the appropriate instruments for public sponsoring of digital TV, government interest in the transition hardly subsided. Quite the contrary, the transition was established as a legitimate item of government concern and intervention.

When in the early 1990s the hype about HDTV as the key driver of electronics markets subsided, the transition became part of a wide-reaching policy agenda that called for governments to sponsor the development of new communications and information technologies in order to secure long-term economic growth and promote social inclusion. This policy agenda, which I call the information revolution agenda, diffused rapidly among policy elites in the industrialized world. The key claim was the need to fashion policies aimed at extending the benefits of the revolution in information processing and transmission technologies throughout the social and economic fabric of nations. This could be done by assembling the separate pieces of the existing communications infrastructure (broadcasting, telecommunications, and computer networks) into an interconnected, broadband, multiservice network based on digital technologies. The Clinton administration quickly embraced the new paradigm and created an Information Infrastructure Task Force (IITF). In Europe, the European Commission (EC) followed soon after with a comprehensive action plan to take Europe into the information society (EC, 1994). Digital TV fit nicely into the new agenda. By eroding the technological barriers between broadcasting, telecommunications, and the computer industry, the transition would facilitate industry convergence and enhance competition across services and platforms. Furthermore, because far more people owned a TV set than a PC (particularly in Europe), why not turn the TV set into a home gateway for digital services? The new agenda thus legitimized public leadership in upgrading television to meet the economic and social challenges of the twenty-first century.

A third factor that fueled government interest in the transition was the radio spectrum crunch created by the explosive growth in mobile telephony and other wireless telecommunications services. By the mid-1990s, it became clear that the innovation cycle in information and communication technologies would soon hit a wall. While demand for spectrum-dependent services was growing exponentially, the availability of radio frequencies increased at a much slower rate. Before long, there would be simply no more room for new services, and the quality of existing ones (as operators attempted to accommodate more usage) would deteriorate significantly. The transition to digital TV promised to alleviate the spectrum shortage by streamlining the use of radio spectrum for broadcasting. Continued innovation in digital compression and decreasing prices for processor components made it possible to squeeze several digital channels within a single frequency channel. In theory, digital TV would make it possible to transmit the existing stations as well as several new ones using less than half of the frequencies occupied by analog TV (as we shall see, the engineering proved more complicated than that). The transition would thus free up "prime real estate" frequencies for new wireless telecommunications services. Furthermore, these newly available airwaves could be sold to the highest bidder, helping to combat public deficit. Digital TV was thus perceived as a magic bullet: it would help combat the "twin deficits" (trade and spending) and at the same time create a bridge for millions of citizens into the information society. For both American and British policymakers, these propositions were hard to resist.

Summing up, I suggest that the answer to the paradox of market-oriented reforms and strong government involvement in the transition to digital TV lies in the combination of three forces: the steady decline of the American and European consumer electronics sector, the international diffusion of the information revolution agenda, and the spectrum shortage created by the rapid growth of mobile telephony and other wireless telecommunications services. Together, these forces created incentives for governments to formulate and implement an action plan for the migration from analog to digital TV, which I call their *transition strategy*. As discussed in the next chapter, these forces varied considerably in form and strength from country to country. Spectrum shortages have been more acute in the United States. The weakening of the consumer electronics sector was more problematic for the Europeans because of the presence of large manufacturers like Thomson and Philips (Americans thus had less at stake to begin with). The point is that each of these forces offers a partial explanation to the paradox of digital TV. They help us understand why policymakers were preaching the retreat of the state and yet bullying the broadcasting industry into a complex reorganization process.

WHAT TRANSITION STRATEGIES HAVE GOVERNMENTS ADOPTED?

The second research question is concerned with the transition strategies adopted in the United States and Britain. The forces just discussed compelled governments to promote digital TV but left the door open for a variety of ways to do so. Policymakers soon realized that the task involved difficult choices between different policy instruments, rival interest group demands, and competing government priorities. For example, could market forces alone provide coordination between network operators, programmers, and equipment manufacturers, or was government intervention necessary to jumpstart the transition? Should digital broadcasting licenses be awarded to incumbents or new entrants (or some combination of both)? Should these licenses be sold or given away in return for certain obligations? Who should pay for the cost of equipment upgrading? Should the government help shoulder viewers' switching costs in order to accelerate the reallocation of analog spectrum?

This study reveals that the answers to many of these questions varied greatly between the United States and Britain. Consider for example the question of licensing. The U.S. Congress made a clear choice to secure the survival of free local TV by privileging incumbent local stations in the allocation of DTT licenses. Each incumbent received, at no cost, a second frequency channel in order to transmit both analog and digital signals during a specified migration period, after which one of the channels would be returned to the government. In Britain, by contrast, only the British Broadcasting Corporation (BBC) received full control of a second frequency channel for DTT. The other incumbents were instead forced to share capacity on two other channels, which opened room for licensing new operators. Consider also the choices made with respect to the governance of standards. Initially, the European approach was to force adoption of a standard called MAC (multiplexed analog components), developed by a group of large European electronics manufacturers (notably Philips and Thomson). After this approach failed, EU officials decided to hand over the development of standards for digital TV back to the industry. Since then, European authorities have effectively rubberstamped the decisions of private industry consortia such as the Digital Video Broadcasting (DVB) group. The United States traveled the opposite route. The government initially took a rather hands-off approach: it let firms develop different standards and convened an advisory board to help it select the winner through extensive technical testing. As the transition progressed, however, it became clear that without more thorough involvement by the FCC and the threat of legislation by Congress, agreement between parties would be hard to attain.

Behind the common goal of promoting digital TV thus lies an array of policies aimed at adapting the transition to domestic concerns and distinct industry trajectories. Their differences reflect the policy trade-offs that policymakers in the United States and Britain have made with respect to investment incentives, cost allocation, and programming obligations, among others. Both nations initiated their transition at about the same time, triggered by the efforts of NHK in the late 1980s to gain worldwide adoption of its HDTV system. They also faced very similar circumstances: a growing trade deficit in consumer electronics, a growing demand for radio spectrum, public spending deficits, and multiple pressures to enact market reforms in the broadcast sector. These nations, however, responded differently to these common challenges by fashioning transition strategies that varied considerably in their priorities, their instruments, and their timing. In a few words, they have created different rules of the game for the reorganization of the sector.

The British transition strategy (discussed at length in Part III of the book) has been one of aggressive implementation of procompetitive industry reforms, premised on the vision that digital TV demanded a unified approach to broadcasting and telecom regulation. The transition was perceived as a unique window of opportunity to accelerate the reorganization of the industry initiated by the Thatcher administration in the early 1980s and to initiate regime reforms in consonance with industry convergence. Policies were often designed to tilt the market in favor of new entrants and restrain dominant operators, particularly in the pay-TV market. This makes the United Kingdom a prime case study to understand the political economy of digital TV: it is not only the nation where the transition is most advanced but also where the most interesting experiments in new ways of organizing the market and regulating its players in a post-transition world have taken place. The exception to the rule has been the continued support to the BBC. The ideological foundations of broadcasting as a public service are well rooted in Britain; at the same, Britain was the first European country to introduce commercial TV, and many have argued that the programming output of the two systems differ little. With the arrival of digital TV, critics claim the justification for the BBC has simply vanished. Yet, despite these critics and the manifold challenges faced by European public service broadcasters during the 1990s, the BBC has emerged stronger than ever from the transition.

The American strategy (discussed at length in Part II) on the other hand has privileged continuity over reform. Digital TV was implemented in a way to create minimal disruption to the existing political-economic arrangements in the industry. A smooth migration built on the analog regulatory edifice and led by the market incumbents has been the guiding principle of American policies, despite the costs in terms of foregone spectrum efficiencies and media access. Ultimately, the goal has been to extend the organization of the industry around small local oligopolies into the digital era. These remarkable differences between the American and British approaches to digital TV are not trivial. In each case we find that certain stakeholders, certain business models, certain market arrangements, and certain policy goals have been favored over others. Different implementations have thus had real implications for the way television has evolved in each of these nations. The comparison also reveals that the character of the new technology has not dictated government policy; but neither have the common challenges with respect to spectrum management, macroeconomic stability, and the promotion of information and communication industries discussed previously. These forces created incentives to promote the transition but, as noted, offered an array of possible courses of action. Digital TV offered similar opportunities and threats for the United States and Britain, and yet these nations have made unique implementation choices. The question thus becomes: how can we explain the remarkable differences in the transition strategies adopted in the United States and Britain?

HOW TO EXPLAIN THE DIFFERENT STRATEGIES ADOPTED?

This study builds upon the framework of the so-called new institutionalism to explain the variations in digital TV policies between the United States and Britain. The basic theoretical assumption is that policy choices can be explicated by tracing back the nature of policy formation and the set of institutional constraints within which they emerge. Public policies do not emerge ex nihilo. They are made by individuals whose authority stems from the institutional positions they occupy and whose decisions are affected by the information available to them, the instruments at hand, the way interest groups are organized and exercise pressure, the costs and rewards associated with alternative choices, and the legacy of past policies (Hall, 1986; Cowhey and McCubbins, 1995). As these policy-making structures vary from country to country, so does the way governments tend to approach problems of industrial adjustment and growth. Institutional analysis thus privileges state actors and organizational arrangements in explaining policy choices (March and Olsen, 1984). It assumes that elected officials and regulators are relatively autonomous and have agendas that are not reducible to those of interest groups (although such autonomy varies greatly across nations). This is not to say that market forces and interest group pressure are not important policy determinants. The argument is that a complex web of domestic institutions mediates between these forces and government officials, filtering information and pressure in specific ways. These institutions determine whose voices are heard, whose interests are weighed, and which proposals are deemed acceptable. Therefore, in order to understand why certain stakeholders are consistently more effective than others, why certain governments are capable of imposing losses on powerful incumbents and others are not, and why diffused interests are represented in some cases and not others, we need to examine the institutional fabric that underlies policymaking.

This perspective presents numerous advantages for comparative policy analysis. Basically, it internalizes cross-national differences as intervening variables. Policy inputs (in our case, demands for different digital TV policies) and outputs (e.g., the transition strategies adopted) are linked differently across nations. These variations result in distinct national regulatory patterns. A number of studies have demonstrated that such patterns hold remarkably well across sectors and issues (Zysman, 1994; S. Vogel, 1996). In other words, because domestic institutions link policy inputs and outputs in unique ways, they define predictable national regimes for industry governance and determine how these regimes are likely to change in response to technology innovations or new policy agendas. I suggest we can explicate the variations in transition strategies adopted in the United States and Britain by examining a number of institutional factors that have stacked the deck in favor of different choices in the regulation and promotion of digital TV. This analysis is undertaken in Part IV of the book. The focus is on three factors.

To begin with, we examine the organization of the state. This is the classic realm of institutional analysis, with an extensive body of work dedicated to the motivational effects of different constitutional, legislative, and administrative arrangements. For simplicity, the analysis focuses on three determinant variables: regime type, electoral system, and formal rule-making procedures. Regime type is concerned with the fundamental distinction between presidential (e.g., the United States) and parliamentary (e.g., Britain and Japan) democracies. Policy scholars have long observed the distinct effects of these regimes on government capabilities. For our purposes, the key factor is how the formal division of powers between the executive and the legislature has affected the formulation and implementation of a transition strategy. The second variable refers to the structure of the electoral system. In all representative democracies political leaders need to mobilize and retain support. As a result, the rules that dictate how they are elected (and reelected) necessarily affect the policy choices they make. This is particularly relevant for our analysis because of the importance of television in shaping public opinion and mobilizing voters. Third, formal rule-making procedures refer to the rules for making and enforcing regulations in the communications sector. A key question here is whether authority is centralized in one or a few policymaking bodies or dispersed across a number of executive, legislative, and judiciary or quasi-judiciary agencies.

We next turn attention to normative models guiding broadcasting policy in each nation. Ideas permeate policymaking, not only because they define how policy actors interpret the issues at stake but also because they alleviate uncertainties and help define "acceptable" courses of action (North, 1990). These road maps (or "shared scripts" in sociological jargon) have been particularly relevant in our case as policymakers faced difficult policy choices in a context of conflicting predictions about the demand for digital TV services and the evolution of the technology. Normative paradigms provided the basic cognitive template through which decision makers interpreted the challenges associated with digital TV and assessed the validity of different possible solutions. It is important not to confound these models with party ideology, although the two are certainly related. Accepted beliefs about the role of the state in the regulation and promotion of industries, about the proper balance between different economic and social goals, or about the appropriate regulatory instruments for government action generally transcend party lines and show remarkable continuity over time in any given nation (Weir, 1992). They are typically embedded in routine bureaucratic procedures and in the traditions of government agencies (e.g., recruiting practices). Though certainly prone to change, these normative models are remarkably resilient.

Lastly, we examine the implications of differences in the preexisting broadcast regime – commonly referred to as "path-dependency" effects. The argument is that the room for maneuvering in the formulation and implementation of a transition strategy was constrained by the existing arrangements in the analog TV sector. The reasons are well established in the public policy literature (Krasner, 1989; North, 1993). Individuals and organizations make long-term commitments (e.g., investments in particular broadcast technologies or services) based on the existing rules of the game. Because these commitments often represent sunk costs, these market agents tend to resist policies that significantly alter those rules. This facilitates policy choices consistent with the existing regime and inhibits those deflecting from it. Changes are possible at the margin, but major shifts require the mobilization of considerable political resources and often payments to compensate the losses incurred by individuals or organizations. The results are policies that tend to outlive their creators. Our model thus takes into account how the preexisting industry arrangements facilitated certain courses of action and inhibited others in the transition to digital TV.

THE MAIN ARGUMENT IN BRIEF

The transition to digital TV is the outcome of a long process of technological innovation and industrial restructuring that began as far back as the mid-1960s, when broadcasters first started experimenting with ways to improve the picture quality offered by analog TV. By the late 1980s a number of forces catapulted the transition to the forefront of the communications policy agenda of the United States and several European nations. Electronics manufacturers effectively seized on the growing concerns about industrial competitiveness vis-à-vis Japan and the newly industrialized nations of Asia to demand government action on HDTV and later digital TV in defense of the domestic high-tech sector. With the decline in the U.S. and European share of the world high-tech market, a trade deficit running in the several billion dollars range, and the lingering unemployment problem, those demands found many receptive ears among government officials. The transition also promised to pave the way into the information society by accelerating digital convergence and alleviating disparities in access to information services (the "digital divide" problem). Finally, digital TV would help alleviate spectrum shortages, thus clearing the way for an entire new generation of wireless telecommunications services. In the process, the state would raise billions of dollars by auctioning the frequencies made available by the transition. All of these forces created incentives for government action – or, at least, conscious inaction.

In response to these forces, governments in the United States and Britain have created an action plan to implement digital TV. These plans involved a number of policy instruments. Governments introduced new legislation aimed at providing a legal framework for the introduction of services and adapting the broadcast regime to the new industry parameters. The plans also involved the use of public credit and the allocation of resources (e.g., radio spectrum) to provide incentives for companies to undertake R&D efforts related to digital TV and make investments in equipment upgrading and services launch. Different study groups, oversight committees, and government task forces were established to coordinate and monitor execution. In short, these nations have adopted what I call a transition strategy. These strategies, however, have been remarkably different in terms of their priorities, their selection of policy instruments, their underlying assumptions, and hence their outcomes. Each represents a unique way to reorganize the industry and modernize the broadcast regime. Their variations reflect fundamental differences in the organization of the political system, the normative orientation of broadcasting policies, and the legacy of the analog TV regime between the United States and Britain. In other words, common pressures inducing government action on digital TV have been mediated by nation-specific factors affecting policy formation and execution, thus resulting in transition strategies of different nature. Figure 1.1 summarizes the argument in diagram form.

The aggressive implementation of a transition strategy characterized by procompetitive reforms in the allocation of terrestrial broadcasting licenses and in the regulation of access to digital TV network facilities was facilitated by the arrangements of the British political system. The centralization of authority within the cabinet, an electoral system that favors clear-cut parliamentary majorities and breeds party discipline, and the lack of checks and balances on government behavior allowed the Major administration rapidly to translate into action a policy agenda that imposed losses on several incumbents and brought significant reforms to a politically sensitive sector. In less than two years, the administration's proposals for the introduction of DTT were transposed into legislation and new licenses awarded. Although the government did not attempt to micromanage the transition, it nonetheless used its control over spectrum allocation and the level of the BBC license fee to secure the well-being of the public broadcaster in the post-transition environment. A cross-party normative orientation in support of a mixed public-commercial broadcasting system facilitated the BBC's efforts to

---

Why promote digital TV?

1. Decline of electronics sector, growing trade deficit
2. Diffusion of information revolution policy agenda
3. Spectrum shortage, government revenues through spectrum auctions

---

Nation-specific intervening factors:

1. Organization of the state (regime type, electoral system, formal rule-making procedures)
2. Normative orientation of media policy
3. Legacy of analog TV regime

United Kingdom	United States
• Aggressive promotion of competition in TV services	• Reinforcement of existing local oligopolies
• Extensive broadcast regime reforms	• Minimal broadcast regime reforms
• Defense of public service broadcasting	• Policy gridlock

Figure 1.1. Diagram of the main argument.

secure such exceptional treatment. Finally, a legacy of mostly national operators in the terrestrial sector and vertically integrated players in the pay-TV market created favorable conditions for the government to play a coordinating role and address market failures rapidly as the transition progressed. In addition, the fresh legacy of the market reforms adopted in the British telecommunications sector since 1982 provided both the normative model and a readily available set of administrative tools for policymakers to tackle the transition.

As Weaver and Rockman argue, "the constitutional order bequeathed by the Framers of the American Constitution was not designed for efficient government. It was designed to counter ambition with ambition and to inhibit tyranny" (1993: 2). The U.S. political system militates against large-scale reforms by splitting policy authority between the executive, two equally important legislative bodies, and the judiciary. In addition, the electoral system creates incentives for legislators to cultivate a personal vote and nurture friendly relations with local broadcasters within their districts. The numerous veto points that government initiatives have to overcome, particularly when they challenge entrenched interests, stacked the deck in favor of policies aimed at implementing digital TV within the existing industry arrangements of the broadcast industry. Particularly important was the protection of the historical compact between legislators and incumbent broadcasters. The legacy of an analog TV regime that fragmented terrestrial TV into hundreds of local markets and limited integration into programming by network operators exacerbated coordination problems by creating multiple players with distinct agendas who more often than not disagreed on key regulatory issues. Policy decentralization and industry fragmentation bred gridlock. Finally, a deep-seated regulatory orientation in favor of arm's-length government discouraged policymakers from using administrative tools to address market failures, notably in producing technical standards for digital TV. The result has been a transition fraught with poor coordination and timid government action that developed in fits and starts rather than a smooth progression.

TWO

Why Digital TV?

During the past few decades the broadcasting industry has undergone a period of unparalleled changes. In Europe, where public stations once dominated the television landscape, governments have either privatized or forced public broadcasters to operate under commercial standards of profitability and ratings (Noam, 1991; Siune and Hultén, 1998). In the United States, where public stations have historically played a minor role, the changes have been no less dramatic. Gradually, programming obligations, ownership restrictions, and other regulations concerning the operation and renewal of terrestrial TV licenses were either relaxed or scrapped altogether. This wave of changes has been typically described as deregulation, a process whereby governments have progressively yielded control of the broadcasting industry to market forces (e.g., Mosco and Schiller, 2001; McChesney, 2003). The argument is that these changes have reduced the scope of government control over who offers what kind of services using which technologies in the television sector. There is certainly no shortage of examples to support this argument. Whether one looks at historical trends in the regulation of market entry and exit, funding, or programming over the past two decades, it is clear that the locus of industry control has shifted from the state to the private sector. This shift ran parallel to new macroeconomic policies adopted in response to the economic slowdown of the early 1970s. Following the oil crises, the governments of industrialized nations started combating stagflation and a growing public deficit by slashing public spending and reducing government control over market entry and investment across industrial sectors (Gourevitch, 1986). The paradigm of smaller government, liberalized markets, and fiscal responsibility spread rapidly among policy elites. It was not long before broadcasting, a sector in which government control was pervasive – whether through direct operation or regulatory straitjacket – became the target of market reforms.

When one concentrates attention on the transition to digital TV, however, the picture that emerges is quite different. Since the mid-1980s, governments in the United States and the EU have forced the industry into a major technological transition, a transition that requires a complete retooling of the production, transmission, and reception infrastructure at a price tag of several billion dollars in each market. Although little of this cost has come from public coffers, governments have used several instruments at hand to prod market actors to cooperate. They have selectively provided funding for R&D initiatives in digital video compression, high-definition displays, and other components of digital TV systems. They have used their control over funding for public broadcasters to line up these stations behind the government's plan and provided tax incentives for commercial broadcasters to introduce digital services. They have implemented spectrum policies that offered broadcasters increased flexibility in the use of the airwaves in exchange for investment commitments. They have used their authority over technical standards to rally support and enforce compliance. In some cases, they have passed intrusive legislation that specified a timetable for the shutdown of analog operations at the risk of license forfeiture. This is not to say that private interests have lacked influence over the transition process. Rather, the argument is that at the same time long-established industry rules were being relaxed, critical decisions about digital TV standards, the timing for the introduction of equipment and services, and the allocation of radio spectrum, to mention a few examples, emerged from a political rather than a market-driven process. I call this the digital TV paradox.

To resolve the paradox, we need a hypothesis that reconciles deregulation with the case of digital TV. In other words, we either need to revise our understanding of the regulatory changes in the industry over the past decades or else provide an explanation of why digital TV policies escaped deregulation. In this chapter I undertake the latter task, leaving the larger discussion about how to interpret such changes in the relation between the state and the broadcasting industry for the conclusion of this book. I suggest that the digital TV paradox can be explained through the examination of three political-economic forces that encouraged governments to promote, in some cases very aggressively, the migration to digital TV:

1. The decline of the consumer electronics sector in the United States and the EU, and the related growth in the trade deficit of these nations with Japan and the newly industrialized countries (NICs) of Asia (Singapore, Hong Kong, South Korea, and Taiwan).
2. The international diffusion of the information revolution policy agenda, which led to high-profile initiatives to stimulate the development of digital communications networks and services.
3. The radio spectrum shortage created by the explosive growth in mobile telephony and other wireless telecommunications services since the early 1980s, which forced policymakers to rethink the existing spectrum regime and search for ways to accommodate this growing demand.

These interrelated forces have taken a peculiar form and strength in each nation, mediated by the structure of the communications sector, the way in which the interest groups affected by these forces are organized, and the permeability of state institutions to new policy agendas. They have interacted with domestic factors that have made some of these forces more relevant than others in each case. These forces have also varied in intensity over time. Concerns about the competitiveness of the consumer electronics industry peaked in the United States and the EU in the late 1980s but tended to ease throughout the 1990s as innovation shifted toward high-tech sectors in which European and in particular American firms had an advantage over international rivals (e.g., networking infrastructure and applications). The information revolution agenda emerged most prominently in the early 1990s accompanied by political changes at the White House and the European Commission. Spectrum shortages became apparent in the late 1990s, encouraging different interest groups to rally in favor of spectrum policy reforms. These forces have thus had different implications over time and across nations. They each offer a partial explanation to the digital TV paradox. This chapter examines each of these forces separately, underscoring how they encouraged the formation of political coalitions in favor of the transition and, most important, legitimized government activism in digital TV.

SALVAGING THE CONSUMER ELECTRONICS INDUSTRY

In the late 1980s America was on the verge of demise as the world's leading economic power – or, at least, so thought many academics and policymakers concerned about the lack of competitiveness of America's firms, particularly in high-tech sectors:

> We have succeeded beyond our wildest dreams, emerging as the world's only military superpower. But we are no longer the world's economic superpower. Indeed, in the full flush of geoeconomic triumph, we are teetering over the abyss of economic decline. The signs are everywhere: anemic productivity growth, falling real wages, a woefully inadequate educational system, and declining shares of world markets for many high-technology products. (D'Andrea Tyson, 1992: 1)

From the vantage point of a decade later, and the impressive growth of the U.S. economy throughout the 1990s, it is hard to imagine that such alarmist views about the health of the American high-tech sector were being seriously considered. But they were, and the debate was not about whether the decline of the U.S. economy was real but about how to address it. Similar concerns were widespread in the EU:

> The EC has also experienced a persistent and progressive decline with respect to the striking gains made by the Asian region in most electronic products. Since the mid 1970s, losses in EC market shares have been very substantial for data processing machines, electronic components and office electronics on both domestic and external markets. Furthermore, in each of these three product groups, the EC as a whole and all its major member countries (Germany, France, the United Kingdom, and Italy) registered significant deficits over the course of the 1980s, exhibiting highly negative trends which clearly indicate a deterioration in EC competitive position over time. (Guerrieri and Milana, 1991: 12–13)

Trade figures corroborate that the American and European postwar lead in the high-tech sector was progressively eroding. In the course of two decades, the U.S. share of world exports in high-tech products declined from about 30 percent in the early 1970s to about 20 percent in the late 1980s (Table 2.1). Similarly, the European share decreased from 46 to 37 percent over the same period. These losses came at the hands of Japan and the Asian NICs, which went from a relatively weak position in the early 1970s to become world-class competitors in electronics, industrial equipment, and other technology-intensive products, overtaking both American and European rivals through a combination of

Table 2.1. *Share of World Exports of High-Tech Products (%)*

	1970–73	1973–76	1976–79	1979–82	1982–85	1985–87	1988–89
United States	29.6	27.4	24.4	25.1	25.2	22.3	20.6
EU (9)	46.4	47.5	47.5	44.1	39.3	38.6	37.4
Germany	16.6	17.1	16.5	14.7	13.0	13.1	12.5
France	7.2	8.1	8.8	8.1	7.3	7.1	6.8
United Kingdom	10.1	9.5	9.7	9.9	8.4	7.5	7.6
Japan	7.1	7.5	9.2	10.1	12.9	15.0	16.0
Asian NICs	1.3	2.3	3.2	4.1	6.0	7.6	8.8

Source: Guerrieri and Milana (1991).

product manufacturing innovations, lower production costs, and, most disturbing, aggressive industrial and trade policies.

The deterioration in the competitive position of American and European technology firms was troubling for a number of reasons. First, it is widely acknowledged that technology products can create a virtuous cycle of R&D investment, innovation, productivity growth, and high-wage employment that ripples across other industries and produces long-term gains in domestic economic welfare (Sandholtz, 1992). During the 1980s, several academics validated the importance of strategic investments in knowledge-intensive industries as a key determinant of long-term wealth creation (Romer, 1990; Krugman, 1990). Second, the gains made by Japan and the Asian NICs were widely perceived as the result – at least in part – of domestic market restrictions and government export subsidies targeted at strategic sectors such as semiconductors and telecommunications equipment. In the eyes of many, these gains were illegitimately acquired through neomercantilist trade policies and public spending. National governments in the United States and EU were called upon to match such efforts from rival trading partners and become more actively involved in defending the interests of domestic high-tech firms (Cohen and Donow, 1989; Beltz, 1991). Third, the competitiveness of the high-tech sector was recognized as having important national security implications. In the early 1990s, a U.S. Department of Defense review of twenty-two "critical" technologies found that domestic producers were significantly lagging in at least eight of them (D'Andrea Tyson, 1992). Secretary of Defense Casper Weinberger was appalled when he learned that the F-16 American jet fighters were using Japanese chips. According

Table 2.2. *Trade in Consumer Electronics, 1988*
(in U.S.$ billions)

	Imports	Exports	Balance
United States	11.2	0.9	−10.3
EU (9)	9.3	1.2	−8.1
Japan	0.7	16.8	16.1
South Korea	0.5	5.2	4.7

Source: EC (1991).

to a U.S. congressional report, "the broad loss of US leadership in semiconductor and other electronic technologies, particularly in their manufacture, raises significant concerns for US defense capabilities in the future" (Office of Technology Assessment, 1990: 16).

The weakening of the high-tech sector also contributed to the rapid increase in the trade deficit of the United States and the EU members during the 1980s. The U.S. trade deficit in consumer electronics alone (which includes video and audio equipment such as TV sets, VCRs, video cameras, CD players, and radios) was up from about $2 billion in 1972 per year to about $10 billion in 1988 (Table 2.2). The situation was only slightly better for other electronics sectors such as semiconductors, telecommunications equipment, and computer displays. In the critical semiconductors market, the global share of European firms fell from 16 percent in 1978 to 10 percent in 1988 (Sandholtz, 1992). Similarly, the U.S. share dropped from 44 percent in 1980 to 31 percent in 1988, while that of Japanese firms rose from 29 to 40 percent (D'Andrea Tyson, 1992). The consumer electronics sector was considered the poster child of the demise in the competitive edge of American and European technology firms. By the end of the 1980s, once-dominant firms had lost much ground to the Japanese and Asian manufacturers. The TV set market offered a troubling example. In 1964, American firms controlled 94% of the domestic color TV market. By 1987, after the purchase of RCA/GE by the state-controlled French electronics giant Thomson, the only remaining U.S. manufacturer (Zenith) controlled a mere 16 percent (Table 2.3). The number of workers employed had declined from about 100,000 in 1966 to 33,000 in 1984 (MIT Commission on Industrial Productivity, 1989). A 1990 report described the state of the sector in the following terms: "[C]onsumer electronics manufacturing is nearly dead in the United States. Much of what remains is domestic 'screwdriver

Table 2.3. *Share of the U.S. Color TV Market by National Origin of the Manufacturer (%)*

	1964	1975	1987
United States	94	67	16
Japan	–	14	34
Netherlands	–	7	10
France	–	–	24
South Korea	–	–	3
Others	6	12	13

Source: MIT Commission on Industrial Productivity (1989).

assembly' of components and subassemblies produced abroad" (Office of Technology Assessment, 1990: 1).

Numerous reasons have been cited for the rapid weakening of the American consumer electronics industry. They include lack of adequate financing to commercialize innovations, the failure to incorporate new manufacturing processes, insufficient investment in R&D, and the failure to recognize new growth opportunities in advanced audio and video equipment (Dupagne, 1998). However, regulatory advantages in the domestic market and strong government support for concerted export efforts were often cited as advantages that most American firms lacked. In Japan, for example, local markets were by and large closed to foreign electronic manufacturers through a combination of tariff and nontariff barriers as well as restrictions on foreign direct investments, while official trade policies aggressively supported penetration of Japanese firms into international territories. During the 1970s, several American manufacturers filed a series of antidumping lawsuits alleging that Japanese manufacturers, with the acquiescence of the government, were fixing artificially high prices in Japan in order to sell below cost in the United States. After years of litigation, the U.S. Supreme Court dismissed the case in 1986. At the same time, the Carter administration negotiated a voluntary restriction of consumer electronics exports with Japan, but the agreement failed to reverse the downward trend of U.S. firms. As both private litigation and managed trade proved of limited value to counter strategic government support of consumer electronics manufacturers overseas, many started demanding a more proactive government role in defense of U.S. interests in high-tech manufacturing. In a word, the

31

stakes were too high to let a highly imperfect market dictate winners and losers.

In Europe, the major consumer electronics manufacturers were able to ward off the Asian challenge better through a variety of commercial and policy instruments designed to raise the entry barriers for foreign firms in the European electronics market. By 1986 Japanese manufacturers controlled only 14 percent of the European color TV market, while Asian NIC firms held 16 percent; the rest was still in the hands of European makers (Cawson et al., 1990). One of these instruments involved restrictions to the licensing of patents for the two European color TV standards, PAL (used in all Western Europe except for France) and SECAM (used in France and Greece). The two European manufacturers that controlled the PAL technology (Telefunken and Thorn) initially refused licenses to Japanese manufacturers. After the Japanese government threatened trade retaliations, licenses were granted but only for small-screen sets (less than twenty inches). The small market for SECAM sets created a natural disincentive for foreign manufacturers, as well as the notorious tariff and nontariff trade barriers imposed by the French government in defense of domestic electronics giant Thomson (eventually nationalized in 1981). Despite these barriers, Asian firms made important gains in Europe as some of the original PAL and SECAM patents began to expire and new products such as VCRs began to drive the market. In the United Kingdom, eight of the ten color TV manufacturers that existed in 1967 (when color TV was introduced in Britain) were British-owned. By the late 1980s, none remained in local hands (as we shall see, the lack of British-owned set manufacturers would decisively influence the government's attitude toward European Community initiatives in digital TV).

The weakening of the electronics sector on both sides of the Atlantic inflicted a sense of a looming crisis for Western industrialized nations. There was an uncomfortable sensation that the competitive edge that the United States and Europe had enjoyed over the rest of the world since World War II had come to an end. Worst of all, the firms gaining ground in high-tech markets were aided by concerted government initiatives in terms of generous R&D subsidies, aggressive trade policies, and preferential treatment at home. In America, the "competitiveness" issue became the subject of several widely read books, think tank policy papers, and electoral campaigning. Many began advocating a larger role for the government in high-tech markets as the most effective response to the competitiveness problem. If governments in Japan and the NICs were implementing policies to promote their electronics sector, the order was to wage battle on the same grounds, that is, with a concerted effort to help revitalize the ailing domestic electronic manufacturers (Hart and D'Andrea Tyson, 1989). In the case of Europe, where several national governments already engaged in industrial policymaking, the sense was that the challenge could only be tackled if such efforts shifted from the national to the regional level. This environment provided a fertile ground for advocates of government activism in the high-tech sector.

The transition to digital TV originated precisely during this period of heightened sensitivity about the consumer electronics sector. The issue initially centered on the development of analog TV services of increased picture quality, so-called high-definition TV (HDTV). HDTV was perceived as the new technological frontier in consumer electronics and related components such as video compression microprocessors, broadband telecommunications networks, and high-resolution displays. The problem was that a consortium of Japanese firms led by public broadcaster NHK was at the forefront of HDTV development. Almost overnight, HDTV became the emblem for the precarious state of the U.S. and European technology sectors and the rallying point for advocates of government-led initiatives to close the "technology gap" with Japan. The case about the strategic importance of local HDTV development was based on three main arguments. First, the market for HDTV equipment (from studio facilities to TV sets) was projected to be large and thus have substantial effects on employment, production, and trade performance in the electronics sector. A series of widely circulated reports released in the late 1980s presented different estimates as to the size and value of the market for HDTV products.[1] The most optimistic forecasted an HDTV market worth $18.5 billion by 2000 in the United States alone. The estimated impact on trade balances was also substantial. Another report forecasted that the failure of American firms to participate in HDTV production would add approximately $100 billion (in 1989 dollars) per year to the U.S. trade deficit over the 1990–2010 period. Contrastingly, successful participation in HDTV (i.e., a 50 percent share of the worldwide market) would result in a trade surplus in electronics of about $90 billion over the same period. The same report forecasted that the U.S. economy could lose more than 750,000 jobs if local firms did not develop a strong presence in HDTV. As the report concludes, "the trade deficits and job losses resulting from the decline in traditional industries could be a mere shadow of the losses that might result

---

[1] These reports are discussed in Webre (1989).

if the US fails to develop a strong HDTV industry" (Cohen and Donow, 1989: 4).

The second argument was that HDTV provided a way for Europeans and American firms to regain strength in the consumer electronics market. Because manufacturers in the Asian NICs were focused on low-end products, the new generation of broadcasting services offered several opportunities in high-margin products such as HDTV sets and flat-panel displays. By developing domestic standards, and initially restricting the licensing of the new technology, local firms could offset the Japanese head start in HDTV. In this case, governments would use their authority over broadcasting standards to sway the market in favor of domestic manufacturers. While the low-cost Asian manufacturers would eventually license the technology and manufacture products to any specification, strategic maneuvering could buy the local industry time to adjust and rebuild competitiveness.

The third and arguably strongest argument in support of government activism in HDTV involved the expected spillover effect of HDTV research and manufacturing on a variety of related electronic sectors. HDTV was a key component in the electronics food chain. It involved the use of complex integrated circuits such as digital signal and image processing chips, which could have broad applications in other product lines ranging from medical imaging devices to satellite communications. Demand for HDTV components would drive developments in semiconductor design and manufacturing, which could translate into gains for other downstream sectors such as computers and telecommunications equipment. HDTV would also drive innovation in flat-panel displays, used for both civilian and important military applications from warplane controls to intelligence analysis. Moreover, the larger bandwidth required to transmit HDTV signals would stimulate investments in fiber optics and other high-bandwidth telecommunications networks. The case about the strategic value of domestic HDTV production became even stronger with the evolution from analog HDTV systems (such as that developed by NHK) to fully digital HDTV in the early 1990s. Now that broadcasting, information technology, and the telecommunications sector spoke the same binary language, overlooking HDTV could prove fatal to the domestic electronics complex. Congressman Mel Levine aptly summarized the argument:

It will not simply be "painful" if we do not develop a United States–owned HDTV industry. It will be disastrous. HDTV will drive the development of semiconductors and other components in many industries in the 1990s. These include not only newer industries like computers and VCRs, but older ones as well. Electronics will, for example, comprise 30% of the cost of an automobile in the year 2000. If ceding HDTV development helps foreigners monopolize the next generation of electronics components, it will not be long before America becomes a second-rate manufacturing power.[2]

The dynamics of international policy imitation also fueled the flames of HDTV in the United States and the EU. That Japan had chosen to target HDTV and spend more than U.S.$700 million in a program led by NHK corroborated the strategic position of HDTV in the electronics food chain. The Japanese efforts in the late 1980s to gain worldwide adoption of the NHK system set off an international arms race to develop HDTV. On both sides of the Atlantic, a coalition of electronics manufacturers and activist policymakers endorsed the need to reclaim competitiveness in the high-tech sector through a government-led effort to stimulate domestic production and the introduction of HDTV services. In order for local firms to compete in this promising new market, government support was necessary to match foreign HDTV initiatives. The NHK program provided these coalitions with powerful ammunition against industrial policy skeptics. The weakening position of European and American electronics manufacturers – and the fears that such decline was symptomatic of a more generalized crisis of industrial competitiveness in the West – thus helped establish the transition to advanced broadcasting services, including HDTV, as a legitimate agenda item for government action.

THE INTERNATIONAL DIFFUSION OF THE INFORMATION REVOLUTION AGENDA

In the early 1990s a new communications policy paradigm took shape. This paradigm, which I call the information revolution agenda, drew on a number of existing ideas about the role of computers and communication technologies in modern societies. The new paradigm combined these ideas into a powerful vision that explained the evolution of economic and social systems and prescribed specific strategies for policy action. The cornerstone of the new agenda was the belief that the technologies to create, manipulate, and, most important, distribute information

[2] "Letter: On U.S. Industrial Future," New York Times, November 28, 1988, A24.

were of strategic importance to the future well-being of nations. Much like the steam engine in the first Industrial Revolution, electronic networks and their associated applications were poised to become the main drivers of growth in the twenty-first century. If the engine behind economic progress was now information, building the capacity to share and manipulate data better was a natural precondition for success. The development of a so-called national information infrastructure (NII) would allow companies, governments, and citizens to use and share information at a speed and scale never imagined in the past. In a networked society, the opportunities were endless. Productivity would rise as firms, large and small, used information to manage inventories across the supply chain, coordinate geographically dispersed activities, monitor resource availability, and track demand. These productivity gains would translate into better products at lower prices, helping domestic firms compete in global markets. Higher productivity would also translate into more and better-paid jobs, inducing noninflationary growth (Kahin, 1997).

The benefits associated with the development of a NII were also predicted to extend across the social fabric of nations. Telecommuting would change working relations and transportation patterns, reducing traffic congestion in urban centers. Educational opportunities would multiply through distance learning and ongoing labor training: "[T]he best schools, teachers, and courses will be available to all students, without regards to geography, distance, resources, or disability" (IITF, 1993: 1). Health care would be better and more uniformly provided through the use of telemedicine applications. Government bureaucracies would be reduced as citizens accessed government services online. Entertainment and information would be more easily available and tailored to specific tastes. Increased cultural exchange would enhance social inclusion and promote tolerance and respect. The opportunities for political participation would expand exponentially, as citizens organized in virtual interest groups and exercised free-speech opportunities unavailable within the present organization of media industries (Drake, 1995). As the OECD summarized it,

> Industrial economies are at the threshold of potentially radical structural changes in their economic structures. Communication networks and interactive multimedia applications are providing the foundation for the transformation of existing social and economic relationships into an information society. . . . The development of an information society is expected to have important beneficial

impacts on economies and society; it is expected to stimulate economic growth and productivity, create new economic activities and
jobs. As well, a number of social benefits are expected to develop
through an information society, including improved education opportunities, improved health care delivery and other social services,
and improved access to cultural and leisure opportunities. (OECD,
1997a: 6)

The promises of the information revolution agenda were indeed high.
But so were the stakes. The new paradigm emerged at a time when the
United States and its Western European allies faced serious economic
challenges. Unemployment affected more than 10 percent of the work
force in Europe, and was particularly troublesome in countries with
rigid labor markets. Although unemployment was lower in the United
States, GDP growth had been declining since the mid-1980s, leading
to a recession that cost millions of jobs and forced the restructuring of
entire industrial sectors. As discussed, concerns about the weakening
of the high-tech sector were pervasive. With the end of the Cold War,
the industrial-military complex would no longer function as a driver of
technological innovation. Policymakers and voters on both sides of the
Atlantic were looking for a coherent cognitive framework that would
help understand these ongoing changes and prescribe recipes for growth
in the new geopolitical scenario. The information revolution agenda
provided just that.

The new agenda called for public leadership in upgrading communication networks to meet the demands of the emerging knowledge-based
society. This did not mean that governments were supposed to take on
themselves the task of modernizing the existing infrastructure. The new
agenda, whether in its European or American incarnation, had a strong
antidirigiste tone that warned against traditional industrial policymaking. Coordinating efforts, clearing regulatory hurdles, providing seed
R&D funding, promoting investment through regulatory reforms such
as dismantling entrenched telecommunications monopolies, and generally leading the way for the private sector – those were the proper government tasks in promoting the information revolution. However, as the new
paradigm disseminated internationally, and policymakers embraced and
translated it into specific policy initiatives, the line between public leadership and industrial policymaking soon became blurry. Several Asian
NICs announced ambitious plans to become "wired nations," which
included generous government expenditure in telecommunications

infrastructure upgrading, applications development, and human resources training (Kahin, 1997). The fact that the Internet – widely perceived as one of the founding pillars of the information revolution – had sprung from a program funded by the American government did not go unnoticed. While the new paradigm preached private investment, market reforms, and arm's-length guidance by public authorities, in the real world of beggar-thy-neighbor trade and strategic public investments such hands-off rhetoric often went unnoticed.

For governments to pilot the modernization of the broadcasting sector and manage the introduction of digital TV services seemed a legitimate task in face of the stakes at play. In a sense, the new paradigm shifted the lenses through which the broadcasting industry was perceived. In the past, television policy was dominated by sociocultural concerns such as programming diversity, localism, and cultural sovereignty. Now, as the information revolution progressed, this pervasive medium would become a core component of the emerging information infrastructure. With digital TV, broadcasting networks would become in many ways indistinguishable from other electronic networks, advancing the new agenda in several ways. Competition between broadcasters and telecom operators could spur innovation and lower prices for customers. More important, upgrading a network with almost universal penetration to offer access to advanced information services would extend, in a single stroke, the benefits of the information revolution to millions of households. This was particularly important in Europe where computer penetration lagged far behind that of TV sets. In other words, governments could help bridge the so-called digital divide by transforming the TV set into a home gateway to the information revolution. As an early advocate of the information revolution agenda explained it, "digital TV doesn't just mean yelling at the television when the referee makes a bad call. It means holding a business meeting without leaving your living room. It means that people at home can use their television not just as entertainment but as an active tool."[3]

The 1992 elections in the United States gave a major push to the new agenda by choosing an administration explicitly committed to an aggressive NII plan. This commitment was embodied by Vice President Al Gore, who for many years in the Senate spearheaded legislation related to the advancement of new communication and information technologies. Such activism differed sharply from the preceding administration's

---

[3] Remarks by Vice President Al Gore at the National Press Club, December 21, 1993.

high-tech policies. The new government soon embraced several items on the information revolution agenda as key policy priorities. Shortly after his inauguration, President Clinton created the Information Infrastructure Task Force (IITF), charged with articulating the administration's vision of the information revolution and recommending a NII action plan. The government's NII initiative was officially launched on September 15, 1993. The initiative did not include any significant new resources. In fact, several bills that authorized federal funding for NII-related projects died in Congress during the first Clinton administration. Rather, it was an ad hoc program to help coordinate policies and the allocation of existing resources by federal agencies such as the Advanced Research Projects Agency (ARPA) and the National Science Foundation (NSF). From the start, the IITF recognized digital broadcasting as a core objective of the government's initiative and mapped a course for the integration of broadcasting and video applications into the NII. According to the IITF, the possibilities opened by digital broadcasting extended well beyond traditional entertainment services. Digital TV would play a key role in distance learning, e-government, access to health care, and other advanced information services. The ubiquity of television and the familiarity of the terminal represented critical opportunities for policy action:

> Digital video will be a major driver towards universal NII access. Without interoperability, traditional broadcasting could become an increasingly isolated industry, able to deliver entertainment products in essentially a single direction but lacking the capabilities to participate in two-way information transfer or the interactive video applications envisioned by NII futurists. This prospect is a serious concern because it is an important part of the economy and a crucial communications medium with more televisions in US homes than telephones. (IITF, 1995: 1)

The breadth of the American NII initiative incited a wave of policy imitation in other nations. Visionary reports and ambitious programs aimed at capturing the promises of the information revolution (and, of course, matching the American NII plan) sprung up across Europe and Asia.[4] The EU soon followed in the footsteps of the American NII program. Released in December 1993, the Delors White Paper (named after the president of the European Commission, Mr. Jacques Delors) presaged

---

[4] For a critical evaluation, see Melody (1996).

the embrace of the information revolution agenda in the European Community.[5] While the paper categorically supported the main tenets of the new paradigm, the concern for matching the initiatives of the United States and other nations was explicit:

> Government decisions in the USA and Japan aim at organizing and speeding up the process, by supporting companies' efforts. The emphasis has been on establishment of the basic infrastructure and support for new applications and technological development. The US programme to establish the "National Information Infrastructure" provides for a total investment of ECU 85 billion. It is in Europe's interests to meet this challenge since the first economies which successfully complete this change, in good conditions, will hold significant competitive advantages. (EC, 1993: 2–3)

The €85 billion figure (then about U.S.$94.4 billion) was a gross overestimation of the American program (in reality, the funding included in the Clinton administration's 1994 budget for NII-related projects amounted to only about $1.8 billion). However, the NII initiative created a sense of urgency among European leaders about not being left behind in the new industrial revolution (Sauter, 1999). The European Council enthusiastically endorsed the Delors White Paper and requested that an action plan be prepared for its next meeting. The resulting Bangemann Report (named after European Commissioner Martin Bangemann) became the bedrock of Europe's information revolution agenda (EC, 1994). The report essentially Europeanized the Clinton administration's NII plan and formulated a series of recommendations for the Community and its member states to welcome what it called the "Information Society" (Marsden and Verhulst, 1999). Much like in the United States, the new action plan gave coherence to a wide range of existing Community programs, among them the completion of reforms in the telecommunications sector and the recently launched Fourth Framework Programme, a U.S.$14.7 billion R&D initiative that included considerable authorizations for work on new information technologies. Yet the breadth of the information revolution agenda also allowed Community policymakers to address a sensitive topic in European politics: television.

---

[5] It is interesting to note that the Nora-Minc report, commissioned by French President Giscard D'Estaing in the late 1970s, articulated many of the themes that would later resurface in the European debate about the information revolution almost two decades later (Nora and Minc, 1980).

Until the early 1990s, Community action on broadcasting had been limited by its contested authority over cultural issues and a general sentiment among European leaders that these matters were best left to member states. The new agenda promoted a different Community approach to broadcasting by underscoring the importance of the sector in the production and distribution of information, as well as its job-creation potential (Levy, 1999). The Delors White Paper estimated that revenues in the European audiovisual sector (a broader term that also included the film industry) would double within a decade to U.S.$45 billion and that 2 million new jobs could be created if appropriate policies were implemented: "[T]he stakes are high. The audiovisual sector is no longer a marginal one in economic or employment terms. On the contrary, it will be one of the major service sectors in the twenty-first century and should be given corresponding attention" (EC, 1993: 21). In order to play this role, however, the European broadcasting sector needed to undertake a major regulatory overhaul. The Bangemann Report identified several problems, including financial weakness and different national media rules that "tend to distort and fragment the market" (EC, 1994: 18). As a remedy, the report prescribed the extension of liberalization measures adopted in telecommunications to the broadcasting sector. With the endorsement of the European Council, information revolution advocates led by Commissioner Bangemann began to exercise considerable authority over broadcasting policies, shifting the concern from traditional media issues (e.g., programming diversity and the promotion of European content) to the development of a Pan-European information infrastructure. Bangemann considered that the necessary reforms, if left to be implemented by national authorities, could take decades and result in yet another patchwork of rules inconsistent with the single-market objective. This was the lesson drawn from the telecommunications reform process. The European Commission thus began pressing for a larger role in the reconfiguration of the television sector to ensure that national policies were consistent with the action plan set in the Bangemann Report.

The publication of the Bangemann Report catalyzed the formulation of similar action plans at the national level. The new agenda received in Britain a most enthusiastic welcome. In November 1994 the Major administration released its first outline of an information revolution action plan (DTI, 1994). The document endorsed the main conclusions of the Bangemann Report and praised the early liberalization of the British telecom market initiated under the Thatcher administration and continued under John Major as a "real advantage over its main international competitors" (DTI, 1994: 1). The fact that since 1991 British cable operators were allowed to offer integrated voice, data, and multimedia services was cited as evidence of Britain's head start in the information revolution race and of the government's commitment to the vision outlined by the Bangemann Report. The report was soon followed by a consultative document about how to adapt the existing regulatory regime to the new policy agenda (OFTEL, 1995). In this document, the digitization of broadcasting networks is explicitly identified as a key government goal, setting the stage for the introduction of the administration's digital TV proposals shortly after. With the Labour victory in the 1997 general elections, the new agenda gained even more strength. The idea of a new industrial revolution powered by information technologies fitted nicely with the New Labour's platform to modernize Britain based on a new compact between industry and labor (Negrine, 1998). The new government soon embraced a vision for the communications industry that demanded an active government role in dismantling the regulatory barriers for the convergence of sectors, promoting investments, expanding network access, and promoting adoption. As we shall see, digital TV would become one of the cornerstones of the Blair administration's plan to advance the information revolution in Britain in a way that built on the strengths of the British television sector and accommodated key Labour constituencies.

In retrospect, the ambitious rhetoric of the information revolution initiatives launched in the United States and Europe during the mid-1990s did not match their rather modest level of funding. Rather, the importance of these initiatives lay in their ability to set the policy agenda, mobilize private resources, and provide a credible vision to support the package of reforms implemented in the telecommunications and broadcasting sectors. The flurry of major communication legislation adopted in the United States (e.g., Telecommunications Act of 1996) and Europe (e.g., UK Broadcasting Act of 1996) in the late 1990s was a direct result of these initiatives. From the start, however, it was clear that governments would not directly fund the development of the new communications infrastructure. This was a task for the private sector. Communication and information technology companies became instrumental in promoting the new paradigm. Their executives formed the task forces and consultative bodies sponsored by governments. Their trade organizations produced many of the ideas and figures that fed official speeches. In a sense, the diffusion of the information revolution agenda reflected the growing political clout of the information and communications technology sector. But behind the eloquent visions of the future came the reality of financing and managing these changes. Building the highways of the future was no minor task, and many firms balked at the risks involved. It soon became clear that doing away with established monopoly privileges was not enough to advance the new agenda in the timing and manner expected by policymakers. Elected officials were impatient, particularly when considerable commitments in the form of public resources or electoral claims had been made. As some of the initiatives associated with the information revolution fell behind schedule, many became convinced that a hands-on approach was needed to move them forward. As we shall see, the transition to digital TV would prove one of the most problematic.

THE GREAT SPECTRUM CRUNCH

"The history of radio has been one of rapid and continuing progress. No letup is in sight. Each generation sees major advances over the previous art. Yet throughout the history of radio, scarcity of spectrum has been a fact of life." (Baran, 1995: 1). With these words Internet pioneer Paul Baran opened his address to the 1995 Marconi Centennial Symposium celebrating the first century of radio. The address was calculated as a wake-up call to an audience of technologists about how the scarcity of radio frequencies could severely slow down future progress in wireless communications. Debates about spectrum management date back to the early twentieth century when progress in radio applications revealed the commercial value of radio frequencies and the need for a coordination system to avoid airwave congestion (Pool, 1983). The politics of spectrum, however, are unlike those of other natural resources because of the peculiar nature of radio frequencies. The radio spectrum is a finite but reusable resource that provides a conduit for a broad range of communication activities, from commercial television to military communications. Not all parts of the radio spectrum are equal: because of the propagation and the data-carrying characteristics of the signals, some frequencies are more valuable than others. Television broadcasting typically uses two frequency bands: very high frequency (VHF) and the ultra high frequency (UHF). Both (in particular the UHF band) are suitable for a variety of purposes, which creates intense demand. When a user no longer utilizes a portion of the spectrum, it becomes readily available for other users. Scarcity stems from the fact that at any given point in time and place the use of a specific slice of the spectrum (i.e., a specific frequency range) typically precludes alternative uses.[6] Without coordination, interference can distort transmissions to a point that effectively prevents reliable communication.

Such need for a coordinating mechanism legitimized government apportioning of the radio spectrum – or more precisely, of the rights to use specific frequencies in a specific geographic location for a specific period of time and for a particular use, which are called licenses. Scarcity provided the justification for a regime whereby governments allocated highly restricted licenses through administrative procedures. This regime has been long criticized by economists (Coase, 1959; Noam, 1997), political scientists (Pool, 1983), technologists (Baran, 1995), and legal scholars (Robinson, 1998; Benkler, 1998). These spectrum management reformists have argued that all economic resources are scarce and that there is nothing in the nature of radio frequencies that requires government administration to replace market mechanisms in the allocation of spectrum. By handing out broadcast licenses for free, governments essentially priced spectrum well below cost: the result, as expected, was that demand for licenses far exceeded supply. Thus, the scarcity of radio frequencies simply reflects the way in which governments have mismanaged this resource by consistently underpricing the use of spectrum.

Until the 1980s, however, these debates were confined to academia, because political pressure to enact spectrum management reform was mitigated by slow innovation in new wireless applications and technical advancements that enabled the use of previously unusable frequencies as well as the more intensive use of existing bands. Although tensions between competing users occasionally surfaced, the growing supply minimized conflict. For example, when black-and-white TV was shutdown in Europe in the late 1970s and early 1980s, those frequencies simply fell into disuse. The situation began to change in the 1980s with the introduction of the first generation of mobile telephony services. As demand for these services surged, the battle for spectrum intensified. Conflict escalated throughout the 1990s, as the take-up of mobile telephony exceeded even the most optimistic expectations. In the United Kingdom, the number of subscribers grew from less than 2 million in 1994 to 35 million in 2000 (Table 2.4). During the same period, American subscribers climbed from 19 million to 97 million. Furthermore, competition between providers brought significant price reductions, which

---

[6] New technologies are increasingly challenging this assumption, but they are yet to be deployed commercially.

Table 2.4. *Mobile Telephony Subscribers (in millions)*

	1994	1995	1996	1997	1998	1999	2000	(Penetration Rate, 2000)
United States	19.2	28.1	38.2	48.7	60.8	76.3	97.0	(35.2%)
United Kingdom	1.9	3.5	5.7	7.1	9.0	14.9	35.0	(58.6%)

Sources: CTIA, OFTEL, ITU.

translated into more intensive use of services. In the United States, for example, while the number of subscribers grew by 646 percent between 1993 and 2000, the number of billable minutes grew by 1,300 percent. While the roll-out of the second generation of mobile services (so-called personal communication services, or PCS) allowed operators to serve more subscribers with the existing resources, industry growth far outpaced spectrum availability, slowing network development and frustrating customers. The problem was particularly acute in the United States. With subscribers growing at an exponential rate, the amount of spectrum available for mobile telephony increased, in comparison, rather slowly, from 50MHz in 1993 to 189MHz in 2000. This translated into far more customers being served per unit of spectrum than in Europe or Japan, inevitably reducing service quality and limiting market expansion.[7] If spectrum reforms were not enacted, warned industry leaders, the United States would continue to lag in mobile telephony penetration.

With the development of the third generation of wireless telephony services, the fight for the airwaves turned into an all-out battle, "the twenty-first century's equivalent of the nineteenth century's wars between ranchers and farmers – a struggle for a crucial and limited natural resource as vital to the expansion of the information age as water and land were to the development of the West" (Labaton, 2001). These so-called 3G services promised to combine mobile telephony and the Internet into a single platform. Existing wireless systems were able to carry voice and brief text messages but were ill-prepared to handle

[7] According to the wireless telephony trade association (Cellular Telecommunications and Internet Association, or CTIA), more than 500,000 mobile customers were served per MHz in the United States in 2000. By comparison, British operators served only 85,000 customers per MHz, while Japanese operators served 200,000.

multimedia and other data-intensive content. The new generation of services, by contrast, would offer high-speed mobile communications capable of supporting Internet access and a plethora of new applications combining voice, text, sound, and video. The future of telecommunications and information technology firms, it was argued, hinged on successful participation in 3G. A widely circulated report prepared by the U.S. Council of Economic Advisors for the Clinton administration forecast that 3G services would generate billions of dollars in economic activity (somewhere between $53 billion and $111 billion), as well as significant technological spillovers. The report urged the government to accelerate the introduction of the new technology: "[E]ach year of delay in introducing 3G will deprive consumers of the surplus that technology will generate. Producers, of course, will also lose the potential profits from providing 3G devices and applications. Finally, the U.S. treasury will lose the interest on delayed auction revenue, which could be substantial" (Council of Economic Advisors, 2000: 14). Similarly, the European Commission reminded its member states that "3G will also have significant impact on job creation in the European Union. . . . A prompt introduction of 3G services will support European competitiveness and leadership in this sector" (EC, 2001: 9).

Much like HDTV a decade before, the deployment of 3G came to be seen in the late 1990s as critical for the global competitiveness of domestic high-tech firms. Moreover, widespread deployment of 3G networks was conceived as a key component of the emerging NII. After a decade of continued growth, the gloomy forecasts for the first generation of mobile telephony services had given way to upbeat calculations about future demand for the new services. The commercial hype that surrounded the development of 3G services and other radio applications such as wireless Internet access turned the spectrum crunch into a national concern. The main problem was to find the frequencies over which the new services could be deployed. The International Telecommunications Union (ITU) estimated that a minimum of 230MHz was needed to deploy 3G networks. In the case of the United States, this meant more than doubling the spectrum allocated to mobile telephony.

Because of its favorable propagation and transmission characteristics, the bands below 3GHz (including the UHF band) were particularly attractive for 3G deployment (OTA, 1995). Policy efforts to maximize spectrum use efficiency thus centered on two heavy users of these desirable frequencies: the government itself and TV broadcasters. Government agencies and in particular the military are the largest users of spectrum and occupy some of the most valuable frequencies for a variety of functions such as national defense, public safety, scientific research, and air traffic control. In the United Kingdom, for example, the military occupies about 30 percent of the currently useable spectrum, including some of the most commercially attractive frequencies (Cave, 2002). In the United States, the government controls only about 15 percent of the spectrum on an exclusive basis but shares another 55 percent with the commercial sector. In both nations, however, efforts to reallocate spectrum from government to commercial users faced numerous obstacles. Reducing resources for national security and law enforcement activities is hardly an easy political sell. The spectrum needs of the armed forces and other law enforcement agencies have also increased as a result of advances in military and public safety technology. Relocation costs can be significant. A U.S. Department of Commerce study estimated the cost of vacating the 1700MHz band to accommodate 3G services at $4.6 billion. It soon became clear that spectrum demand would not be met by simply transferring frequencies from the government to the commercial sector. If the next generation of wireless services were to become a reality, something else had to give.

As the military and other government users proved hard to displace, policymakers turned attention to the second largest group of users of frequencies below 3GHz: TV broadcasters. Analog TV occupies considerable slices of spectrum. Each TV channel occupies 6MHz in the United States and 8MHz in Europe. Moreover, because analog systems are relatively unsophisticated, they require that significant spectrum intervals be left between channels (the so-called taboo channels). In Paul Baran's words,

> The major spectrum hog is analog broadcast TV transmission. In the U.S. and to an extent in other countries a spectrum analyzer will find much of the allocated VHF and UHF TV spectrum unused, even in big cities. The UHF television band is punctuated with vast empty holes called "taboo channels." These channels are left unoccupied because of the frequency selectivity limitation of early era television receivers. Today we know how to build far better receivers than when this early rule was adopted and when those frequencies were set aside. We should never forget that any transmission capacity not used is wasted forever, like water over the dam. And, there has been water pouring here for many, many years, even during an endless spectrum drought. (Baran, 1995: 3)

Just how much spectrum has been "pouring over the dam" is revealed by the utilization ratio of the spectrum assigned in the United States and Europe for analog TV services. In America, while 402MHz of prime spectrum (i.e., below 3GHz) is allocated to analog TV broadcasting (more than double the amount allocated for mobile telephony), the average U.S. local television market has only seven analog stations.[8] In Britain, the spectrum allocated for television services comprises forty-six channels, each 8MHz wide for a total of 368MHz. Yet, there are only five national stations, some of them with less than complete coverage.

Digital broadcasting, by contrast, utilizes spectrum much more efficiently. As noted in the previous chapter, advanced digital compression and signal processing technologies not only allow several stations to be transmitted within a single frequency channel but also permit stations to broadcast much closer to each other, reducing the need for large vacant intervals between stations. Digital broadcasting thus generates significant economies in the spectrum utilized by terrestrial broadcasters, even if advanced applications such as HDTV are deployed. The exact amount of spectrum available for reallocation after the transition to digital TV is completed depends on a number of technical choices.[9] In digital broadcasting, there is a trade-off between signal strength and data capacity: essentially, better geographical coverage comes at the expense of number of channels or services carried. The configuration of digital TV networks is thus a critical choice for policymakers, because it determines the number and quality of the digital services offered and the number of frequency channels released for other uses. In the United States, for example, the current plan calls for the release of 108MHz out of the 402MHz currently designated for television services. Similarly, the British government has estimated that after the switch-off of analog stations between twelve and twenty frequency channels could be reallocated for other uses (between 96 and 160MHz in total), depending on the final configuration of the digital terrestrial network (DTI, 2002). In both cases, these frequencies represented prime real-estate spectrum that could help alleviate the spectrum drought and foster the deployment of advanced wireless applications.

The transition to digital TV thus became entangled with the politics of spectrum management and the urgency to make available frequencies

---

[8] The household-weighted average is larger (thirteen stations) because large markets tend to have more stations. See Hazlett (2001).

[9] For a nontechnical discussion, see BIPE (2002).

for new services such as 3G mobile telephony. The faster the migration proceeded, the earlier these valuable frequencies could be put in the hands of more innovative companies. The spectrum crunch of the late 1990s helped advance the transition to digital TV by encouraging governments to implement policies to accelerate the switch-off of analog stations and the subsequent recovery of spectrum. Expediting completion was all the more important because, technically speaking, the need to introduce digital TV alongside existing analog services to allow for a gradual replacement of household equipment (the so-called simulcasting period) in fact increased spectrum congestion. As a result, once digital broadcasting was introduced, the pressure to speed up the migration increased, because simultaneous transmission of similar programming in both analog and digital formats exacerbated the spectrum drought. In short, the longer the transition, the more water would pour over the dam in the form of duplicate signals. The problem was that the collective benefits of a rapid migration could not be internalized by any particular broadcaster because, as discussed, the existing regime neither monetized nor taxed the use of spectrum for broadcasting. In other words, the incentives motivating particular viewers and broadcasters to adopt digital TV did not include the benefits to society as a whole of more efficient spectrum use (BIPE, 2002). To correct this market failure, government action was perceived as critical to lead the transition to completion in the most beneficial manner.

By the end of the 1990s, expediting the transition became a top policy priority for policymakers on both sides of the Atlantic. Even those who rejected the idea of market intervention acknowledged the need to take a proactive approach, oftentimes in stark contradiction with efforts to reduce government regulation of the industry. For them, the existing transition strategy was the unwelcome legacy of misguided industrial policies aimed at reviving the domestic electronics sector by previous administrations. HDTV had clearly not turned out to be the driver of innovation and growth in the consumer electronics industry. What the transition was really about was to make room for new wireless applications. Yet, without the proper incentive structure, wasteful duplication of analog and digital services could last for decades. Both economic theory and the slow pace of the migration justified intervention. These policies were supported by coalitions of industrial interests, academics, and media advocates assembled around a common goal: to facilitate access to the airwaves by new actors, whether 3G operators

Table 2.5. *General Government Financial Balance as a Percentage of Nominal GDP*

	1989	1990	1991	1992	1993	1994	1995	1996	1997	1998	1999	2000
United States	−3.2	−4.3	−5.0	−5.9	−5.0	−3.6	−3.1	−2.2	−0.9	0.3	0.8	1.7
United Kingdom	0.8	−1.6	−3.1	−6.4	−7.9	−6.7	−5.8	−4.4	−2.2	0.4	1.1	1.9

Source: OECD.

or community broadcasters. Such coalitions would provide key political support for the use of aggressive command-and-control instruments to expedite the transition and implement spectrum management reforms. Similarly powerful coalitions, however, were assembled against such policies. As we shall see, accelerating the shut off of analog stations faced several political obstacles. In particular, incumbent broadcasters refused to vacate their analog frequencies (or relocate to others) without compensation of some sort. They were theoretically committed to the transition, yet at their own timing. If the government wanted to bend the market and reclaim their analog licenses ahead of time, this would have to come at a price.

As radio frequencies became a hot commodity, a related factor encouraged policymakers to drive the transition forward: the need to combat public deficit. By the early 1990s, government finances were deteriorating steadily in the United States and Europe (Table 2.5). After somewhat declining in the late 1980s, the U.S. public deficit edged up to 5.9 percent (as a percentage of nominal GDP) in 1992. In Britain, it peaked at 7.9 percent in 1993. According to the new economic consensus, deficits threatened long-term growth by increasing the cost of capital to the private sector. Balancing the public budget was imperative to put industrialized nations on the track of economic growth once again. Governments thus scrambled to find new ways to raise money without raising general taxes. In this context, spectrum reform advocates suddenly found receptive ears for their pledges to introduce market mechanisms in the allocation of licenses. By replacing administrative procedures with spectrum auctions, governments found they could raise fiscal revenues through a noncontroversial, easy-to-administer tax on mobile operators and other spectrum users. The spectrum drought provided a golden opportunity to patch holes in the public budget. They thus initiated reforms long-advocated by academics to monetize the use of spectrum, allowing regulators to allocate licenses through competitive bidding.

Spectrum auctions proved to be a revenue windfall for governments beyond any bureaucrat's wildest dreams. The U.S. Congress first authorized competitive bidding in the allocation of licenses in 1993. By 1997, over $22 billion had been raised. In the United Kingdom, spectrum auctions were formally introduced by the Wireless Telegraphy Act of 1998 (although since 1990 some tenders for commercial TV licenses had included a cash bid component). In early 2000, the auctions held for 3G licenses fetched an eye-popping U.S.$35.4 billion, more than seven times the amount originally expected by administration officials. The success of the spectrum auctions (in terms of government revenues raised) had a twofold effect on the politics of the digital TV transition. On the one hand, it increased the pressure to expedite the transition so that new frequencies could be sold – or, rather, rented – to the highest bidder. Several key policy choices about the transition have been made in the context of budget-related debates and legislation. Government activism was often justified on the need to balance the public budget rather than on broadcasting policy considerations. On the other hand, the auctions revealed the hidden value of the frequencies that terrestrial broadcasters had been using at no cost for decades. Once this value was revealed, it would become much harder to justify the extension of the analog broadcast regime of zero-priced licenses into the digital era. New policy coalitions started demanding that governments either impose more stringent programming obligations on digital broadcasters or extract payments to compensate the foregone auction revenues. In any case, now that the specter of license auctions loomed large, the existing broadcast regime needed to be bargained anew.

Each of the forces discussed here helps explain the paradox of government activism in digital TV during times of market-oriented reforms in the broadcasting industry. They represent common challenges to which governments in the United States and the European Union had to respond, motivating the adoption of a national transition strategy. These forces not only provided common incentives for policy intervention but offered a common rhetoric around which policy actors could gather in support of a government-managed transition. In a sense, digital broadcasting became a silver bullet with which governments hoped to accomplish a diverse array of fiscal and industrial policy goals. Revitalizing the electronics sector, combating the twin (trade and budget) deficits, leading the nation into the information revolution age – all of these seemed possible by accelerating the migration to digital TV. As we shall see in the following chapters, governments in the United States and Britain responded differently to these challenges depending on how national factors mediated these forces and the policy instruments available for action. The outcome of the interaction between the international forces discussed in this chapter and domestic institutions and interests is what I seek to describe in the remainder of the book.

PART II

The American Road
to Digital TV

THREE

The Genesis of Broadcast Regulation
in the United States

Policymaking in the United States does not come about easily. For any new law, policy initiative, or regulation to be passed, legislative and judicial obstacles have to be overcome, and side payments made to opponents in transparent ways. In this respect, the very existence of a government plan to migrate from analog to digital TV is noteworthy. The American broadcasting system, unlike those of Europe and most other nations, has historically functioned on a commercial basis. The state certainly organized the structure of the market and regulated services, but operational decisions were always left to private companies, partly because of a general distaste for government-run corporations in America, and partly because of long-running concerns about state propaganda and the separation of government and the media. While these structural factors militated against government implementation of a transition strategy, the political context of the mid-1980s made it even more improbable. Following a general trend of market reforms in telecommunications and other industries, broadcasting regulation was progressively scaled back in most areas since the first Reagan administration. But if one would expect to find minimal government involvement in the switchover to digital TV in the United States, quite the contrary has happened. Administrative decisions about technological standards, resource allocation, equipment design, and the timing of the switchover have critically shaped the American migration path, probably more so than in most other industrialized nations.

In the previous chapter we explored several possible answers to this apparent paradox. This provides the starting point for the examination of the American transition. As discussed, concerns about the competitiveness of the American electronics industry, an administration keen to promote a policy agenda based on new information and communication

55

technologies, and the new political and economic challenges of spectrum management created a fertile ground for policies that in several ways contradicted the market-oriented communication legislation of this period. We are also interested in how the peculiar, long-lasting regulatory organization of the American broadcasting system has shaped the transition. As we shall see, a major determinant of the transition policies adopted has been the preservation of the essential political arrangements of the analog broadcast regime. From this perspective, to characterize the American transition simply as an ill-fated case of industrial policy is to ignore both the motivational and the institutional factors underpinning digital TV policies in the United States. Some of the obstacles faced by the American transition emanate from the inflexibilities built into its political system that favor the inertia of existing regulatory and economic arrangements. Yet other obstacles have been deliberately introduced to minimize change and protect economic and political rents.

This chapter examines the historical origins of the commercial broadcasting system and the political-economic basis for the regulation of analog broadcasting that emerged in the 1920s. This regime has proved surprisingly resilient to both political and technological changes. It has functioned as a mold to which every new generation of broadcast technologies, no matter how disruptive, needed to be adapted. The following chapters reveal how this has also been true for digital TV. For convenience, they are organized following the three determinant variables discussed in the previous chapter, which roughly coincide with three different administrations. Chapter 4 narrates the origin of the policy-making process leading to the adoption of a formal transition strategy by the FCC despite the refusal of the George Bush administration to endorse a rescue plan for the struggling American electronics manufacturers based on HDTV. Chapter 5 discusses the reconfiguration of the transition strategy during the first Clinton administration as digital TV was accommodated to the ambitious NII initiative launched by the administration in 1993. Set within this larger policy framework, the strategy underwent significant changes that required a new round of bargaining between government, incumbent broadcasters, and other policy actors involved. Finally, Chapter 6 turns to the final years of the Clinton administration, when transition policies were again subsumed within larger initiatives to maximize efficiency in the use of spectrum and balance the federal budget. This period reveals the numerous coordination problems involved in the migration to digital TV and illustrates the dynamics of the struggle between agents to apportion the economic and political costs that emerged as the pace of the transition slowed to a crawl.

THE PUBLIC INTEREST STANDARD

An unambiguous link exists between the American model for the regulation of analog broadcasting as originated in the late 1920s and the digital TV policies adopted since the late 1980s. Of course, much has changed since the early days of radio. Yet the fundamental principles of broadcast regulation and the institutional structure through which these principles translate into legislation and administrative rules have remained, after over six decades, largely unchanged. The bedrock of the regime is the concept of the private broadcaster as a public trustee, first instituted by the Radio Act of 1927 and later consolidated in the 1934 Communications Act. Radio broadcasting began in the United States in 1920 and expanded quickly throughout the nation. Under the Radio Act of 1912, the Department of Commerce issued licenses and determined the appropriate frequency, power, and time period in order to minimize interference (Pool, 1983). As radio became popular, more commercial entrepreneurs jumped in and the frequencies initially allocated were soon exhausted. The nascent broadcasting industry quickly organized – forming the National Association of Broadcasters (NAB) – to prevent new entry. The NAB demanded a freeze on new licenses and proposed a system whereby in exchange for the exclusive right to use a portion of the radio spectrum broadcasters would be subject to "public interest" obligations to be defined by legislators. In essence, the industry demanded government regulation to secure incumbency rights. Under existing legislation, however, the Department of Commerce did not have the authority to refuse licenses. To make matters worse, a 1926 court ruling held that the government lacked the authority to enforce the existing frequency assignments.[1] What ensued was a period of widespread interference as broadcasters jumped frequencies in an attempt to assert rights to the most desirable bands (McChesney, 1993). This became known as the period of broadcasting "chaos,"[2] triggering congressional action to regulate the emerging radio industry.

Interested parties proposed different solutions to the problem of interference and apportioning of the radio spectrum. In this formative period,

---

[1] *U.S. v. Zenith Radio Corp.*, 12 Fed. (2) 614 (1926).
[2] As described by the U.S. Supreme Court in *Red Lion Broadcasting Co. v. FCC*, 395 US 367 (1969).

several models for the organization of the industry were available. Some proposed to nationalize the entire system and let a government-owned corporation run radio as a public service, along the lines of the solution enacted in Britain and other European countries. However, besides the navy and the small Socialist Party, this solution had few advocates and was rapidly discarded (Pool, 1983). With the rejection of nationalization, the organization of broadcasting as a commercial enterprise and funded by advertising began to take shape (Krasnow and Longley, 1978). Yet the problem of spectrum allocation remained. A solution floated by AT&T – already the dominant telecommunications operator and at the time an important player in the radio sector – was to impose common carrier regulation on broadcasters, with radio time being leased on a regulated basis to programmers. The plan was reminiscent of the agreement reached between AT&T and the government in the telecom sector. The NAB and Congress – wary about an even larger AT&T – rejected the plan. Legislators wanted a solution that gave the government more control over programming and possibly licensing. However, First Amendment concerns were raised about giving too much control over radio to Congress and the executive branch. The regime thus had to be crafted so that legislators lacked direct control over programming but could impose significant content obligations on broadcasters given the alleged need to limit the number of licensees.

The solution that emerged has characterized the American regime of broadcast regulation ever since: in return for the exclusive use of a portion of the radio spectrum, broadcasters would be regulated as trustees of the public airwaves and thus be required to act "in the public convenience, interest, or necessity" as codified in the 1927 Radio Act. An independent federal agency under congressional supervision (the Federal Radio Commission, later Federal Communications Commission) was created to assign licenses and enforce the public interest obligations as defined by Congress. Prominent among these obligations were those related to access by political candidates. Licensees were granted editorial freedom, yet within the parameters dictated by the act because the spectrum could not accommodate all those who wished to exercise their free-speech rights. Such speech regulation was not construed as censorship but rather as a necessary First Amendment compromise for the orderly operation of the new medium. As Horwitz describes it, "broadcast regulation essentially represented an uneasy compromise between formal First Amendment protections and a narrow form of common carrier obligations" (1989: 120). Over the years, as broadcasters challenged these obligations before courts increasingly sympathetic to their First Amendment pledges, the public interest principle was deprived of much substance (Hoffman-Riem, 1996; Geller, 1998); yet broadcasters were still exempted from fees, rate regulation, universal services mandates, and other obligations imposed on common carriers. Broadcast licenses only accorded the right to utilize a specific radio frequency for a particular service in a particular geographical area over a specific time period. Yet for most purposes they embodied de facto property rights over the radio spectrum, which could be bought and sold in the marketplace (Shelanski and Huber, 1998). As the regime solidified, privileged access (at zero cost) to spectrum came to be perceived by incumbent broadcasters as a question of natural rights.

The 1927 Radio Act was a remarkable regulatory achievement. It codified a political compromise between legislators and the emerging radio interests that has lasted for more than seventy-five years and created the conditions for the explosive growth of the industry that followed (Barnouw, 1968). The compromise benefited both parties (Hazlett, 1998). On the one hand, broadcasters were protected from direct government censorship as well as from competitive entry. Licenses in the most desirable markets (i.e., wealthy urban areas) were limited, and preferential treatment was given to existing incumbents in the initial allocation process (McChesney, 1993). The new agency was now given clear authority to enforce assignments and penalize trespassers. On the other hand, incumbent legislators could leverage public interest obligations and the threat of a possible investigation at the time of license renewal to ensure good behavior by those who controlled the airwaves on behalf of the public. In a sense, legislators were acting defensively to prevent abuses in the use of a new medium that many considered a powerful propaganda tool. As Barnouw (1968) shows, fears about the power of radio in shaping public opinion and influencing electoral outcomes permeated the debate about the new regime. Given the First Amendment restraints on speech regulation, the compromise at least ensured legislators that radio would not be overtly used in favor or against particular candidates or viewpoints and that commercial broadcasters were likely to comply for risk of losing their valuable spectrum rights. The compromise was later ratified by the U.S. Supreme Court in a series of cases that legitimized the authority of Congress to limit broadcasters' editorial freedom based on the alleged physical scarcity of the new medium.[3]

---

[3] In particular *National Broadcasting Company v. U.S.*, 319 US 190 (1943) and the aforementioned *Red Lion* case (1969).

The scarcity argument upon which the regime was built soon encountered manifold challenges. Starting in the 1950s, several economists began arguing that the scarcity of radio frequencies did not differ from that of all other economic resources and that a price clearance mechanism for the allocation of spectrum was preferable to the existing system of administrative allocation (Coase, 1959). Furthermore, the development of new radio technologies that made possible the use of new spectrum bands and the more efficient use of existing ones challenged the natural limitation argument (Pool, 1983). Yet the regime survived through a peculiar interpretation of its original intent: the regulation of broadcasting was not only necessary to prevent interference and ensure that the "scarce" airwaves were used in the public interest; it was also in the public interest to restrict entry in broadcasting (even when physical scarcity no longer existed) to guarantee the commercial viability of existing operators who served as public trustees. In other words, the regulatory goal of preventing abuses by those who controlled a scarce public resource became the justification for creating scarcity through regulatory means. The technical argument was turned on its head to justify a political pact that helped reelect congressional incumbents and kept the market closed for broadcasters. The 1934 Communications Act (which replaced the 1927 Radio Act) ratified this marriage of convenience between legislators and radio incumbents, as well as the settlement reached between the government and AT&T for the regulated monopoly organization of the telecommunications industry (the newly created Federal Communications Commission took over regulation of telegraph and telephone from the Interstate Commerce Commission). In the telecom case, the regime was gradually eroded by new technologies and court challenges until it formally collapsed with the break-up of AT&T in 1984 (Brock, 1994). In the case of broadcasting, on the contrary, it has withstood decades of both technological and political changes.

The regime created the conditions for long-term investments in radio and a related new technology, television. The new technology presented the FCC with a unique opportunity to shape the organizational structure of a new communication service (in the case of radio and telephony the commission was simply tasked with enforcing agreements reached beforehand). Yet industry pressure and the conservatism embedded in the commission's own rule-making procedures stacked the deck in favor of television policies that duplicated the structure of the radio sector. Television broadcasting thus evolved along similar lines: a commercial oligopoly by a handful of national networks protected by spectrum and licensing rules that artificially restricted entry, with the commission unable to extract any significant content obligation from its licensees. Early experiments in television broadcasting were undertaken in the 1930s by the Radio Corporation of America (RCA), which operated two national radio networks through its National Broadcasting Company (NBC) subsidiary, as well as by several other firms including Columbia Broadcasting System (CBS), the main NBC competitor. The FCC was initially reluctant to allow full-scale commercialization of services because of industry disagreements about technical standards. It insisted on the creation of an industry forum to reach consensus on a single standard to be used by all television broadcasters and manufacturers. The National Television Systems Committee (NTSC) achieved this goal, and in April 1941 the FCC ratified the NTSC recommendations for a television system of 525 interlaced lines per frame over 6MHz channels on the VHF band. The commission soon began issuing licenses, but the entry of the United States in World War II interrupted the development of the new service. With the end of the war, the FCC reengaged in efforts to create a framework for the growth of television. CBS proposed to revise the NTSC standard and relocate services to the UHF band, which would allow for more licensees and the use of its new "high-definition" mechanical color TV system. Due to strong opposition from RCA and fears that relocation would further delay service roll-out, the commission rejected the CBS proposal and proceeded to allocate licenses based on the prewar plan.[4] Most of the 108 licenses granted fell to the incumbent radio operators, considered most apt to operate the new services because of their technical and commercial expertise. Yet the limited frequency bands assigned for television and the rapid growth in consumer adoption of equipment created intense demand for the new licenses. The plan soon proved inadequate to accommodate demand and prevent interference.

The FCC responded quickly with a temporary freeze on license assignments that lasted from September 30, 1948, to July 1, 1952. During the freeze, two different solutions emerged. The first was backed by Du Mont, the smallest of the four existing TV networks (the others were operated by NBC, CBS, and the American Broadcasting Company, or

---

[4] It is interesting to note that at the same time the commission did relocate the nascent FM radio service, which had begun competing with the incumbent AM stations before the onset of World War II. According to Barnouw (1968), postwar relocation imposed a tremendous cost on station owners and rendered half a million receivers obsolete, essentially preventing FM radio from competing with AM incumbents for several decades (see also Krasnow and Longley, 1978).

ABC, a smaller network that the FCC forced RCA to spin off from its NBC subsidiary in 1941). At the time of Du Mont's proposal, it was clear that the economics of advertising-funded broadcasting favored the formation of national networks in order to aggregate large audiences, reduce transaction costs between broadcasters and advertisers, and distribute the fixed costs of content production (Noll, Peck, and McGowan, 1973). Du Mont found difficulties in obtaining national coverage because local licensees preferred to affiliate with the larger networks. Its proposal was to have each station cover a larger geographical area so that there would be fewer cities with their own local TV stations but more stations per market. In essence, this spectrum plan would have allowed for more competition between national networks but less localism in television services. The commission nonetheless rejected the Du Mont plan on the basis of a naive Jeffersonian vision of television as a local service to be distributed evenly across the nation's communities – a vision that ran against the basic economics of advertising-supported broadcasting. Localism prevailed in the famous Sixth Report and Order of 1952 that lifted the license freeze.[5] The new plan reserved channels even for communities that could not support more than one station, thus depriving others (because of interference protection) from additional services. Localism in practice meant that television stations would exist in as many congressional districts as possible but that fewer stations would be licensed in each market (Hazlett and Spitzer, 2000). As a result of the plan, the Du Mont network went dark in September 1955.

While rejecting the Du Mont plan, the FCC made a timid attempt at opening the market by authorizing the use of the UHF band for television services. This inaugurated the so-called intermixture policy, or the allotment of stations in both the VHF and the UHF bands in the same market. It soon became clear that the newly licensed UHF stations were at serious disadvantage against their prefreeze VHF competitors. First, UHF signals were more difficult to receive (particularly in metropolitan areas), even with the purchase of special antennas. More important, the installed base of TV sets was not equipped with tuners for UHF broadcasting. After a decade, an estimated 94 percent of the existing sets could not receive UHF signals (Horwitz, 1989). Advertisers naturally preferred the incumbent VHF stations, and manufacturers catered to the VHF transmission and reception equipment market. UHF licensees were trapped in a chicken-and-egg problem that would later reappear

---

[5] Sixth Report and Order, 41 FCC 148 (1952).

with digital TV: a small receiver base translated into low advertising revenues and few attractive programming, keeping consumer interest low, and thereby preventing economies of scale in equipment manufacturing (Krasnow and Longley, 1978). Various proposals were floated to remedy this situation.

UHF licensees demanded de-intermixing so that all local stations competed on the same footing. Naturally, the VHF incumbents rejected the plan. The FCC admitted that a complete shift of the system to the UHF band was, technically speaking, the optimal solution to the problem. Nonetheless, given the installed base of receivers and transmission equipment for existing VHF system, this solution was considered too radical, and the risk-averse commission rejected it. Instead, the FCC asked Congress for the authority to force manufacturers to include both VHF and UHF tuners in all new TV sets sold. This would at least alleviate some of the obstacles for UHF stations in the long term, without imposing conversion costs on viewers or VHF stations.[6] The result was the All-Channel Receiver Act of 1962, which translated into statute a deal between Congress, the FCC, and the VHF operators: the commission would get the authority to mandate UHF tuners, but in return de-intermixture plans were abandoned. In practice, the act did little to improve the situation of UHF stations, which were still unable to compete with VHF stations in reach and signal quality (Krasnow and Longley, 1978). Ultimately, the combination of intermixture and localism in the Sixth Report solidified a system of market oligopoly by the early entrants, which, with the notable exception of the reemergence of a fourth, smaller national network in the 1980s (News Corporation's Fox), has endured for more than five decades. Over this period, and in spite of manifold advances in broadcasting technology, the FCC would be instrumental in defending the basic industry structure – and hence the commercial and political interests – created by the Sixth Report.

Color TV represented one of the first major breakthroughs in television technology. While it did not challenge the order established by the Sixth Report, color TV did require substantial investments by station owners and consumers, as well as a way to coordinate those investments so that the transition from the existing black-and-white to the new color TV system did not create major service disruptions. As noted, CBS had developed a color TV system in the early 1940s, and following

---

[6] The replacement cycle of TV sets is estimated to be about ten years, although older sets are often kept in the household as second or third receivers.

the resumption of activities in commercial TV after World War II, the company urged the FCC to adopt it as an American standard. Although the commission rejected the petition, it opened a round of technical tests between two competing color TV systems: the one presented by CBS and a competing system being developed by RCA. The CBS system performed better, but it was not backward compatible (i.e., it could not be received on existing black-and-white sets). The RCA system was backward compatible but was not fully developed at the time of testing. In October 1950 the FCC voted to adopt the CBS system as the U.S. color TV standard (Farrell and Shapiro, 1992). CBS had no significant manufacturing capabilities, however, and the leading equipment makers (including RCA) continued to produce and sell black-and-white sets. Color TV was brought to a brief halt with the onset of the Korean War; in the meantime, RCA completed the development of its system and amassed political support within the NTSC. By 1953 there were 23 million TV sets, of which only a slim minority were equipped to receive the CBS color TV signals. The FCC was unwilling to oppose the new industry consensus, and in December 1953 it reversed its decision and endorsed the RCA color TV system.

Despite the FCC endorsement, the advantages of a backward-compatible system, and the fact that RCA controlled both a large network and a leading TV set manufacturing operation, adoption of color TV was slow. Broadcasters – in particular the NBC and the CBS affiliates – were quick to make the necessary investments to transmit color signals: by 1954, more than 60 percent of the VHF stations in the top forty markets were ready for color TV (Farrell and Shapiro, 1992: 55). Appealing color TV programming, however, was much slower to come. Not surprisingly, after a decade only about 3 percent of American households owned a color TV set, which remained far more expensive than black-and-white sets. Sales of color sets only took off after a significant volume of programming was made available (and even color-themed programming such as *Walt Disney's Wonderful World of Color*). Penetration surpassed the 50 percent mark in the early 1970s, almost two decades after color services were first introduced. The transition to color TV provides interesting parallels with the case of digital TV, although the comparison needs to be made carefully. At the time, the industry was far less complex, with considerable integration between networks and equipment manufacturers and with less peripheral equipment such as VCRs and cable set-top boxes. The introduction of digital TV services has taken place in the context of a more mature, less integrated industry, with a far larger number of market agents involved. Overcoming coordination problems and reaching standards agreements will prove significantly more problematic in the new context.

NEW TECHNOLOGIES AND REFORM

Cable TV represented the first technological challenge to the arrangements laid down by the Sixth Report. Cable was originally conceived as a way to improve reception in areas with poor coverage, where a large community antenna could pick up the terrestrial signals and send them through coaxial cables to households. Local stations initially welcomed the new technology as a way to reach viewers who would otherwise receive poor or no service. Cable operators soon realized that the technology also enabled them to provide additional services of two types. The first comprised local services produced by the cable operator, initially consisting in rudimentary feeds with time or weather information. These did not raise as many concerns as the second type of services, which were out-of-town terrestrial signals imported via microwave relays (Owen, 1999). Local broadcasters protested that distant signals reduced the value of their programming and lowered advertising revenues, thus making it more difficult to meet their public interest obligations. Up until this point, the FCC had largely ignored cable. The only significant action had been the rejection of a petition to regulate cable operators as common carriers. Not surprisingly, the petition was filed by thirteen local broadcasters (Powe, 1987). When the issue of distant signals arose, the commission realized it lacked clear jurisdiction, as cable was a local service (not interstate) that did not utilize radio spectrum. The commission however had authority over the microwave relay links that cable operators used to import distant signals. Starting in the early 1960s, the FCC utilized this authority to restrict the development of cable TV. In a controversial 1962 decision, the commission denied a permit for a microwave carrier to construct facilities for the relay of television signals to cable systems.[7] The justification was that the microwave relay would create economic injury to local broadcasters, threatening their commercial viability and thus the fulfillment of their public trustee obligations. The decision again reversed the logic of the regime: it safeguarded the instrument for addressing the spectrum scarcity problem, even when this exacerbated the alleged problem.

---

[7] Carter Mountain Transmission Corp., 32 FCC 459 (February 14, 1962).

Economic injury to local broadcasters thus became an official doctrine for justifying the restrictions on the operation of cable TV. Several so-called antisiphoning rules were imposed: a "must-carry" requirement that forced cable operators to carry all local stations; tight restrictions on the import of distant signals and the purchase of rights for sports and first-run movies (which ensured the availability of premium programming on free TV); and a virtual freeze on the development of cable in the top 100 markets to protect UHF stations (despite evidence that cable retransmission could in fact help UHF broadcasters by equalizing reception with the VHF incumbents).[8] Industry pressure and the commission's reluctance to reevaluate its own instruments and interpretations of the statute in the face of new technologies fostered its restrictive cable policies. Congress had little interest in revising the existing regime, and cable operators had little political clout to wield. As a former FCC commissioner explained, "since the advent of cable, the Commission's first concern has been the impact of cable, not on the public, but on the broadcast industry" (Robinson, 1978: 246).

Cable policies were later relaxed by the twin forces of court challenges and a new deregulatory orientation within the FCC that accompanied the larger regulatory reform movement of the late 1970s. New FCC commissioners recognized the historical bias of the agency in favor of local broadcasters and started to redress it by lifting restrictions and encouraging the deployment of new communication technologies such as cable, satellite TV, and low-power terrestrial services. The new orientation was championed by a heterodox political coalition that included public interest groups pushing for better citizens' access to the airwaves, free-market economists who condemned the FCC's protectionist policies, educators advocating noncommercial broadcasting, and new White House officials armed with a broad deregulatory agenda (Horwitz, 1989). The coalition embraced new broadcasting technologies as a way to reform the existing market oligopoly and create more opportunities for new voices in entertainment and political speech on television. In the meantime, despite the restrictions, the cable industry was growing steadily, and increasing consolidation improved the industry's lobbying power. The National Cable and Telecommunications Association (NCTA) became an important political force in Washington. Broadcasters opposed any changes to the antisiphoning rules but ultimately settled in return for reforms that significantly relaxed content obligations, raised ownership

[8] For a discussion of the antisiphoning rules, see Crandall and Furchtgott-Roth (1996).

caps, and facilitated license renewals. Starting in 1974, the FCC began gradually relaxing restrictions on imported signals and cable deployment (Crandall and Furchtgott-Roth, 1996). The commission also authorized the use of satellite technology to deliver programming to cable operators, which opened the market for specialized cable networks with nationwide coverage.

The burden of proof was now on the broadcasters, and the commission was less willing to accept economic harm as a justification for protectionist rules. In 1977 a court struck down the restrictions on pay-TV programming in a strongly worded decision that questioned the FCC's authority to regulate cable content and the lack of evidence demonstrating how its cable rules promoted the goals of the 1934 Communications Act.[9] In 1979 the Supreme Court struck down FCC rules that required cable operators to make available channels for educational, governmental, and public access.[10] The Court ruled that such access rules violated the 1934 act by imposing common-carrier status on cable operators and encroaching on operators' First Amendment rights as electronic publishers. The case set an important precedent for the strict separation between telecommunication and broadcasting regulation, limiting the application of common-carrier rules on cable operators and programming distributors in general (Pool, 1983). Decades later, despite increasing technological convergence and the blurring of industry boundaries, telecom and broadcast regulation continued to evolve along different tracks.

Following these cases, the commission abandoned its antisiphoning rules, and the cable industry experienced sustained growth. In 1980 only 20 percent of households subscribed to cable. By 1985 penetration had grown to 42 percent, and by 1990 it was close to 60 percent. Much of the regulatory void left by the FCC was filled by local franchising authorities, which since the start of cable had been extracting both cash and non-cash payments from operators in return for monopoly privileges. Large operators began to complain about the burden inflicted by obligations that differed considerably from city to city, and they lobbied Congress in favor of federal rules that established a uniform regime and preempted state and local authorities. The Cable Act of 1984 finally laid down federal policy on cable services. While the act imposed numerous rules on the operation of cable TV, the legislation was deregulatory by virtue of

[9] *Home Box Office v. FCC*, 567 F.2d 9 (1977).
[10] *United States v. Midwest Video Corp.*, 440 US 689 (1979) (*Midwest II*).

its attempt to create minimal federal rules and curb the discretion of local franchising authorities. The act codified the prohibition against the regulation of cable as a common carrier and preempted local authorities from requiring specific services or regulating cable rates. Yet the act also imposed general access obligations that continued the long judicial and political battle between the cable industry, local broadcasters and other programmers, and both local and federal authorities.

At the heart of the battle was the extent to which access obligations could be imposed on cable operators in light of the firm separation between the regimes for common carriers and publishers established by the Supreme Court in *Midwest II*. The 1984 act established two types of access obligations. First, local franchising authorities were granted power to demand that operators set aside capacity for educational, governmental, and public access channels. Second, the act forced operators to lease a certain share of their capacity to unaffiliated commercial parties. These rules were both clarified and expanded by Congress in the 1992 Cable Act, which also codified the third and most controversial type of access rule: must-carry obligations that forced cable operators to carry upon request, at no charge, local VHF and UHF stations for up to one-third of their total channel capacity.[11]

The 1992 Cable Act was passed by a two-thirds majority in Congress, overcoming President Bush's veto. The act represented a major political victory for local broadcasters, which seized on the growing public discontent about the increase in cable prices since the 1984 act deregulated rates. In an election year, Congress proved ready to respond and slapped the cable industry with rate regulation and must-carry obligations. Must-carry was justified on grounds that cable operators had an economic incentive to refuse carriage to local stations in favor of affiliated cable programmers, thus threatening information plurality and the continued viability of free local television service on which at the time about 40 percent of American households relied (Aaron, 2000). Within days, cable operators challenged must-carry in court. After a long judicial battle, in March 1997 the Supreme Court finally upheld the constitutional validity of must-carry obligations.[12] The Court agreed with Congress that imposing an allegedly content-neutral access requirement on cable operators was justified because, despite the obvious harm to cable's

---

[11] More precisely, the act establishes that local broadcasters can either request mandatory carriage under must-carry rules or negotiate retransmission fees with the cable operator (see 47 U.S.C. § 534, 535).

[12] *Turner Broadcasting System, Inc. v. FCC*, 520 US 180 (1997) (*Turner II*).

editorial freedom, it advanced other important government goals such as the preservation of free local broadcasting. Disguised in procompetition and information diversity language, must-carry rules were an attempt to extend a regulatory edifice crafted to address the problem of spectrum scarcity into an era of spectrum abundance. This paradox was to come under new scrutiny in the context of the transition to digital TV as the new technology also drastically expanded channel capacity for both cable and terrestrial operators.

The *Turner II* decision reversed a trend of increased judicial challenge to the analog broadcasting order. Interestingly, at the time the Supreme Court upheld the validity of must-carry rules in favor of local broadcasters, only about a quarter of American households relied on terrestrial signals for TV service. While cable growth slowed in the 1990s, satellite TV experienced sustained expansion, partially eroding the de facto cable monopolies. The start of satellite TV is paradoxically linked to the expansion of cable. The first commercial satellites designed for television were used by cable programmers such as HBO to deliver signals to cable operators across the country (Owen, 1999). As the price of receiving equipment dropped, some viewers acquired satellite dishes to receive the programming for which others paid (through the cable operator). The problem was rectified with the development of signal encryption technology, but the episode revealed that significant demand existed for direct-to-home satellite services, particularly in rural areas with poor or no cable services. Satellite TV nonetheless remained a niche market (in part because of the large size of the dish required for reception) until the launch of a new generation of satellite systems in 1994. Despite being late market entrants, the use of digital technology put the new satellite operators a step ahead of cable in terms of channel capacity and new services. The problem was how to fill the available satellite capacity with valuable content. Interestingly, Congress stepped in to ensure that content be made available to the new market entrants. Concerns about cable operators with interests in programming withholding their channels from satellite to deter competitive entry led legislators to establish rules that prohibited exclusivity contracts between cable operators and their affiliated programmers. Later, Congress moved to lift restrictions on the carriage of local stations on satellite, which essentially replicated the must-carry requirements imposed on cable.[13] Content availability

---

[13] Although in this case must-carry obligations are only triggered if the satellite operator decides to offer any local station (the "carry one, carry all" principle). See

and the poor commercial performance of many cable operators unaccustomed to competition created the conditions for digital satellite to grow rapidly. By the year 2000, satellite TV reached 15 percent penetration, bringing the number of households served by terrestrial TV below the 20 percent mark.[14]

Whereas satellite became a viable competitor to cable, policies in support of entry into the programming distribution business by telecom operators have largely failed.[15] Nonetheless, such policies signaled the inclination to dismantle gradually the regulatory barriers between industry sectors – barriers erected by Congress and the FCC since the Radio Act of 1927 to prevent telecom operators from controlling the content that traveled through their pipes. At the time of the 1927 act, Congress was essentially ratifying a corporate division of labor between RCA and AT&T, whereby the two companies exchanged assets and promised to keep out of each other's main turf (Neuman, McKnight, and Solomon, 1997). The transition to digital TV would invite fresh scrutiny of these barriers. After all, regardless of whether the bits flowed over copper wires, fiber optic lines, or radio waves, the underlying technologies and the equipment utilized were increasingly similar. But if the new technology invited major regime reforms, existing political arrangements induced otherwise. As we shall see, American communication policymakers would often face the unenviable task of patching up a regime based on obsolete technological principles and dubious economic logic – but robust political foundations.

Implementation of the Satellite Home Viewer Improvement Act of 1999, CS Docket Nos. 00-96, 99-363, Report and Order, 16 FCC Rcd 1918 (2000).

[14] Annual Assessment of the Status of Competition in the Market for the Delivery of Video Programming, Seventh Annual Report, CS Docket No. 00-132, 16 FCC Rcd 6005 (2001).

[15] The first initiative, undertaken by the FCC in 1992, created a framework for the entry of local carriers into video distribution called Video Dialtone. Under this framework, telephone companies were allowed to provide video programming but required to allow other content providers to serve subscribers using the same video platform as used by the telephone company, on a nondiscriminatory basis, up to 75 percent of the platform capacity. This framework spurred little investment, and was later replaced by a somewhat relaxed framework called Open Video Systems (OVS) that allowed common carrier control of up to a third of the video platform capacity (the rest would still be reserved for third-party programmers). Again, telecom operators were unenthusiastic about the hybrid common-carrier–publisher model and only a handful of OVS operators were licensed.

FOUR

HDTV Comes to America

The American transition to digital TV grew out of political maneuvering by incumbent local broadcasters in the mid-1980s in defense of the industry arrangements sanctioned by the Sixth Report of 1952. As discussed, the report inaugurated the intermixture policy whereby both VHF and UHF stations were licensed in the same market, putting UHF stations at great technical disadvantage. As a result, UHF stations struggled, and many frequency channels reserved for UHF broadcasting remained unused (Hazlett and Spitzer, 2000). In 1985 a number of parties petitioned the FCC to relax restrictions on the sharing of UHF channels by land mobile operators.[1] The coalition was led by Motorola, which manufactured the two-way radios used by land mobile operators such as public safety organizations and commercial delivery companies. Since the early 1970s, land mobile and analog TV had been sharing a small portion of the UHF spectrum (channels 14–20). The coalition demanded that the sharing agreement be extended to other unused UHF channels and that interference-prevention rules be relaxed.

Incumbent broadcasters vehemently opposed the proposal. However, a credible claim was needed to prevent police departments and ambulances from utilizing frequencies that essentially lay unused. Otherwise, local broadcasters were headed for a public relations disaster. NAB executives considered different options and eventually decided on a course of action that hinged on the argument that these frequencies needed to be preserved for the impending deployment of advanced television services, including HDTV.[2] At the time, HDTV was not being discussed

---

[1] Amendment of the Rules Concerning Further Sharing of the UHF Television Band by Private Land Mobile Radio Services, GEN Docket No. 85-172, *Notice of Proposed Rulemaking*, 101 FCC 2d 852, 861 (1985).

[2] Interview with John Abel (May 2001), former executive vice president of the NAB.

in the United States beyond small working groups established by different companies and professional associations. In Japan, by contrast, an HDTV system had already been developed by public broadcaster NHK. The system, called Hi-Vision MUSE, was a result of more than twenty years of research undertaken by NHK and several Japanese electronics manufacturers (Seel, 1998). NHK had shown prototypes of its HDTV system in the United States in the early 1980s but found little interest before the filing of the UHF sharing petition by land mobile operators in 1985. The technical characteristics of Hi-Vision MUSE fit well with the NAB's strategy. The system was designed for 8.1MHz frequency channels and thus required an additional 2MHz per station for deployment. It was therefore reasonable to request that the vacant UHF frequencies be reserved for the future implementation of HDTV. Moreover, while largely based on analog technologies, Hi-Vision MUSE was not backward-compatible, thus ensuring that the commission would proceed cautiously. HDTV provided the perfect ammunition against the land mobile petition (Brinkley, 1997). In February 1987 several industry organizations led by the Association for Maximum Service Television (MSTV, a smaller trade organization representing network-owned affiliates) requested that the UHF sharing proposal be halted pending further studies about HDTV deployment.

Shortly after, the commission opened an inquiry inviting public comment on advanced television systems – an inquiry that formally commenced the long policymaking journey of digital TV in the United States.[3] Two initial steps were taken. First, the commission imposed a freeze on all new UHF assignments and agreed to defer action on the UHF sharing proposal, blocking entry once again on behalf of local incumbents.[4] Second, the commission decided to form an advisory committee to recommend policies on advanced TV systems, including HDTV. The Advisory Committee on Advanced Television Service (ACATS) was established with representatives of broadcasters, cable operators, equipment manufacturers, and government officials. In practice, the committee was controlled by incumbent broadcasters.[5] Richard Wiley, a former FCC chairman and an influential communications

[3] Advanced Television Systems and Their Impact on the Existing Television Broadcast Service, MM Docket No. 87-268, Notice of Inquiry, 2 FCC Rcd 5125 (1987).
[4] Amendment of the Rules Concerning Further Sharing of the UHF Television Band by Private Land Mobile Radio Services, GEN Docket No. 85-172, 52 FR 43205 (1987).
[5] Of the twenty-five members of ACATS, eleven were CEOs of broadcast corporations, while five others had strong ties to incumbent broadcasters (see Dupagne, 1998).

lawyer whose law firm represented various broadcasters groups, was chosen to chair the new committee. The membership of ACATS overlapped significantly with the Advanced Television Systems Committee (ATSC), an industry forum established a few years before by the NAB and other industry and professional organizations to develop technical standards for HDTV. ATSC and ACATS were supposed to do for HDTV what NTSC had done for black-and-white and color TV: rally industry consensus around a specific set of standards for the production, transmission, and reception in terrestrial TV. Yet the industry as a whole had changed significantly since the early 1950s. As a result, the new committees would face challenges far greater than those of NTSC.

One of the first questions addressed by ACATS concerned the nature of the transition to HDTV. Two main proposals were floated: first, the augmentation approach, whereby analog stations would transmit an NTSC-compatible signal plus the necessary enhancements for HDTV; second, the simulcasting approach, whereby stations would transmit their regular analog signal and a new, noncompatible HDTV signal simultaneously. Not surprisingly, both implied allocating additional spectrum (between 3 and 6MHz) to incumbent broadcasters. In a preliminary decision issued in September 1988, the commission did not favor either but determined that HDTV services would have to be accommodated within the existing broadcast spectrum and that the existing NTSC services should continue to be provided to viewers during the transition period. Clearly, the commission felt that implementation of HDTV would have to proceed without substantial disruption to the existing industry arrangements: "[T]he public would benefit from terrestrial broadcast use of the ATV [advanced TV] techniques by the existing system of freely available entertainment and non-entertainment programming provided by privately-owned and operated stations. We conclude that the public could reap the benefits of ATV technology most quickly if existing broadcasters are permitted to implement it."[6] As the commission acknowledged, this would most likely imply providing each broadcaster additional spectrum, whether for augmentation or simulcasting.

More immediately, the September 1988 decision rendered the Hi-Vision MUSE system unviable. Support for the Japanese system was in any case waning. As the prominence of HDTV gradually rose from an issue of technological improvement in the broadcast industry to a question

---

[6] Advanced Television Systems and Their Impact on the Existing Television Broadcast Service, MM Docket No. 87-268, Tentative Decision and Further Notice of Inquiry, 3 FCC Rcd 6520 (1988).

of international leadership in the next generation of electronics, several policy actors coalesced around the need for a coordinated government response that included the development of an indigenous HDTV system. As discussed, the late 1980s provided a fertile ground for advocates of government activism in defense of national interests in technology-related industries. The consumer electronics industry had experienced a formidable decline, and there were widespread concerns about the competitiveness of the nation's high-tech sectors. Moreover, many perceived that the gains made by some of America's fiercest competitors like Japan were a result of trade promotion and subsidy programs established by the government (Hart and D'Andrea Tyson, 1989). Such aggressive policies demanded an equally aggressive response by the U.S. government in support of its industry constituencies.

The attempt by the Japanese delegation to the CCIR (the French acronym for International Radio Consultative Committee) to gain international adoption of the NHK-developed HDTV system fueled these concerns. The CCIR was an organ of the ITU that recommended international broadcasting standards (it was later renamed ITU-Radiocommunications, or ITU-R). At the Dubrovnik meeting in May 1986, the Japanese delegation proposed the adoption of the NHK system as the worldwide HDTV standard. Interestingly, on recommendation from the ATSC, the U.S. delegation initially supported the Japanese proposal. The decision was based on the benefits that a worldwide HDTV standard would bring to the American television industry by reducing nontariff barriers for trade in programming. American electronics firms were poorly represented in the ATSC, and because the issue was largely perceived as technical, the U.S. Department of State acted upon the ATSC recommendation that essentially reflected the interests of broadcasters and programmers.

The Japanese proposal was ultimately blocked by the European front, and the CCIR failed to produce recommendations on HDTV. This gave time for the American electronics industry to assemble a coalition in support of a government-led program to develop HDTV technology locally that would match similar initiatives under way in Japan and most recently Europe. The American Electronics Association (AEA), a trade group composed mainly of U.S.-owned electronics manufacturers, played a central role in pushing the case for an American HDTV program and in spreading the panic about the HDTV initiatives under way in Japan and the EU. In November 1988 the AEA released a report that forecasted a market for HDTV sets as large as the market for color TV within the next fifteen to twenty years (Webre, 1989). According to the report, because of technological spillovers into R&D and manufacturing, the failure of U.S. firms to participate in HDTV would significantly affect their ability to compete in the market for related electronic components such as semiconductors and advanced displays. If the world market share for U.S. companies in HDTV stood at about the same level as the existing share in conventional TV (around 13 percent), the report predicted that the United States could lose up to 50 percent of its world share in the critical semiconductor market. Only by capturing at least half of the American HDTV market could the United States expect to maintain its current market share in semiconductors (about 35 percent) and advanced workstations (about 70 percent). The report was widely commented on in the media, which framed the story as an example of the widening technology gap between the United States and its international rivals.

The Democrats seized the opportunity to turn HDTV into an electoral issue against the George Bush administration. Among the most vocal were Representative Edward Markey, chairman of the Subcommittee on Telecommunications and Finance of the House Committee on Energy and Commerce, and senators Al Gore and Ernest Hollings. These Democrats felt strongly about the need to support local HDTV development. Interestingly, some support for a government-led HDTV initiative also emerged from within the Bush administration, particularly among officials in the Department of Commerce (most prominently Alfred Sikes, head of the National Telecommunications and Information Administration, or NTIA, who would later become FCC chairman) and the Defense Advanced Research Projects Agency (DARPA). DARPA, a Pentagon agency initially established to fund military R&D, had also been involved in a number of successful dual-use projects, among them the development of packet-switched networks that would form the basis for the Internet (McKnight and Neuman, 1995). The alleged connections between HDTV and national security interests resonated with Pentagon officials. In June 1989 the agency awarded $30 million to support research in high-definition displays and microprocessor research (Beltz, 1991). At the same time, Markey and others introduced a series of House bills to stimulate local HDTV research and manufacturing. The bills essentially provided tax incentives for R&D in HDTV, relaxed antitrust laws to facilitate the formation of industry consortia (one bill proposed the formation of a SEMATECH-like consortium called TV Tech), and provided federal assistance in the funding and coordination of HDTV-related programs. Gore and Hollings introduced similar bills in the Senate. By 1990 a grand total of nine bills had been introduced, and both the House and the Senate held numerous hearings on HDTV.

Having successfully installed HDTV in the national policy agenda, the AEA decided it was time to collect the rewards. At a May 1989 congressional hearing, the trade group proposed a comprehensive plan to advance American interests in HDTV. The plan essentially gave national champion treatment to U.S. firms involved in HDTV research and manufacturing. A federally chartered development corporation would be created to administer the plan and channel both public and private funding to HDTV. Between grants, discounted loans, and loan guarantees, the total bill for the federal government was a staggering $1.35 billion. The George Bush administration, which had so far expressed cautious skepticism about the HDTV activism campaign, reacted angrily to the AEA proposal. Even Commerce Secretary Robert Mosbacher, who had earlier expressed some support for a federal role in revitalizing the electronics industry through HDTV, reprimanded the industry for requesting what essentially amounted to a government bailout. A growing public deficit made Republicans even less likely to endorse any industrial policy scheme. The audacious AEA proposal eroded what little support existed for a government-led HDTV initiative in the White House. Even worse, it backfired against HDTV advocates (Dupagne, 1998).

Despite a solid Democratic majority in Congress, the HDTV-related bills stalled in committees and subcommittees. Clearly, few congressmen were ready to endorse an expensive program that the administration vehemently opposed. As Banks, Cohen, and Noll (1991) argue, incumbent congressmen tend to be impatient and risk-averse. Costly R&D initiatives that have considerable risks of failure and only long-term rewards are thus difficult to pass. In the case of HDTV, there was much uncertainty about a plan based on inconclusive market projections in a sector with minimal U.S. presence (at the time, Zenith was the only remaining U.S.-based TV set manufacturer). A congressional staff report released in July 1989 bolstered these concerns. The report questioned many of the optimistic assumptions presented by the AEA about the expected size of the HDTV market and the positive spillover effect of local research and manufacturing on the electronics complex. According to the report, "even the most optimistic market growth would be unlikely to affect other electronic industries in the way suggested by proponents of

HDTV" (Webre, 1989: v). A subsequent congressional report released by the Office of Technology Assessment (OTA) in June 1990 was more optimistic about the "strategic" importance of HDTV, but the report acknowledged the difficulties in predicting how fast and from which technologies the market for HDTV would evolve (OTA, 1990). Secretary of Commerce Mosbacher abandoned his support even for a modest government role in HDTV, failing to release a previously announced HDTV plan. DARPA was instructed to cut its HDTV research budget by a third (to $20 million), and when Director Craig Fields later decided to fund additional research out of discretionary funds, the White House had him transferred out of the agency. As the prospects for a rescue package from Congress waned, however, HDTV gained steam at the FCC with the nomination of Alfred Sikes as chairman in August 1989. The development of HDTV was one of Sikes's top priorities. Under his leadership, the commission would create the blueprint for the transition strategy cemented several years later by Congress in the 1996 Telecommunications Act.

THE STANDARDS RACE

The new FCC chairman made a strong case in favor of the simulcasting approach. Despite the considerable risks involved in pursuing a strategy that would render the existing base of about 240 million NTSC receivers obsolete, Sikes believed that this approach was superior to augmentation. In June 1990 General Instrument announced that it had developed an all-digital HDTV system. The company's engineers succeeded in compressing an HDTV signal into a standard 6MHz frequency channel. This engineering breakthrough sent shockwaves across the world, as Japan and the EU had made considerable investments in HDTV initiatives based largely on analog components. In a sudden turn of events, the nation previously considered an HDTV laggard was at the forefront of a new generation of broadcasting technology. Sikes welcomed the breakthrough and announced that the commission would abandon work on NTSC-compatible HDTV. The decision was formally adopted with the release of the commission's First Report and Order on Advanced Television Systems.[7] The report simply established that the commission intended to select an HDTV system that worked independently of the

---

[7] Advanced Television Systems and Their Impact on the Existing Television Broadcast Service, MM Docket No. 87-268, First Report and Order, 5 FCC Rcd 5627 (1990).

existing NTSC system but, at the same time, was compatible with the existing 6MHz frequency allocation plan.

The importance of the First Report and Order cannot be overstated. While addressing a seemingly technical issue, it laid the foundations for the U.S. transition strategy based on temporarily loaning a second channel to incumbents for simulcasting a noncompatible signal. The commission was aware of the risks involved. The lessons from the transition to color TV were clear: a compatible system provided a much smoother migration path; even so, penetration, driven by content availability, was slower than anticipated. Achieving coordination in the introduction of programming and equipment would be more difficult today given the absence of vertically integrated firms. Yet the possibility of leapfrogging the Europeans and Japanese with a digital HDTV system was hard to resist. Sikes had been a champion of American HDTV interests at the NTIA, and now, as head of the FCC, he swayed fellow commissioners and the ACATS into a more challenging path, a path that he believed would ultimately prove rewarding for broadcasters and equipment manufacturers.

There was by no means consensus among broadcasters that simulcasting was preferable over augmentation. Having achieved their goal of preventing UHF sharing, incumbents were now apprehensive about HDTV (Brinkley, 1997). Implementing a more advanced TV system demanded considerable costs in new studio and transmission facilities. However, HDTV was not expected to bring higher advertising revenues, and a noncompatible system could even produce a temporary revenue drop if consumers failed to upgrade their receiving equipment. Many small station owners claimed that a forced conversion would put them out of business. Wiley nevertheless pushed simulcasting through the advisory committee by reminding incumbents that this approach significantly increased the likelihood that the government would loan each broadcaster a second 6MHz channel, locking out competitors for several decades. Once broadcasters got their spectrum, they could later negotiate more favorable migration terms in Congress, where local incumbents knew they could still count on broad cross-party support. Legislators were persuaded that, without significant technical enhancement, terrestrial broadcasters would not survive competition from cable and satellite. Without local broadcasting, incumbent congressmen would be more vulnerable to electoral challenges, particularly the members of the House of Representatives who were elected in local electoral districts. Thus, the survival of free local TV was also a question of political survival.

The release of the FCC's proposals for the allocation of the new licenses in October 1991 confirmed the approach outlined by Sikes.[8] These proposals became the blueprint for the American transition strategy and, despite several challenges, would be ratified several years later by Congress with only minor alterations. The heart of the plan was to limit the allocation of digital TV licenses to incumbent broadcasters. Each existing licensee would receive a second frequency channel to launch digital services. After a period of simulcasting, analog operations would be shut down and the analog channels would be returned to the government. This would allow for the co-location of digital and analog facilities by the incumbents. Potential new entrants would be allowed to apply for the new licenses only after allocations were made to all existing licensees, or in the case an incumbent failed to apply for a digital TV license or initiate construction of facilities within a specified time period (the commission suggested a three-year period for applications and a two-year period for construction). It was thus a "use it or lose it" approach. DTT licenses would be awarded for periods concurrent with the associated analog license and would not be independently transferable. According to the commission's own studies, available frequencies would be exhausted after a second 6MHz channel was allocated to all incumbents. Even worse, in the most crowded markets some low-power stations would have to be displaced to make room for new HDTV allotments to full-power commercial incumbents, and the commission proposed to do so if needed.[9]

The commission took great care in presenting the plan as an enhancement of the existing TV service rather than as the development of a new video distribution service: "[O]ur objective in this proceeding is to effect a major technological improvement in television transmission by allowing broadcasters to implement ATV, and not to launch a new and separate video service" (FCC, 1991: 3). Framing HDTV as a mere improvement of existing services was critical for two reasons. First, it gave political legitimacy to a strategy that openly benefited incumbents and in some cases even reduced competition in TV services. According

---

[8] Advanced Television Systems and Their Impact on the Existing Television Broadcast Service, MM Docket No. 87-268, Notice of Proposed Rulemaking, 6 FCC Rcd 7024 (1991).

[9] Low-power stations were authorized by the commission in 1982 on a secondary basis. They are allowed to operate as long as their signal does not interfere with full-power stations and must accept interference from primary licensees. Moreover, the commission may force a low-power station to yield to a new licensee.

to the commission, existing broadcasters had invested considerable resources and expertise in the present system, and therefore giving them the first opportunity to deploy HDTV appeared to be "the most practical and expedite way" to bring the new services to the public. Giving incumbents the opportunity to remain competitive with the use of the latest broadcasting technologies was critical to guarantee the continuity of free local TV. Furthermore, the commission did not believe it prudent "to accompany a major change in technology, such as conversion to ATV, with a change in the ownership structure of the entire broadcasting industry. Initially restricting eligibility for ATV frequencies to existing broadcasters thus would appear to serve the public interest by hastening and smoothing the transition to ATV transmission" (FCC, 1991: 3). Once again, the commission was turning the regime on its head to justify protection for incumbents. Diversity and effective market competition were the first casualties of the plan.

Second, framing HDTV as an improvement over existing services provided critical defense against possible judicial challenges to the plan. The legal question was whether the commission could restrict eligibility to existing broadcasters in the licensing process. Excluding other potential licensees raised concerns under the doctrine established by the Supreme Court in *Ashbacker*.[10] In this case, the Court held that the FCC must conduct a comparative hearing whenever there were before it mutually exclusive applications for a broadcast license. Allocating all available DTT licenses to incumbents locked out prospective market entrants at least during the simulcasting period – which by most estimates could extend for several decades. If HDTV was a new service, comparative hearings would be required. According to the commission, the plan did not violate *Ashbacker*, because the rules simply set licensee eligibility standards, which the commission was authorized to do if it considered that restricting eligibility was in the public interest. Furthermore, by requiring 100 percent simulcasting on the digital channel, the commission could reinforce its case that HDTV was part of the same license and did not represent a new video service. In any case, argued FCC officials, new entrants would be able to apply for DTT licenses if incumbents failed to apply for licenses or construct facilities in time (the "use it or lose it" doctrine), or through the regular process of challenging incumbents at the time of license renewal. But as Butler argued, these alleged opportunities

---

[10] *Ashbacker Radio Corp. v. FCC*, 326 US 327 (1945).

for entry were largely illusionary:

> NTSC licenses applying early for HDTV licenses would have at least six years in which to construct an HDTV broadcast facility. In the event that a broadcaster failed to meet the deadline, the FCC could conceivably grant a hardship extension upon the showing of a good faith effort. Nor is there any security in the prospect of an aspiring broadcaster acquiring a channel when the license of an existing broadcaster comes up for renewal. The history of the FCC reveals a strong preference for license renewal of incumbent licensees, and statistics overwhelmingly indicate that an existing broadcaster's application for license renewal will be approved. (1992: 170–171)

The proposals also addressed the switchover issue. The commission argued that setting a firm date for broadcasters to surrender their analog frequencies appeared necessary to provide credible signals about the transition to broadcasters, the public, and other potential users of spectrum. The proposals considered several possible alternatives about how to select such a date: first, to specify a certain nationwide penetration rate of digital TV receivers that would trigger the start of the switch-off process; second, to establish similar criteria but on a market-by-market basis so as not to impose hardships on broadcasters in less affluent markets; and, third, to establish a firm date by which broadcasters would have to surrender their analog channels and complete the transition, independently of the level of equipment penetration achieved. After a period of consultation, the commission issued rules on the allotment of DTT licenses in April 1992.[11]

The final rules deviated little from the proposals presented a few months before. The commission reaffirmed that restricting the initial eligibility for DTT licenses to existing broadcasters advanced the public interest by expediting the transition. Such initial period was estimated to last for two years, although the commission expected few DTT licenses to become available thereafter in the most desirable markets. The "use it or lose it" period remained at five years, with extensions granted only under strict guidelines and for reasons "beyond the permittee's control" (inability to obtain adequate financing would only be considered

---

[11] Advanced Television Systems and Their Impact on the Existing Television Broadcast Service, MM Docket No. 87-268, Second Report and Order/Further Notice of Proposed Rulemaking, 7 FCC Rcd 3340 (1992).

under "extraordinary circumstances"). The commission explicitly refused to make equipment penetration a factor in granting extensions,
noting that availability of programming was the key factor to drive penetration. In other words, the commission expected incumbents to lead
the transition. According to ACATS estimates, while the cost of a complete upgrade for a local station could be up to $15 million (a figure
that exceeded the value of several small-market licensees), the necessary
equipment simply to pass through an HDTV network signal could be
bought for as little as $1 million.

As noted, skepticism about the commercial prospects of HDTV was
growing among incumbents, who were still reeling from the effects of
the advertising market downturn that followed the economic slowdown
of the early 1990s.[12] Many began to wonder whether the additional frequency channel would be put to more profitable use by broadcasting several standard-definition (SDTV) channels in digital format rather than
a single HDTV signal. After all, digital compression enabled incumbents
to squeeze as many as four SDTV channels of resolution similar to the existing NTSC signals in a single 6MHz channel. Unlike HDTV, additional
channels would bring additional advertising revenues. Increasingly, NAB
officials talked about the need for "spectrum flexibility," which essentially meant allowing broadcasters to utilize the second channel as they
saw fit as long as they transmitted in digital format. The idea infuriated Sikes and his fellow commissioners. This was not the bargain that
the FCC was brokering. Besides, if the commission allowed flexibility,
the plan would be prone to *Ashbacker* challenges because broadcasters would clearly offer new services. This was explicitly written in the
new DTT license rules: "[T]he reason broadcasters are being allowed a
second channel is to permit them to move to an improved technology
without service disruption. If a broadcaster chooses not to broadcast in
ATV, there is no reason for awarding that broadcaster an additional license."[13] Accordingly, the commission asserted the intention to impose
a 100 percent simulcasting requirement "at the earliest possible point"
in the transition, tentatively no later than four years after the initiation
of HDTV services (the commission estimated that the transition would
take fifteen years to complete).

---

[12] According to the Television Bureau of Advertising (TVB), advertising expenditure in
broadcast TV contracted 4.3 percent in 1991.

[13] Advanced Television Systems and Their Impact on the Existing Television Broadcast Service, MM Docket No. 87-268, Second Report and Order/Further Notice of
Proposed Rulemaking, 7 FCC Rcd 3340 (1992), at 4.

Incumbent broadcasters were lukewarm about the new license rules. On the one hand, the rules cemented their control of broadcast spectrum. On the other, many feared that HDTV might turn into a Pyrrhic victory as the commission forced the industry into a technological transition with few rewards accruing to those supposed to implement it, particularly in the absence of spectrum flexibility. The suggestion that the transition could be completed in fifteen years was also a source of concern. This would require large investments in the coming years in an untried technology, independent of the pace of consumer adoption of reception equipment. The NAB and other trade organizations insisted on several changes. In particular, they demanded spectrum flexibility and a staggered approach to the construction requirement, with large markets implementing first and small markets last, with enforcement being subject to equipment penetration benchmarks. The commission, however, rejected these demands in an order released just weeks before the November 1992 elections.[14] Sikes was an uncompromising enthusiast of HDTV, and he firmly believed that the construction and simulcasting requirements imposed were more than justified by the opportunity to develop HDTV that the commission was granting to incumbents. The uncompromising attitude of the commission was a source of increasing concern for incumbents. Yet the NAB and other trade organizations decided to wait for the outcome of the November 1992 general elections. A change of government would most certainly change the composition of the commission (out of the five commission seats two were to be filled by the incoming government) and bring a new chairman (the new president was entitled to designate the chairman among the five commissioners). Without Sikes at the helm, HDTV would lose much steam.

These calculations proved partially right. The triumph of the Bill Clinton–Al Gore formula brought significant changes to the digital TV policies adopted. Yet this did not mean that broadcasters would be left to adopt the new technology at their own pace and liking. As discussed in Chapter 2, digital TV was an important component of the NII agenda brought in by the new administration. The digitization of the existing terrestrial broadcast network became part of the larger effort to deploy new communication infrastructure and service across the nation. Vice President Al Gore championed these efforts. As a senator, Gore had sponsored several of the HDTV bills vetoed by the Bush administration. He

---

[14] Advanced Television Systems and Their Impact on the Existing Television Broadcast Service, MM Docket No. 87-268, Memorandum of Opinion and Order/Third Report and Order/Further Notice of Proposed Rulemaking, 7 FCC Rcd 6924 (1992).

nominated an old-time friend, Reed Hundt, for the top FCC post. Hundt was certainly much less enthusiastic about HDTV than his predecessor. In fact, he was publicly cautious and privately cynical about the transition strategy created by the salient FCC leadership and the ACATS. As he later recalled,

> I never met anyone who truly believed that the broadcasters would give back the analog channels. In the foreseeable future, Americans were not about to throw away their 200 million analog televisions, so broadcasters would not stop sending signals to them. Nor did anyone truly think high-definition televisions would supplement analog television – not at several thousand dollars a set to watch the exact same shows available on existing televisions, albeit in a sharper resolution. We had inherited a crazy policy. (Hundt, 2000: 65)

However, Hundt did not intend to grant incumbent broadcasters those valuable frequencies without strings attached. With the new leadership at the White House and the FCC, the focus of the transition would change from bringing sharper pictures to the American public to bringing new information services (e.g., health care, government services, distance learning) into every U.S. household. Upgrading to a digital network with near universal penetration seemed a logical way to proceed. In other words, the focus was now on digital TV and so-called ancillary services but not HDTV. Broadcasters welcomed the policy turn. Few believed that HDTV would be a profitable venture under the terms of the plan advanced by the previous commission, and so broadcasters were happy to kill – or at least move to the backburner – a creature of their own making. If the new administration wanted to create an ubiquitous platform for the delivery of new information services, broadcasters were ready to take on the job. But, of course, the terms of the bargain had to be renegotiated.

AN IMPERFECT ALLIANCE

Despite a small Democratic majority in the Senate, Hundt's nomination was tied up by Republican opposition for several months. Meanwhile, the race to develop the American digital TV standard coordinated by the ACATS was in full steam. The commission wanted to ensure that significant industry consensus existed before the adoption of the final technical specifications. This was precisely what the ACATS was supposed to achieve. Also, the recent experience of AM stereo had demonstrated that market forces alone do not necessarily produce timely standards to enable coordination in the introduction of complementary products (i.e., programming and receiving equipment). Without standards, AM stereo failed to develop. The commission had taken its share of criticism for the fiasco.[15] The stakes were much larger in the case of digital TV. It involved reequipping 240 million analog TV sets and the facilities of about 1,500 broadcasters. The commission was unwilling to take risks. From the very start, FCC officials took an active role in the standardization process. Given the failed policy experiment with AM stereo and the high-profile that HDTV had taken, it was clear that the commission would have the final word on the selection of the system and closely monitor the progress of the race.

Wiley initially encouraged companies to develop competing systems but gradually prodded competitors to cooperate under the framework of the National Cooperative Research Act of 1984. The act had been passed in response to concerns about public sponsorship of R&D programs abroad and provided antitrust relief to joint research ventures. Given that national governments in Japan and Europe were aggressively sponsoring HDTV consortia, it seemed logical for Sikes and Wiley to encourage companies to cooperate on the design of the American standard. In February 1993 ACATS released the results of the last round of tests. Interestingly, the tests were not conducted by the FCC but by a nonprofit corporation set up by broadcasters, the Advanced Television Testing Center (ATTC). The commission was keen to avoid any litigation based on test results and preferred to delegate the task to broadcasters. According to ACATS, the results showed no substantial differences between four of the five systems tested, yet none performed flawlessly. The committee recommended that the four systems be perfected and sent back to the ATTC for an additional round of tests (Brinkley, 1997). Facing the prospects of expensive retesting and possible litigation by losing proponents, the competing consortia accepted the terms of a truce brokered by Wiley: the four systems would be merged into a single proposal that would combine "the best of all" systems. The commission blessed the agreement: a concerted effort seemed to obtain the sort of industry consensus needed to expedite the transition. In May 1993 the so-called Grand Alliance was formally announced.

[15] See, for example, Besen and Johnson (1986). In fact, the FCC initially planned to define a standard for AM stereo but later reversed course amid protests from some broadcasters and fear of litigation by losing contenders.

The new consortium was hailed as a success of the American standardization approach in high-technology industries. Led by the FCC at arm's length, the race had resulted in significant innovation, while at the same time producing an agreement backed by major equipment manufacturers (e.g., Zenith, Thomson, General Instruments, and Philips), information technology developers (e.g., Bell Labs and Sarnoff Research), and broadcasters (e.g., ACATS). The benefits of standards coordination had been achieved while avoiding the heavy hand of government picking winners and losers in the market, an approach that left Europe and Japan stuck with an analog HDTV system. Moreover, without engaging in overt protectionism, the process resulted in significant participation by American companies that would at least hold substantial interests in HDTV patents. It appeared that, in the end, the United States had emerged as the winner in an international race in which only a few years ago it was a distant third. Nonetheless, optimism soon receded as the Grand Alliance faced the challenging task of accommodating the interests of a wide variety of participants. Two main camps emerged: on the one side, TV set manufacturers and existing broadcasters; on the other, the computer industry.

A relative newcomer to the HDTV proceedings, the computer industry was significantly underrepresented in the ACATS and the ATSC. Yet it had suddenly become a key player with the development of a digital HDTV system based largely on information technology components. Furthermore, Silicon Valley interests had close connections with the Clinton administration and started pressing the government for more participation in the HDTV standardization process. Finally confirmed in November 1993, Hundt personally encouraged firms such as Microsoft and Apple to become involved. He hoped this would counterbalance the overwhelming power wielded by broadcasters and help the commission steer the transition in a direction less favorable to incumbents' interests and more in tune with the new administration's NII agenda.

The two camps soon clashed over the picture format to be adopted by the Grand Alliance.[16] Computer industry representatives aggressively pushed for a system that utilized progressive scanning, a method typically used in computer monitors and that would better serve for the display of applications other than video programming. Broadcasters

---

[16] The picture format is determined by three main factors: the picture aspect ratio (e.g., the conventional 4:3 or the widescreen 16:9), the number of lines per picture frame (e.g., the more conventional 420 lines of SDTV or the 1,080 lines of true HDTV), and the scanning method used (e.g., interlaced vs. progressive).

and TV set manufacturers opposed progressive scanning and favored the conventional interlaced scanning system used in existing analog sets. They argued that progressive scanning would unnecessarily add to the cost of receivers without rendering better images. At the heart of the debate were opposing views about the future evolution of the industry. While computer interests argued that the new system needed to accommodate the inevitable convergence of the computer and the TV into a single device, broadcasters and manufacturers claimed that convergence would ultimately be limited by the different functionality of the TV (used primarily for entertainment) and the PC (used for task-oriented purposes). In the end, a compromise was reached whereby the system would accommodate several different picture formats (eighteen in total) based on different scanning methods, aspect ratios, and lines per frame. This flexibility would allow broadcasters to select between different formats according to the specific applications they favored, and equipment manufacturers could offer a wide variety of receivers to match the public's demands better. On the other hand, flexibility came at the expense of coordination problems in the introduction of services and equipment (as different broadcasters in the same market could well make different picture format choices) and greater confusion for consumers. Although this was not what Wiley and the broadcasting community had in mind for the Grand Alliance, it was as good a compromise as could possibly be reached, given the increased political power of the computer industry and the new White House orientation.

In November 1995 ACATS voted to approve the system developed by the Grand Alliance and recommended to the FCC that the system be adopted as the American digital TV standard. In due course, the FCC opened a period of public consultation about the system.[17] During this period, the computer industry launched a last-ditch effort to block the use of interlaced scanning, which according to its representatives would severely delay the convergence process as well as the realization of the administration's NII goals. The consultation provided a better arena for bargaining than ACATS, where the industry remained considerably underrepresented. Industry lobbyists had now assembled a larger coalition under an organization called the Computer Industry Coalition on Advanced Television Services (CICATS) that included several heavyweights

---

[17] Advanced Television Systems and Their Impact on the Existing Television Broadcast Service, MM Docket No. 87-268, Fifth Further Notice of Proposed Rulemaking, 11 FCC Rcd 6235 (1996).

such as Microsoft, Apple, Compaq, Hewlett-Packard, Intel, and Oracle. Riding on a wave of public enthusiasm about the Internet and other innovations, CICATS representatives testified before the Senate Commerce Committee against adoption of the ACATS system and suggested voluntary standards for digital TV. According to CICATS, a receiver capable of supporting the eighteen formats of the system would be costly, thus retarding consumer adoption. This would create disincentives for the introduction of advanced information services based on the convergence of computers and the television. Other parties, such as the cable industry and several Hollywood film celebrities, joined CICATS in opposing an FCC mandate.[18] The commission became reluctant to proceed with the recommendations of the ACATS in face of the considerable opposition to the adoption of the ACATS system. Instead, it decided to attempt to bring the parties together in support of a baseline system. While not a Grand Alliance advocate, Chairman Hundt worried that the CICATS coalition would obstruct the adoption of any standard, leading to a delay of the transition for several years.

FCC Commissioner Susan Ness led the task of attempting to mend fences. After four weeks of intense negotiations at the end of 1996, the parties came to an agreement: the FCC would adopt the ACATS recommendations but not the table that specified the eighteen picture formats. Broadcasters and equipment manufacturers would therefore be completely free to choose what picture format to support. The commission welcomed the agreement as advancing the transition while eliminating unnecessary government regulation of video formats, and moved expeditiously to rubber-stamp it.[19]

After almost a decade of intense commercial negotiations, countless technical tests, and several lobbying battles, the United States finally seemed to have a digital TV standard on which industry players and consumers could make long-term investment plans for the transition. However, the reality would prove more complex than that. It soon became clear that the agreement was incomplete as it addressed the concerns of only the main three parties involved (broadcasters, equipment manufacturers, and the computer industry) for a single distribution

---

[18] The main concern voiced by Hollywood's artistic community was that the Grand Alliance standard would prevent the broadcast of movies in their original aspect ratio. Yet this was not supported by the Motion Picture Association of America (MPAA), the trade organization for the major film and TV studios.

[19] Advanced Television Systems and Their Impact on the Existing Television Broadcast Service, MM Docket No. 87-268, Fourth Report and Order, 11 FCC Rcd 17771 (1996).

platform (digital terrestrial TV, or DTT). The American television industry of the late 1990s was in fact much more complex than that, and as the transition got under way new issues emerged and new players would come to demand that their interests and concerns be addressed. In other words, the adoption of the ACATS system was only the beginning of a long standardization process that would later demand a more proactive approach by the commission as new standards battles threatened to derail the government's entire transition strategy.

FIVE

A New Bargain

ACATS was originally expected to produce recommendations on an HDTV standard. Ironically, when the FCC finally adopted the ACATS recommendations in December 1996, interest in HDTV had almost completely waned among broadcasters and the FCC alike. Since 1987, when the FCC started the HDTV proceeding at the request of incumbent broadcasters, the stakes had shifted considerably. The transition was no longer about sharper pictures or the competitiveness of the electronics sector. Digital TV offered opportunities never imagined by HDTV advocates back in 1987. The problem was that the transition strategy inherited from the Sikes commission was centered on HDTV: incumbents would get a second frequency channel because, based on their control of resources (e.g., popular programming) and technical expertise, they were the most likely to succeed in implementing HDTV. Sharply divided about the commercial opportunities offered by the transition, broadcasters split into two camps. Some felt it was imperative to migrate as soon as possible to match in quality and services what other platforms (i.e., cable and satellite) would provide. Others deemed the upfront costs unjustified – at least until a significant percentage of the population could actually receive the new services. Yet everyone agreed that it was vital to keep potential competitors off the DTT market. In a sense, as HDTV faded, the policymaking process returned to its point of origin: a struggle by incumbent broadcasters to retain spectrum control and defend a regulatory edifice founded half a century ago.

The Clinton administration supported the transition efforts for reasons closely associated with its NII agenda. Digital video broadcasting was identified as a key application that could drive demand for advanced communications infrastructure and facilitate the universal availability of new information services. Notwithstanding the picture format controversy, the standard developed by the Grand Alliance was largely based on computer technologies that made it flexible enough to accommodate a broad range of data delivery applications and allowed possible extension to other transport platforms (e.g., broadband telecom networks). Moreover, if nothing else, the transition would eventually release valuable frequencies that could be redeployed for other uses and, best of all, at a price.

Under the Sikes plan, about 72MHz would be freed up after the fifteen years that the transition was expected to last. Gore and Hundt wanted more spectrum to be released, and sooner. Fifteen years was an eternity for an administration that had campaigned on the urgent need to balance the federal budget. The plan needed to be revised so that at least some of the most desirable frequencies could be auctioned almost immediately. Broadcasters were generally pleased about the lack of reference to HDTV by Clinton administration officials. Yet they feared that complete abandonment would renew questions about the transition strategy developed by Sikes. In other words, if incumbent broadcasters were no longer interested in doing HDTV, then why award them an entire new channel, and not just enough capacity to simulcast their current programming in digital format? Simulcasting all local broadcasters in SDTV would, on average, require only about two frequency channels (and maybe less depending on the number of stations in the market). The flexibility of the ACATS standard allowed for such implementation. Without HDTV, both the political and the legal justification for the existing plan became questionable.

One of the early legislative successes of the new administration was the passage of the Omnibus Budget Reconciliation Act of 1993 (OBRA-1993). Among other things, the act authorized the FCC, for the first time, to assign licenses by competitive bidding.[1] The authorization came at a critical time as the commission was preparing to license the second generation of cellular telephony, the so-called personal communication services (PCS) (the first generation of mobile telephony licenses had been assigned by lottery). Monetizing the use of spectrum for cellular telephony would create an important precedent as policymakers and the industry renegotiated the transition strategy. Broadcasters opposed the OBRA-93 authorization even when it explicitly excluded broadcast licenses. They feared that as auctions revealed the market value of radio spectrum, policymakers would come under pressure to take a second

---

[1] 47 U.S.C. § 309(j).

look at the existing transition plan. Yet, this opposition was mitigated by fears of retaliation from the commission (which strongly favored the authorization) as it prepared to undertake implementation of must-carry and other key provisions of the Cable Act of 1992 (Hazlett, 1998).

The result of the first spectrum auction held in July 1994 confirmed broadcasters' worst fears: the auction of less than 1MHz nationwide (which allowed for deployment of narrowband applications such as two-way paging) produced $650 million. In early 1995 the auction of 60MHz for regional PCS licenses netted a staggering $7.7 billion. Broadcasters were right in opposing spectrum auctions. With the revelation of the hidden value of the spectrum that they had always used free of charge, broadcasters would now have to walk a thin line between advocating flexibility in the use of the second channel for services other than HDTV and undermining the political and legal legitimacy of the existing transition plan. In other words, in pushing for spectrum flexibility, they risked losing, as aptly described by Chairman Hundt, "beachfront property on the Cybersea."

The first official document of the Hundt era on digital TV signaled the intention to introduce significant changes to the existing transition strategy:

In previous orders in this Advanced Television (ATV) proceeding, our focus was on fostering the development of High Definition Television (HDTV). With that focus we made a series of decisions regarding, among other things, the nature of ATV service, eligibility for ATV transition channels, and the transition period. Technological evolution obliges us to revisit some of those decisions and consider new information, which we do in this document.[2]

The new proposals acknowledged a new political reality that resulted in little support for HDTV and that required a new bargaining round between regulators and incumbents to define how digital TV would be implemented. In essence, the proposals suggested the need to revisit the decisions on simulcasting, spectrum allocation, and the transition timetable, in light of the fact that digital broadcasters were likely to offer not one HDTV service but several SDTV channels and possibly ancillary data services. The commission offered the following new compromise: broadcasters would get the flexibility they requested to use the second

[2] Advanced Television Systems and Their Impact on the Existing Television Broadcast Service, MM Docket No. 87-268, Fourth Further Notice of Proposed Rulemaking/Third Notice of Inquiry, 10 FCC Rcd 10540 (1995), at 3–4.

channel in ways they considered most beneficial as long as the programming offered in analog was also simulcast (whether in HDTV or SDTV) on the digital channel. In return, the transition period will be significantly shortened and the spectrum plan modified to allow more frequencies to be reclaimed. To this end, the commission proposed to concentrate the new digital channel assignments on a "core" band within the existing broadcast spectrum. Frequencies outside this core would be recovered in advance of the eventual switch-off of analog TV and in contiguous nationwide blocks. In other words, broadcasters would be loaned a second channel even without doing HDTV. In return, however, they would have to accept a more aggressive plan in terms of construction of facilities and spectrum recovery.

Although confident that the new plan would survive *Ashbacker* challenges, Hundt was aware that broadcasters' use of the second channel to offer several SDTV signals and data services opened a Pandora's box of questions. For example, would the public interest obligations apply to one or all of the SDTV channels provided by a local broadcaster? What ancillary services would broadcasters be allowed to offer? Could they lease out spectrum capacity to third parties? Implementation of must-carry obligations was particularly problematic. Under the 1992 Cable Act, cable operators were forced to carry, "without material degradation," only the "primary video" originated by local broadcasters, as long as this signal did not "substantially duplicate" that of another local station carried by the same operator. The implementation of the statute in a simulcasting environment or when local stations broadcast multiple SDTV channels presented difficult legal questions. It became increasingly evident that Congress would have to be called in to sanction whatever new agreement was reached between the industry and the commission.

At the time, Congress was debating new legislation proposed by the Clinton administration to liberalize market entry both within and across communications sectors. The government expected market competition to be the driving force behind the deployment of the NII. The bill was hotly contested, for it threatened the monopoly rents of several incumbent players that had long benefited from regulatory barriers to entry and from the compartmentalization of the industry into separate sectors. Several versions included spectrum flexibility for digital broadcasters (Goodman, 1997), and such flexibility was consistent with the bill's deregulatory intent. The problem was that the commission was ready to give beachfront spectrum property to incumbent broadcasters for free, while others were being charged hundreds of millions at public auctions.

This required the limitation of spectrum flexibility in order to prevent a public outcry from mobile telephony operators. In other words, flexibility would need to be accompanied with a mechanism that addressed this asymmetry and somehow monetized the additional spectrum given to broadcasters.

What ensued during the 1995–1997 period was one of the most dramatic rent-seeking battles waged in the history of the American broadcasting industry since the formative period of the communications sector in the early 1920s. At stake were property rights over prime spectrum as well as incumbency rents based on regulatory barriers to market entry. The context resembled the early 1970s period when, as a result of the growth of cable, a heterodox political coalition called for revisiting the regime established by the Sixth Report of 1952. This time, a new coalition demanded changes to a transition strategy that carefully preserved a regime that limited to a handful the number of licensees per market, when in fact digital TV opened significant opportunities for increased competition and access to the airwaves. The new coalition was as heterodox as the previous one: it comprised free-market economists calling for efficient spectrum allocation, academics, and media access advocates pressing for more opportunities for community and noncommercial broadcasting, potential market entrants seeking access to the airwaves, and competing spectrum users. Similarly, key allies were found among regime reform advocates within the commission and the White House, as well as political entrepreneurs in Congress. The coalition seized the window of opportunity created by the PCS auctions to create pressure on Congress and the FCC to revisit the second-channel loan plan. For the first time, having broadcasters pay for the use of spectrum was seriously debated in Congress and elsewhere.

The Republican landslide victory in the 1994 midterm elections reshaped the political landscape for digital TV. Particularly important was the change in command of key Senate positions. Senate Majority Leader Bob Dole and the new chairman of the influential Committee on Commerce, Science and Transportation, Senator Larry Pressler, were both fervent advocates of spectrum auctions for broadcast licenses. They were also fervent enemies of federal funding for Public Broadcasting Service (PBS), the small public broadcasting network founded in the late 1960s to link the existing noncommercial stations. In the fall of 1995, Pressler unveiled a radical new proposal that would replace government contributions for PBS (at the time at about $285 million per year) with a trust fund initially financed by the receipts from the auction of digital TV licenses. This was the first time that a high-ranking member of Congress seriously articulated a plan for auctioning digital TV licenses (De Witt, 1995). An alternative plan, introduced by Republican Senator John McCain, required the commission to auction all new spectrum licenses, irrespective of the service offered (Andrews, 1995). In the wake of the staggering amount raised by the PCS license auctions, several congressmen preferred to confront broadcasters rather than pay the political costs associated with funding cuts to popular federal programs in order to balance the budget. Estimates about the expected receipts from auctioning the digital TV licenses varied wildly. The commission predicted the market value of the licenses to be between $11 billion and $70 billion, depending on the future availability of spectrum and the rules attached to the licenses.[3]

The numbers grabbed the attention of the press establishment, which started referring to the licensing plan as a "spectrum giveaway" to incumbents.[4] Hundt also endorsed the idea of digital TV spectrum auctions. As he recalled later, the second-channel loan plan would be hard to justify, particularly because local broadcasters had not developed credible plans for digital TV services:

> Ironically, the spectrum was intrinsically valuable for mobile communications, if not digital television broadcast. It could be auctioned for billions if Congress did not limit its use. But Congress, broadcasters, and previous Commissions were bent on giving analog television stations license holders the gift of the so-called second channel. This would be the largest grant of government largesse since the 19th century donation of 10 percent of the public land in the West to three dozen railroad companies in order to persuade them to build transcontinental railroads. Yet unlike the railroads the recipients had no plausible business plan for using the boon from government. (Hundt, 2000: 65)

The FCC chairman instead favored a plan whereby the new licenses would be auctioned and the collected receipts used to provide Internet service to every public school and library in the country, one of Hundt's

---

[3] Letter from Robert M. Pepper, Chief, FCC Office of Plans and Policy, to Senator Joseph Lieberman, May 5, 1995.

[4] "Congress plans to take $270 billion out of Medicare, almost $200 billion out of Medicaid and about $40 billion out of tax credits for low-paid workers. Yet it apparently has enough cash to send politically powerful broadcasters a gift worth perhaps $40 billion." Editorial in the *New York Times*, October 25, 1995, p. 20.

(and Gore's) pet projects. He actively enlisted the cooperation of broadcasters' traditional and new foes against the spectrum "giveaway," including the press establishment, the computer industry, educators, and media advocates. At a minimum, Hundt wanted unambiguous public interest concessions on the part of broadcasters in return for the digital licenses, including a minimum number of hours of children's programming per week and free airtime for political candidates. While these concessions would not alter the essence of the established regime, they at least imposed enforceable obligations and could eventually reduce the dependence of congressmen on local broadcasters for reelection. Nevertheless, the commission's hands were tied. Because of the prohibition to auction broadcast licenses included in the OBRA-93 authorization, any credible threat about auctions for digital TV licenses would have to come directly from Congress.

The broadcast industry was divided about how to react to this offensive against the DTT licensing plan. The big three networks (NBC, ABC, and CBS) and MSTV considered the threat of spectrum auctions serious enough to warrant a renewed commitment to HDTV. In submissions to the commission, these organizations reaffirmed the centrality of HDTV in their plans for the second channel and even encouraged the commission to set minimum HDTV requirements.[5] Other parties also favored a minimum HDTV mandate. Equipment manufacturers worried that the absence of such a mandate would significantly delay the replacement of older analog sets as viewers opted for relatively inexpensive converter boxes to receive SDTV signals and deferred buying new HDTV sets. The Grand Alliance partners claimed that the opportunities offered by digital TV did not warrant a major shift in the commission's strategy and urged the agency to prevent broadcasters from reneging on their end of the old bargain, namely, to utilize the second channel for HDTV. As they explained, opponents of the plan were rightly questioning its legitimacy in the absence of a credible commitment to HDTV: "[T]hese objections fall away if the Commission adopts policies to ensure that the predominant use of the ATV channel is for free over-the-air television with HDTV as the primary application. Without such assurances, however, the Commission's approach to lend broadcasters a second channel is not sustainable either as good policy or as a matter of law."[6] In this sense,

---

[5] Broadcasters' Comments to the Fourth Notice of Proposed Rulemaking, MM Docket No. 87-268, November 20, 1995.

[6] Reply Comments of the Digital HDTV Grand Alliance to the Fourth Notice of Proposed Rulemaking, MM Docket No. 87-268, January 22, 1996, at 8.

equipment manufacturers concurred with the claims of the pro-auction coalition: without HDTV, the plan amounted to a massive giveaway to local incumbents (Wiley, 1994).

Other incumbents, however, remained skeptical about demand for HDTV services and were confident that Congress would bless the existing plan even without an HDTV mandate. This was the official NAB position:

> HDTV is an exciting technology and NAB enthusiastically encourages its deployment in the marketplace. Unfortunately, predicting winners and losers in mass media services is a difficult and risky proposition. . . . While the vast majority of broadcasters undoubtedly will present a substantial amount of HDTV programming, they and the viewers should be the ones to determine how much and when HDTV programming will be broadcast. Fixed rules about minimum quantity of HDTV are simply unwarranted and potentially could delay the ultimate return of NTSC spectrum by elongating the transition period.[7]

Having won several battles over spectrum before, NAB officials were confident that the auction plan could be blocked either at the commission, in Congress, or in the courts. Their counterarguments stressed the "hidden costs" of auctions. The main alleged cost would be the demise of free local broadcasting, as existing stations would be unable to compete for licenses with the deep-pocketed telephone companies and other potential bidders (of course, there was no mention that the FCC could simply require that licensees offer nonsubscription services). Put differently, the survival of free television was at stake, and the DTT migration was key for local stations to compete effectively with subscription-based services in the digital era. This was the classic "economic hardship" argument successfully used against cable in the late 1960s. Furthermore, argued the NAB, selling the spectrum after the transition in nationwide contiguous blocks made far more sense than selling it in piecemeal fashion before the shutoff of NTSC signals. The existing plan already poses great challenges to broadcasters because it requires stations to provide digital programming before viewers acquired digital reception equipment. With spectrum auctions, concluded the NAB, the transition will simply never happen.

---

[7] Comments of the National Association of Broadcasters to the Fourth Notice of Proposed Rulemaking, MM Docket No. 87-268, November 20, 1995.

THE TELECOMMUNICATIONS ACT OF 1996

Armed with these arguments, the trade organizations, though bitterly divided on minimum HDTV requirements and other issues, lobbied intensively to avert broadcast spectrum auctions. The plans presented by Pressler and McCain failed to pass, but the controversy continued through the fall of 1995, along with debates over the new telecommunications legislation. The issue came to a climax in early 1996, when Congress prepared for a final vote on a new telecom bill that included several important provisions related to the transition. First, the bill ratified the restriction on the initial eligibility of digital TV licenses to incumbent broadcasters. This was critical to prevent *Ashbacker* challenges to the licensing plan. Interestingly, the bill was written so as to avoid a direct license award by Congress: "[I]f the Commission determines to issue additional licenses for advanced television services, the Commission (1) should limit the initial eligibility for such licenses to persons that, as of the date of such issuance, are licensed to operate a television broadcast station or hold a permit to construct such a station."[8] Second, the bill gave broadcasters flexibility to use the digital channel subject to a number of conditions, the details of which were left to be decided by the FCC. The bill authorized – but did not require – the commission to stipulate a minimum amount of HDTV programming per day, and to limit the provision of ancillary services "so as to avoid derogation of any advanced television services, including high definition television broadcasts."[9] Should these ancillary services be subscription-based, the bill authorized the commission to impose a spectrum use fee, the level of which should approximate the amount that would have been generated had the spectrum been allocated through competitive bidding. Finally, the bill did not set a firm date for the switch-off of analog services. Instead, it directed the commission to conduct an evaluation of the transition and the possible reallocation of broadcast spectrum within ten years of the issuing of the digital licenses.

In essence, the new bill met the key demands made by the NAB: the licenses would go to the incumbents with few strings attached, and the date for the return of the analog channels was left unspecified. Combined with a number of other favorable provisions (e.g., raise in ownership caps, extension in the duration of broadcast licenses, and reduced scrutiny for license renewals), there was hardly more than the incumbents could

---

[8] 47 U.S.C. § 336(a).
[9] 47 U.S.C. § 336(b).

have bargained for. Yet, many legislators initially refused to endorse the bill and reacted against what they perceived as a broken promise from broadcasters. The second channel was meant for HDTV; if broadcasters were not interested in HDTV, then those frequencies should be awarded to the highest bidder. Senate Majority Leader Bob Dole lambasted the bill for its generosity to broadcasters and threatened to block passage until the issue of digital licenses and spectrum recovery was properly addressed. A compromise was finally reached whereby the majority leader would bring the bill to a vote but licenses would not be awarded pending further debate about spectrum auctions. The compromise was sealed with a letter from the five FCC commissioners to Senate leaders in which they pledged to postpone the award of licenses until after these congressional deliberations.[10]

As a result, the debate about digital licenses and broadcast spectrum auctions only intensified in the aftermath of the passage of the act in February 1996. Five congressional hearings were held in the following months, and several spectrum allocation plans introduced. The plans hovered around three main alternatives (CBO, 1997). The first was the so-called baseline plan, as outlined by the commission in its July 1995 proposals and further elaborated in a July 1996 document.[11] According to this plan, incumbent broadcasters would get the additional channel for digital TV as required by statute. The great majority of the digital channels would be in a core region of the broadcast spectrum between channels 7 and 51. This would allow for the recovery of 138MHz of broadcast spectrum (as opposed to 72MHz), some of it almost immediately in the lightly used band between channels 60 and 69 (only ninety-seven analog stations and about thirty new digital stations would utilize this band nationwide). Being adjacent to spectrum utilized by wireless mobile services, these frequencies were prime candidates for licensing through competitive bidding or use by public safety authorities.

The Clinton administration proposed an alternative plan whereby the transition period would be reduced from fifteen to ten years and, most important, the spectrum expected to be cleared by the transition would be auctioned as early as 2002 (i.e., three years before the switch-off of analog TV). In order to protect incumbents, the licenses auctioned

---

[10] Letter from FCC Chairman Reed E. Hundt and Commissioners Quello, Barrett, Ness, and Chong to Senator Larry Pressler, February 1, 1996 (142 Cong. Rec. S 684).

[11] Advanced Television Systems and Their Impact on the Existing Television Broadcast Service, MM Docket No. 87-268, Sixth Further Notice of Proposed Rulemaking, 11 FCC Rcd 10968 (1996).

before the completion of the transition would only grant the right to use any unencumbered portion of the spectrum during the simulcasting period (so-called overlay licenses). After the switch-off of analog stations, they would be converted into full-blown licenses. This modest proposal departed relatively little from the baseline plan and had the advantage of generating early auction receipts. The Congressional Budget Office (CBO) estimated that about $10 billion could be collected by 2002 (CBO, 1997), although selling spectrum before it became effectively available raised several questions. What if digital TV penetration fell behind expectations? Would the government still force analog stations to switch off, leaving millions without TV service, in order to make room for the new licensees? A third and more radical plan introduced by Senator Pressler sought to replace a government-mandated transition with a market-based one (Hazlett, 2001). According to the plan, overlay licenses would be auctioned not just in lightly used bands but across the whole broadcast spectrum. Incumbents would receive digital licenses against payment of a deposit (to be refunded upon return of the analog channel) and would be free to use these frequencies for services other than broadcasting, as long as they provided viewers with a "comparable free replacement" for terrestrial TV service (e.g., a prepaid cable subscription). There would be no mandated transition period or a digital TV standard authorized by the FCC. This was a bold departure from the existing transition strategy but still consistent with the letter (though not the intent) of the 1996 act.

Incumbent broadcasters resisted these proposals. Even the modest overlay plan advanced by the administration was rejected. The NAB mounted a formidable lobbying campaign against broadcast spectrum auctions (Snider, 2001). Local broadcasters across the nation ran spots prepared by the NAB that claimed auctions threatened free local TV and urged viewers to mobilize against the "TV Tax" (Brinkley, 1997). In addition, Grand Alliance members formed a group, called Citizens for HDTV, that ran newspaper ads attacking the proposals. Auction advocates, including Senator Dole and Chairman Hundt, were infuriated and claimed the ads presented false information and misrepresented the proposals. But with no significant coverage of the issue on local TV, they had little opportunity to present their case to the public (Hickey, 1996). The main effect of the campaign was to dilute support for spectrum auctions among Republican incumbents. With general elections less than six months away, most legislators refused to support proposals that antagonized local broadcasters even when they might have contributed to balance the federal budget over the long term. In other words, whereas the political credit for having balanced the budget based on receipts from broadcast spectrum auctions could only be redeemed five or ten years down the road, the political threat was around the corner. In May 1996 Senate Majority Leader Bob Dole resigned from Congress to run (unsuccessfully) for president. The issue was finally put to a rest in June 1996 when in a letter to Chairman Hundt congressional leaders urged the commission to proceed "as expeditiously as possible" with the assignment of digital licenses to incumbents (Brinkley, 1996). After two years of passionate public debate and numerous congressional deliberations, the Commission was being directed to proceed with the original plan.

PUBLIC INTEREST OBLIGATIONS FOR THE DIGITAL AGE

The Clinton administration broadly supported the idea of auctioning the digital licenses but realized that changing the cornerstone of the existing regime (i.e., free spectrum) would take a colossal congressional battle. Instead, the administration used the threat of auctions to extract concessions from local incumbents. In return for the opportunity to use an additional frequency channel for an extended period of time, the government expected broadcasters to make significant in-kind contributions in favor of its communication policy agenda. The haggling focused on three issues. The first two related to the idea of creating a more children-friendly television environment, an issue that would play well in the upcoming general elections and was advocated by President Clinton. At the time, broadcasters were fighting against the commission's new implementation of the Children's Television Act of 1990.[12] Hundt wanted to force local stations to provide a minimum of three hours a week of children's programming, but broadcasters logically resisted any attempt at quantifying their vaguely defined public interest obligations. In addition, by threatening a veto, President Clinton managed to include a provision in the 1996 act that mandated the use of parental TV monitoring technology called the V-chip.[13] Implementation of the V-chip required the cooperation of broadcasters in developing and implementing a programming rating system. Broadcasters attacked the V-chip as an attempt to censor programming and threatened to block implementation in the courts.

[12] Policies and Rules Concerning Children's Television Programming, MM Docket 93-48, Report and Order, 11 FCC Rcd 10661 (1996).
[13] 47 U.S.C. § 303(x).

As the various broadcast spectrum auction proposals made their way through Congress, incumbents felt prudent to make concessions on the children's television issue. In early 1996 they dropped opposition to the V-chip and reluctantly agreed to cooperate in developing a voluntary ratings system. A few months later, as Hundt attempted to turn the "kidvid" rule into an election campaign issue, the NAB reversed course and agreed to compromise on a three-hour minimum mandate. Under intense attack from the elite press on the digital channel issue, broadcasters wanted to avoid a public relations debacle on children's programming that would only strengthen the pro-auctions coalition. On balance, these were small concessions to make as the threat of spectrum auctions or the indefinite hold-up of digital licenses by the commission loomed large. The third issue on which the Clinton administration demanded concessions, however, was a more direct challenge to the established broadcast regime. The administration wanted broadcasters to give free airtime to political candidates. The United States is unique among advanced democracies for its lack of speech opportunities afforded to candidates for political office (Norris, 2000). The problem is closer to the Democrats' heart, as they are typically less well funded than their Republican opponents. The free airtime crusade was led by Chairman Hundt, who assembled a coalition of academics, public interest advocates, industry personalities, and congressional entrepreneurs (notably Senator McCain) to support the cause. The idea was to make the award of the digital licenses conditional on broadcasters agreeing to accept a free airtime requirement. According to Hundt, if incumbents were being granted beachfront spectrum property, the least they could be asked to do was to give a modest in-kind contribution in the form of free airtime to political candidates. Broadcasters felt the pressure, and several of them voluntarily offered free airtime during the November 1996 elections. Although by then the threat of spectrum auctions had receded, the FCC had yet to allocate the new licenses. After the elections, allegations about improper fundraising practices by candidates from both major parties fueled the debate on campaign finance reform. The White House fully supported Hundt's plan to extract tangible public interest commitments from incumbent broadcasters in return for the digital licenses, particularly free airtime. As President Clinton explained in a March 1997 speech:

> The move from analog signals to digital ones will give each broadcaster much more signal capacity than they have today. The broadcasters asked Congress to be given this new access to the public

airwaves without charge. I believe, therefore, it is time to update
the broadcasters' public interest obligations to meet the demands of
the new times and the new technological realities. I believe broadcasters who receive digital licenses should provide free air time for
candidates, and I believe the FCC should act to require free air time
for candidates.[14]

With the support from the White House, a compromise was struck
whereby the FCC would proceed with the allocation of the digital licenses, but in return an ad hoc presidential committee would be formed
to advise the government on the public interest obligations to be imposed on digital broadcasters. Broadcasters were pleased with the agreement. They continued to resist free airtime but calculated that, once
the licenses were awarded, there would be several avenues to prevent
the committee's recommendations from ever translating into enforceable obligations. Generally speaking, having to renegotiate the terms of
the existing regime (even with minor concessions such as the "kidvid"
mandate) was a small price to pay for successfully extending such regime
into the digital era.

The Advisory Committee on the Public Interest Obligations of Digital Television Broadcasters (otherwise known as the Gore Committee)
was established on March 11, 1997. Its twenty-two members included
academics, media professionals, public interest advocates, and broadcast industry representatives. Three weeks later, the FCC proceeded to
allocate every local TV broadcaster in America (about 1,600 of them)
a second 6MHz frequency channel, at no cost, in return for the commitment to build digital TV facilities and operate under public interest obligations to be specified at a later date. The commission declined
to mandate a minimum number of hours of HDTV. With the explicit
blessing from Congress, the licensing plan was now much less prone
to judicial challenges even in the absence of an HDTV mandate. The licenses gave broadcasters almost complete flexibility in the use of the new
channel, the only significant requirement being to provide a free digital
service, "the resolution of which is comparable to or better than that of
today's service and aired during the same time periods that their analog
channel is broadcasting."[15] In other words, local stations could provide

[14] Remarks by President Clinton to the Conference on Free TV and Political Reform at
the National Press Club, March 11, 1997.
[15] Advanced Television Systems and Their Impact on the Existing Television Broadcast
Service, MM Docket No. 87-268, Fifth Report and Order, 12 FCC Rcd 12810 (1997),
at 28.

(or, in fact, have third parties provide) everything from data services to subscription TV as long as they broadcast at least one free SDTV channel.[16] According to the commission, spectrum flexibility would allow broadcasters to tailor services to consumer demand, thus encouraging adoption.

On the other hand, the new licenses imposed an aggressive transition schedule in terms of construction of facilities and spectrum recovery. This was the centerpiece of the new bargain crafted by Hundt. The commission adopted the staggered approach to the introduction of services favored by broadcasters: affiliates of the main four national networks (ABC, CBS, NBC, and Fox) in the top ten markets were required to have a digital signal on the air in about twenty-four months (by May 1, 1999), while affiliates in markets 11 through 30 were granted an additional six months (about thirty months in total).[17] All other commercial stations would have about five years (until May 1, 2002) to launch digital services. Noncommercial stations were given an extra year (until May 1, 2003). As a result of this accelerated timetable for the introduction of services, the commission significantly shortened the expected transition period from fifteen to about eight years. According to the new rules, by December 31, 2006, analog transmissions would cease and broadcasters would return one of their two frequency channels. In terms of spectrum recovery, the commission partly ceded to pressure from broadcasters to extend the so-called core band for digital TV. The rules established a new core located between channels 2 and 51 (the July 1996 proposals excluded channels 2–6 from the core). Under the new plan, a total of 108MHz (down from 138MHz, but still more than the original 72MHz) would be recovered after the transition. The lightly used higher UHF frequencies (channels 60–69) would be almost immediately available for reallocation, as only fifteen digital channel allotments were made in this band. The White House wanted these frequencies auctioned by 2002.

The FCC chairman hailed the new rules as a major departure from the transition strategy inherited from the Sikes era. According to Hundt,

---

[16] Following a congressional mandate, the FCC later established a 5 percent fee on gross revenues from any subscription services provided by digital broadcasters. See Fees for Ancillary or Supplementary Use of Digital Television Spectrum Pursuant to Section 336(e)(1) of the Telecommunications Act of 1996, MM Docket No. 97-247, Report and Order, 14 FCC Rcd 3259 (1998).

[17] Prodded by Chairman Hundt, several stations in the top ten markets voluntarily committed to have a digital TV signal on the air by November 1, 1998, in time for the 1998 holiday shopping season. See Letter from NAB and MSTV to FCC Chairman Reed P. Hundt, April 2, 1997.

the new policies represented a move away from a command-and-control
approach toward a more market-oriented transition:

> The Commission has moved from having government determine
> the television format of the future to having industries compete to
> provide the best format; from having government tell broadcasters
> the quality of picture resolution to giving broadcasters the freedom
> to respond to market forces; from having government restrict the
> use of the digital channel through simulcasting and other policies
> to giving broadcasters the flexibility to use the spectrum to respond
> to market opportunities.[18]

In reality, the new plan represented a curious mixture of industrial policymaking and laissez-faire formulas. The revised strategy was aggressively interventionist in terms of the timetable for the introduction of
services and the plans for spectrum recovery by the end of 2006. At the
same time, the new licenses were granted with few strings attached in
terms of programming obligations or service requirements. True, the
commission was making no attempt at guessing what kinds of digital
services would be valued by viewers. Yet it had determined beforehand
who would provide those services, on what frequencies, the roll-out
schedule in each market, and the target date for the switch-off of analog stations. By all counts, the timetable responded more to budgetary
needs than genuine considerations of the transition exercise. There was
widespread agreement that the eight-year transition period was utterly
unrealistic. Many even doubted that the channels 60–69 band could be
auctioned by 2002. Eight years after the beginning of color transmissions
fewer than 2 percent of American households had a color TV set. It was
clear that Congress would not allow the FCC to switch off analog TV
until a significant majority of the American households were equipped
with digital TV receivers. This political reality presaged a transition well
beyond December 31, 2006.

The outcome of the process initiated with the formation of the Gore
Commission in March 1997 vividly reflected the structural flaws of
the American broadcast regime. As noted, the Clinton administration
hoped that, at a minimum, the process would serve to exact mandatory free airtime for political candidates in return for the digital licenses.
The deliberations of the Gore Commission were riddled by controversy

---

[18] Separate Statement by Chairman Hundt Regarding Adoption of Digital Television
Allotment and Service Rules and Orders, April 3, 1997.

between advocates of government regulation and advocates of industry self-regulation. Several commission members supported the imposition of quantitative requirements modeled after the children's programming rule. They demanded that digital stations deliver at least three hours a week of local news and another three hours of educational and public affairs programming, as well as a minimum of five minutes a night of free airtime for political candidates in the thirty days prior to an election. Should stations not comply with these obligations, they would be levied a fee commensurate with the value of the spectrum – the so-called play-or-pay approach. On the other hand, industry representatives resisted these obligations and instead suggested that broadcasters adhere to a voluntary code of "good practices" prepared and administered by the industry. Such voluntary code would avert the First Amendment concerns associated with the imposition of programming obligations while ensuring that digital broadcasters live up to their commitments as public trustees.

After fifteen months of deliberations, the Gore Commission finally released its report in December 1998 (Advisory Committee on Public Interest Obligations of Digital Television Broadcasters, 1998). The report was a mix of insightful legal analysis, vague proposals, and wishful thinking about the potential of digital TV for improving political involvement and education. For example, the commission recommended that broadcasters "seize the opportunities inherent in digital television technology to substantially enhance the diversity available in the television marketplace" (1998: 63), but failed to specify any practical instruments for achieving such a goal. The report advanced the following proposals: the creation of a voluntary code of conduct drafted by the NAB that would specify principles and standards for digital programming; a set of *minimum* public interest requirements adopted by the FCC in the areas of community outreach, accountability, public service announcements, public affairs programming, and closed captioning; and the creation by Congress of a trust fund for public broadcasting and the allocation of a new digital channel after the completion of the transition for noncommercial educational programming. For broadcasters that opted to offer multiple SDTV channels (as opposed to a single HDTV channel), the report suggested a limited play-or-pay scheme whereby stations would either dedicate one of these SDTV channels to public interest programming or pay a fee in lieu of their obligations. However, at the request of industry representatives a third alternative was added: to provide in-kind contributions equivalent in market value to the fee. This option diluted the play-or-pay proposal back into the murky waters of the unenforceable public interest obligations as existing in the analog regime (Sunstein, 2000). On the controversial issue of political advertising, the report made two key recommendations. As a part of a "comprehensive campaign finance reform" to be adopted by Congress in the future, broadcasters would offer free airtime in return for the repeal of the "lowest unit charge" rule, as well as support the creation of a "broadcast bank" to distribute money or vouchers among candidates. Otherwise, broadcasters would voluntarily provide five minutes of free airtime each night in the thirty days before an election.

The final report of the Gore Commission reflected its deep internal divisions. The few recommendations to which the commission arrived on a consensual basis were rather weak and ineffectual, "a vague jumble of voluntary suggestions" as a newspaper editorial described them.[19] Ironically, most committee members publicly critiqued the final report, some for failing to impose enforceable obligations, others for subverting the existing regime with proposals such as the limited play or pay scheme for multiple SDTV broadcasting.[20] The broadcast lobby was nonetheless satisfied with the outcome of the deliberations. The very existence of the Gore Commission helped rebut critics of the "spectrum giveaway" and strengthened the case against auctions. Local stations were not getting additional spectrum for free; rather, they would be subject to additional public interest obligations as proposed in the final report. In effect, the industry managed to avert any enforceable programming guidelines or mandatory payments for the additional capacity received.

By the time the final report was released, political support for serious reform of the broadcast regime, including mandatory free airtime, had waned. Hundt left the FCC in November 1997. Gore and McCain were busy campaigning for president, and President Clinton was fighting impeachment. After a letter from Vice President Gore urging the FCC to act, a proceeding to implement the Gore Commission's proposals was finally initiated in December 1999.[21] Hundt's successor, William Kennard, a former broadcast industry lawyer, was initially cautious about tackling these politically charged issues. Yet, after two of the four major networks declined to air the first presidential debate of the 2000 elections, he

---

[19] Editorial in the *New York Times*, December 26, 1998, p. 26.
[20] See the separate statements of the Gore Commission members in Appendix, Advisory Committee on Public Interest Obligations of Digital Television Broadcasters (1998).
[21] Public Interest Obligations of TV Broadcast Licensees, MM Docket No. 99-360, Notice of Inquiry, 14 FCC Rcd 21633 (1999).

became a vocal reform advocate. Shortly after the debate incident, Kennard delivered a controversial speech titled "What does $70 billion buy you anyway?" in which he strongly criticized broadcasters for failing to live up to their public interest obligations after having received billions worth of spectrum from the government.[22] However, Kennard's efforts proved too little, too late. With the Republican victory in the November 2000 general elections and the nomination of Commissioner Michael Powell, an uncompromising deregulation advocate, as FCC chairman in January 2001, implementation of the Gore Commission's recommendations was summarily put to rest.

The FCC's failure to enact even the rather minor reforms proposed by the Gore Commission revealed the fallacy of the public trustee model upon which the American broadcast regime continues to be based. The obligations of digital broadcasters were never defined not only because of the limitations inherent to the FCC's congressional mandate or the unwillingness of particular commissioners to act against the powerful broadcast lobby. The difficulties in extracting any meaningful concession in return for the digital licenses stem from the more fundamental deficit of a regime that, in face of the prevailing interpretation of the First Amendment and the general lack of support for command-and-control regulations, had long been deprived of any substance. The limited play or pay scheme proposed for SDTV was never seriously considered by the commission. Industry self-regulation also failed as the NAB refused to endorse a voluntary code of conduct and broadcasters largely reneged on their promise to provide free airtime for political candidates (Taylor and Ornstein, 2002). After the licenses were handed out, broadcasters' only meaningful obligation was to introduce digital TV services within the schedule established by the commission. Yet, as discussed in the next chapter, enforcing this end of the bargain would also prove problematic.

---

[22] Remarks by FCC Chairman William Kennard, Museum of Television and Radio, New York, October 10, 2000.

SIX

A Long Journey

By mid-1997 the American transition had entered its third phase. Neomercantilist considerations about the revitalization of the domestic electronics industry had long been abandoned. The building of an NII was still on the agenda, but in practice the government's task was limited to facilitating private investment and filling gaps in commercially unattractive areas. The country was riding a wave of unprecedented growth in the telecommunications and information technology sectors. As a result, the demand for spectrum grew exponentially. Some policymakers, notably FCC Chairman Kennard, challenged broadcasters to join the "Internet revolution" by offering digital TV services that would serve as a bridge for millions of Americans across the so-called digital divide. Yet, as the transition evolved, it became clear that incumbent broadcasters had other plans in mind. In fact, they had initiated the transition to keep spectrum out of the hands of land mobile operators and had successfully steered the process so that the migration created minimal disruption to the existing industry arrangements. The new bargain gave broadcasters flexibility to use the second channel for new services in return for an accelerated spectrum recovery schedule. In reality, few expected incumbent broadcasters to create such services. But at least the government could reclaim some valuable frequencies almost immediately, hand them over to more innovative companies for a price, and use those receipts to balance the federal budget. Spectrum recovery and fiscal receipts, not pretty pictures and new information services, constituted the political reality of digital TV.

As the FCC finalized the allocation of digital licenses, the Clinton administration negotiated with a Republican-controlled Congress to put an end to several decades of public deficits. The administration released its budget proposals in February 1997, which included receipts for about

$5 billion through 2002 from the auction of the broadcast spectrum out-
side the core digital TV band. Incumbent broadcasters recognized that
any auctions held in advance of the statutory switch-off deadline would
significantly increase the likelihood that policymakers would come to
enforce the statute even if millions of households lacked the equipment
to receive digital TV. Industry lobbyists immediately began working on
a strategy that would allow an extension of the transition timetable.
NAB lawyers persuaded Republican representative Billy Tauzin, chairman of the House Subcommittee on Telecommunications, Trade, and
Consumer Protection, that a safeguard provision was necessary to protect analog viewers unable – or, for that matter, unwilling – to purchase
digital TV sets by the December 31, 2006, switch-off deadline. The argument overlooked the fact that the great majority of American households
(about 75 percent of them) received their signals via cable or satellite and,
therefore, did not need an expensive new TV set to receive digital TV (a
low cost set-top box converter – already in use by satellite operators –
sufficed). Tauzin introduced an amendment to the budget bill whereby
local broadcasters would be allowed to keep their analog channel beyond
2006 in markets where more than 5 percent of households lacked digital receiving equipment. In other words, the switch-off process would
be delayed until digital TV reached 95 percent penetration. The NAB
also managed to work in an amendment in the Senate version of the
budget bill that relaxed the build-out schedule established by the FCC.
The amendment made the November 1, 1999, construction deadline for
stations in the top thirty markets voluntary.

This maneuvering generated an outcry from the White House and
spectrum auction advocates. The amendments sealed the spectrum giveaway, they argued, by extending the originally temporary second-channel
loan for an indefinite period. Administration officials accused the industry of reneging on its compromise for an accelerated transition and
claimed that if the amendments passed, not only would the federal budget
not be balanced but the urgent spectrum needs of public safety agencies would not be met (Mintz and Farhi, 1997). With the amendments
about to pass, a last-minute compromise was brokered whereby the
95 percent penetration safeguard was replaced in the Balanced Budget
Act of 1997 by the following formula: an analog broadcaster would be
allowed to request an extension for operating beyond 2006 if one or
more of the major networks' affiliates were not broadcasting a signal
in its local market, or digital-to-analog converters were generally not
available, or less than 85 percent of the households in its market were

capable of receiving at least one digital channel from each local broadcaster either terrestrially or through a cable or satellite operator.[1] Of these three tests, the first two were unlikely to represent impediments for the recovery of the spectrum by 2006. The third, however, was a tall order. Even if the several technical problems that surfaced as DTT services were introduced could be resolved promptly, reaching such level of household penetration was highly unlikely to occur before 2006. As the CBO noted, it took twenty-two years for color TV and fifteen years for VCRs to reach 85 percent penetration (Bazelon, 1999). To believe that digital TV would be adopted by 85 percent of American households in only eight years was not only wishful thinking; it was simply ludicrous.[2]

The budget act also instructed the FCC to auction no less than 55MHz of spectrum located in the most desirable bands (i.e., below 3GHz) in order for receipts to reach the U.S. Treasury by September 2002. Most of these frequencies would be made available as the commission reclaimed the channels outside the digital TV core spectrum (i.e., channels 52–69). More specifically, the act mandated that the 60MHz reallocated from channels 60–69 be divided between public safety services (24MHz) and commercial users (36MHz). The remaining frequencies (48MHz from channels 52–59) would be offered on a second round of auctions, always before September 2002. The statute still afforded full interference protection to incumbent broadcasters in both bands. Potential users would thus be bidding on frequencies that would not become available until December 31, 2006, at the earliest, and given the switch-off safeguards introduced by the act, possibly much later. The act also extended the FCC auction authority introduced by the OBRA-1993 to broadcast licenses. For the first time, the commission could sell licenses for television services. Interestingly, such authorization, which caused a political storm when initially proposed in 1993, now ruffled few feathers. In theory, selling broadcast licenses would challenge the established regime based on hard-to-measure public interest contributions by licensees. In practice, however, after the allocation of a second frequency channel to all local incumbents, most desirable licenses were depleted. With the authorization

---

[1] *Balanced Budget Act of 1997*, Pub. L. No. 105-33, Sec. 3003.
[2] Another problem is that the act contained several ambiguities related to the three tests. In particular, it lacks a definition of local television market (the FCC uses several ones based on different technical calculations) and fails to specify exactly which cable or satellite subscribers could be counted towards the 85 percent mark. For a discussion, see Bazelon (1999).

in hand, there was now only a handful of broadcast licenses for the commission to sell.

Only weeks after the passage of the Balanced Budget Act of 1997, top industry executives suggested that their digital plans did not include HDTV. Once again, the remarks sparked flames in Congress. As a result, the industry would undergo one more wave of criticism for not keeping its end of the original bargain to broadcast at least a minimum amount of HDTV in the second frequency channel. Although Congress failed to introduce a minimum HDTV mandate in the 1996 Telecom Act, several legislators still believed that broadcasters owed it to Congress to air some HDTV. Even some traditional allies like Billy Tauzin were infuriated by the industry's remarks. They had pressured a reluctant FCC to expedite the allocation of licenses and fought hard on behalf of the industry against auctions. At the very least, broadcasters could keep their word on HDTV. The Senate Commerce Committee held hearings in which Senator McCain lambasted broadcasters for having used HDTV as a gimmick to receive the new licenses:

> Broadcasters by dint of their ceaseless efforts to paint HDTV as free TV's passport to the future are being given tens of billions of dollars of public property in digital spectrum, insulated by Congress from claims of competing users and exempt from having to pay what the spectrum is worth on the market. . . . Having first lost the option value of the spectrum, the public now has no real certainty of what they are likely to get in return or when they are likely to get it. I don't think we should accept that.[3]

Put on the defensive, incumbents once again promised that "the vast majority of the broadcast industry" was committed to HDTV but noted the importance of preserving the spectrum flexibility provision in order to launch services in consonance with market demand.[4] In other words, HDTV would eventually happen, but no one was prepared to say when, or how.

After this congressional jawboning, the transition entered a period of relative calm. The fate of HDTV had been sealed long before the 1997 congressional hearings, and the best legislators could ask for was a smooth transition and the prompt recovery of the spectrum. The initial

[3] Remarks by Senator John McCain, Hearing of the Senate Commerce, Science and Transportation Committee, September 17, 1997.
[4] Remarks by Robert Decherd in representation of the NAB, Hearing of the Senate Commerce, Science and Transportation Committee, September 17, 1997.

Table 6.1. *Statutory versus Actual Digital TV Build-out for Commercial Broadcasters*

	May 1, 1999 (Top 10 Markets Affiliates)	November 1, 1999 (Top 30 Markets Affiliates)	May 1, 2002 (All Commercial Broadcasters)
Mandated	40	119	1,240
Completed	32	71	397
Completion rate	80%	60%	32%

Source: FCC.

signs were encouraging. In February 1998 the FCC adopted the final table of allotments for DTT.[5] The construction of the table involved several trade-offs between larger and smaller stations, commercial and public stations, incumbents and new entrants, broadcasting and new services. In a sense, the entitlements once allotted by the Sixth Report and Order of 1952 were being distributed anew. Channel allotments were planned so as to allow licensees to provide digital services to a geographic area comparable with their existing analog service area (the so-called replication principle). This extended the historical advantage of the larger VHF stations into the digital world. Yet, last-minute revisions favored several displaced low-power broadcasters and allowed better coverage for UHF stations. These revisions to some extent redistributed spectrum rights in favor of independent stations, public broadcasters, and affiliates of the smaller networks.

On November 1, 1998, forty-two digital TV stations went on the air. This was almost double the number of stations that originally volunteered to be transmitting before the 1998 holiday shopping season. By the May 1, 1999, deadline for affiliate stations in the top ten markets, there were more than sixty-five digital stations on the air, far more than required by the statutory timetable (Table 6.1). But optimism was short-lived. Soon after digital TV became operational, numerous obstacles surfaced. Some of these obstacles stemmed from fractures within the broadcasting community. The interests of the major national networks, large-station owners, and small broadcasters (not to mention noncommercial stations) often collided. For some, SDTV and ancillary services

[5] Advanced Television Systems and Their Impact on the Existing Television Broadcast Service, MM Docket No. 87-268, Memorandum Opinion and Order on Reconsideration of the Sixth Report, 13 FCC Rcd 7418 (1998).

offered great commercial opportunities. Others still believed in HDTV. Most small stations were skeptical about both. After getting the digital licenses, little agreement existed in the industry about what to do with them. Other obstacles underscored the complexity of the industry in comparison to the period of the transition to color TV. Given that most households received services through cable operators, that a large share of the most attractive programming was produced by third parties (i.e., the Hollywood studios), and that the receiving equipment was marketed by unaffiliated manufacturers, putting the DTT signals on the air was just a small part of a multifaceted puzzle.

TECHNICAL AND LEGAL UNCERTAINTIES

As soon as the first digital stations went on the air, controversy erupted over the poor performance of the ACATS system. At the center of the controversy was the modulation technology used by the system called 8-level vestigial side-band (8-VSB).[6] The technology performed below expectations, thus creating considerable indoor reception problems. As a result, in early 1999 several broadcasting organizations led by the Sinclair Broadcasting Group approached the FCC to request a revision and the possible replacement of 8-VSB with a competing technology called coded orthogonal frequency division multiplex (COFDM). COFDM was already being implemented in Europe and was believed to be superior for mobile data services, which according to the trade press several broadcasters planned to offer. The formal filing of a petition by Sinclair asking the commission to reconsider the modulation technology in the ACATS standard sent shockwaves throughout the industry.[7] The Consumer Electronics Association (CEA), the trade group representing consumer equipment manufacturers, opposed any changes to the system, arguing that engineers were working to solve the reception problems and that any changes would orphan the equipment already sold and send manufacturers back to the design board.[8] In response to the petition, the commission conducted a thorough revision of the technical evidence, concluding that

---

[6] Modulation refers to the process of encoding digital data into carrier waves for transmission.

[7] Advanced Television Systems and Their Impact on the Existing Television Broadcast Service, MM Docket No. 87-268, Petition for Expedite Rulemaking filed by Sinclair Broadcast Group, October 8, 1999 (denied February 8, 2000).

[8] Statement of Gary Shapiro, President and CEO, Consumer Electronics Association, before the Subcommittee on Telecommunications, Trade and Consumer Protection, July 25, 2000.

both 8-VSB and COFDM had certain advantages and disadvantages. Ultimately, the commission endorsed 8-VSB, for the data showed that the relative benefits of switching to COFDM were unclear and would not outweigh the considerable costs of making such a revision in the DTT standard adopted in December 1996.[9]

Although the commission denied Sinclair's petition, the controversy lingered on through 2000. COFDM supporters took their case to Congress and sparred in technical demonstrations against 8-VSB advocates before the House Telecommunications Subcommittee chaired by Tauzin. Legislators were puzzled by the highly technical controversy and urged the industry to resolve the question promptly and proceed with the roll-out of services as scheduled. Tauzin also warned broadcasters against using the digital frequencies for mobile data services that competed directly with those of mobile telephony operators, particularly if provided by third parties:

> The deal was that the 6 megahertz of digital spectrum was to be used for digital transmission including HDTV and that the broadcasters could use it for ancillary services. If they got into any kind of competition with anybody else they'd have to pay for it. That was the deal. It would be a clear deal-breaker for anyone to think they could profit by selling the spectrum off or leasing it off.[10]

The demonstrations provided few answers, and Congress, as expected, sent the issue back to the FCC. Chairman Kennard generally disliked the idea of imposing standards on the rapidly evolving communications industry. Yet the case of digital TV was different. As market agents failed to resolve this and other standards issues, Kennard became increasingly convinced of the need to force parties to agree by threatening to open official commission proceedings. Kennard urged the industry to rally behind 8-VSB, for "a mid-course change to introduce a new modulation technology at this late date could lead to lengthy and unacceptable delays in the DTV transition process."[11] Still, the industry remained divided, and the major broadcasting organizations decided to conduct their own technical tests. The tests revealed that the present system needed urgent

[9] DTV Report on COFDM and 8-VSB Performance, FCC/OET 99-2 (September 30, 1999).
[10] Statement of Representative Billy Tauzin, Chairman, Subcommittee on Telecommunications, Trade, and Consumer Protection, July 25, 2000.
[11] Letter from FCC Chairman William E. Kennard to NAB President Edward Fritts, July 24, 2000.

improvements but that there was insufficient evidence to support a change to COFDM. The controversy was finally put to rest in January 2001, when the NAB and MSTV formally endorsed 8-VSB.[12]

The lengthy resolution of the modulation debate revealed the fragility of the consensus on DTT within a divided broadcast community, as well as the reluctance of the commission to seek compliance of its own decisions in face of divergent industry interests. A similar pattern would emerge in the attempted resolution of other controversies that slowed the transition process. To complicate matters, some of these involved not only broadcasters and equipment manufacturers but two other powerful stakeholders: cable operators and the Hollywood studios. Cable carriage of DTT channels was critical to accomplish the 85 percent penetration target required by the Balanced Budget Act of 1997. This presented two major problems: first, to define the legal framework for the negotiations between cable operators and digital broadcasters, particularly with regard to the implementation of must-carry rules; and, second, to make the two industries agree on the technical standards for the transmission of DTT channels over cable (the "cable compatibility" issue). The application of must-carry rules presented delicate legal questions in light of the variations allowed by the ACATS standard and the flexibility granted to broadcasters in the use of the digital channels. Were cable operators to be forced to carry all SDTV signals originated by local broadcasters? In which picture format? How would digital services entitled to must-carry be separated from other services (Aaron, 2000)?

In July 1998 the commission opened proceedings to address the digital must-carry issue.[13] Particularly important was to define the framework for cable carriage during the simulcasting period. Local broadcasters demanded so-called dual carriage, that is, that cable operators be forced to carry both their analog and their digital channels. Cable operators argued that dual carriage unreasonably burdened them with obligations beyond those authorized by the Supreme Court in *Turner II*. Other programmers also opposed dual carriage for fear of being bumped off cable systems if operators were forced to carry both analog and DTT channels. In a preliminary decision issued in January 2001, the commission dealt a resounding blow to local incumbents by refusing to mandate dual carriage and ruling that, when broadcasters offered multiple SDTV channels,

---

[12] Resolution of the MSTV Board of Directors and the NAB Television Board, January 15, 2001.

[13] Carriage of the Transmissions of Digital Broadcast Stations, CS Docket No. 98-120, Notice of Proposed Rulemaking, 13 FCC Rcd 15092 (1998).

only one of those channels was entitled to must-carry status.[14] Interestingly, the commission also allowed broadcasters to demand that their DTT signal be carried in analog format so that cable subscribers, even without digital TV equipment, could be counted toward the 85 percent penetration target. Having its DTT signal carried in analog format on cable would also make broadcasters more willing to surrender their analog frequencies by the switchover date.

As expected, the debate only intensified after the ruling. Having lost in the FCC arena, broadcasters appealed to Congress. The government had loaned local stations a second channel to introduce digital TV, argued the NAB. Without proper carriage on cable, the American public would only marginally collect the benefits from this considerable spectrum loan. The Republican-controlled House that emerged out of the November 2000 elections proved receptive to these pledges, particularly when coming from small religious broadcasters that served a critical GOP constituency and that lacked bargaining power for carriage vis-à-vis cable operators. By mid-2002 House leaders were urging Chairman Powell to reconsider the issue of multiple SDTV carriage and to force cable operators to carry all nonsubscription DTT channels (McConnell, 2002). The controversy is unlikely to be resolved until the Supreme Court agrees to revisit *Turner II.*

The problem of cable compatibility was significantly aggravated by a little-noticed provision worked into the Telecom Act of 1996 by the consumer electronic retailers that required the creation of a retail market for the set-top boxes used by cable subscribers.[15] The FCC proceeded to implement this mandate based on the "right to attach" principle that guided commission policy on the unbundling of consumer equipment and services in the telecom sector.[16] Because cable operators use different technologies to secure their signals (i.e., different CASs), it was necessary for the FCC to require the unbundling of the security functions from the cable set-top box so that subscribers could buy the decoder at retail and add this component later depending on their choice of operator. The rules adopted required the availability of CAS modules by July 1, 2000,

[14] Carriage of the Transmissions of Digital Broadcast Stations, CS Docket No. 98-120, First Report and Order and Further Notice of Proposed Rulemaking, 16 FCC Rcd 2598 (2001).

[15] 47 U.S.C. § 549.

[16] This was established by two major cases: *Hush-a-Phone Corporation v. U.S.*, 238 F.2d 266 (1956), and In the Matter of Use of the Carterfone Device in Message Toll Telephone Service, FCC 2d 420 (1968). For a discussion, see Brock (1994).

and the complete phase-out of integrated boxes by January 1, 2005. Cable operators were also required to disclose their security interface specifications to assist retailers and equipment manufacturers in developing the set-top box retail market.[17] In order to comply with the FCC rules, the cable industry launched the OpenCable project, an initiative aimed at creating a complete set of interface specifications for cable-ready digital TV sets and set-top boxes.

After several months of negotiations, the consumer equipment manufacturers and the cable industry were unable to reach agreement on two critical issues related to the specifications for digital set-top boxes and cable-ready sets: the labeling of "cable-ready" receivers and the licensing terms for the copyright protection technology developed by OpenCable. Frustrated by these delays, Chairman Kennard "reluctantly" initiated proceedings to resolve these outstanding compatibility issues.[18] The opening of a formal FCC proceeding was more than a jawboning exercise to force agreement. It signaled the increasing cynicism about the ability of market agents to achieve standards agreements among federal policymakers. Without such agreements, achieving 85 percent penetration would take several decades. The threat of government-mandated standards proved real in September 2000, when the commission issued its first ruling on cable compatibility.[19] Yet the ruling only narrowly addressed the labeling issue. Once again, the commission was reluctant to resolve an industry dispute for fear of extensive litigation or even retaliation by Congress. With no cable compatibility agreement in place, penetration of digital TV equipment grew at a snail's pace. Of the 33 million TV sets sold in the United States in 2000, only about 40,000 were equipped to receive DTT signals.[20] With every new analog TV set sold, the switch-off of analog stations inched a step beyond December 31, 2006.

The entry of the major Hollywood studios into the digital TV debate spawned another set of problems. The main concern of this politically

[17] Implementation of Section 304 of the Telecommunications Act of 1996: Commercial Availability of Navigation Devices, CS Docket No. 97-80, Report and Order, 13 FCC Rcd 14775 (1998).
[18] Compatibility between Cable Systems and Consumer Electronics Equipment, PP Docket No. 00-67, Notice of Proposed Rulemaking, 15 FCC Rcd 8776 (2000).
[19] Compatibility between Cable Systems and Consumer Electronics Equipment, PP Docket No. 00-67, Report and Order, 15 FCC Rcd 17568 (2000). The commission established three categories of digital TV receivers that differed on interface components and capabilities for interactive TV services.
[20] Consumer Electronics Association (2001), p. 2.

powerful group was unauthorized redistribution of content. Digitization of video content facilitates illegal copying and redistribution over electronic networks such as the Internet. As losses from unauthorized distribution of copyrighted music mounted, the studios became increasingly concerned about the "Napsterization" of their film and TV properties. DTT is particularly susceptible to piracy as the content travels "in the clear" (i.e., unprotected) between a local station transmitter and a digital TV receiver. Even in the case of cable and satellite, content may be copied illegally as it travels between different components of the digital TV terminal (e.g., between a host set-top box and a CAS module) or between the receiver and peripheral consumer equipment (e.g., an analog VCR). In the absence of a copyright protection scheme, these companies were reluctant to make available their premium programming (i.e., recent film releases) on digital TV networks. Without such programming, the appeal of digital services would diminish considerably, thus discouraging adoption.

The commission initially left to the industry the task of resolving this delicate issue, partly because of Kennard's noted reluctance to mandate standards and partly because of the limited FCC jurisdiction in the area of copyright. In 1996 representatives of the equipment manufacturing, information technology, motion picture, cable, and broadcast industries established a forum to discuss the implementation of a copy protection scheme for digital video. Both Congress and the commission were hopeful that these efforts would result in a solution with wide industry support. Several years of deliberations, however, yielded no agreement beyond the general endorsement of a "broadcast flag" solution for DTT.[21] In addition, equipment manufacturers and consumer groups opposed the licensing terms and enforcement mechanisms demanded by copyright holders, such as the total ban on noncompliant devices. They argued such implementation would curtail the legitimate rights that consumers already enjoyed in the analog world and reduce opportunities for innovation in digital TV equipment. Copyright holders and broadcasters, on the other hand, urged the commission to mandate the broadcast flag solution. The failure of the voluntary industry agreement prompted an angry reaction from congressional leaders,

---

[21] Final Report of the Co-Chairs of the Broadcast Protection Discussion Subgroup to the Copy Protection Technical Working Group, June 3, 2002. The broadcast flag refers to a means for signaling that digital broadcast content is to be protected against unauthorized copying and redistribution. The flag is recognized by technology embedded in the digital TV receiver.

who threatened to impose copyright protection by fiat and urged the commission to address the problem notwithstanding its limited jurisdiction. In August 2002 the FCC initiated proceedings to resolve the copyright protection issue.[22] It remains to be seen whether administrative rule making will more effectively address a complex technological problem involving powerful stakeholders with conflicting preferences. Most likely, this will be the first step in a long policymaking journey through the commission, Congress, and almost certainly the courts. Meanwhile, attractive programming remained conspicuously scarce in DTT services.

The legal and technical puzzles that followed the introduction of DTT services revealed the complexity of the American television industry of the late 1990s. By the fall of 1998, more than half of the U.S. population had access to several local DTT channels. Yet, the obstacles enumerated here created an environment less than conducive to a rapid transition. With no economies of scale in manufacturing, digital TV equipment remained expensive. Lack of agreement about critical technical standards obstructed coordination in the introduction of products and discouraged consumer adoption. Copyright holders withheld their most valuable properties from DTT for fear of widespread piracy. Cable operators were reluctant to agree to long-term carriage contracts given the legal uncertainty about digital must-carry of local stations (in commercial terms, carrying digital stations that significantly replicated analog ones and reached few viewers was hardly appealing). By the same token, local broadcasters could not generate long-term business plans for digital TV due to the outstanding standards issues and the lack of a credible framework for negotiating carriage contracts with cable operators.

In a sense, where American regulators had erred was not so much in imposing an unrealistic transition timetable on local broadcasters but rather in failing to incorporate other key constituencies at the outset of the transition process. Beyond the ACATS system, the arduous task of achieving technical coordination for the introduction of digital TV was largely left to market forces. As documented by several scholars (e.g., David and Shurmer, 1996; Economides, 1996), voluntary standards agreements are hard to come by when multiple players bring different preferences to the bargaining table and the threat of government

---

[22] Digital Broadcast Copy Protection, MB Docket No. 02-230, Notice of Proposed Rulemaking, 17 FCC Rcd 16027 (2002).

Table 6.2. *U.S. Digital TV Penetration by*
Platform (in 000s of households)

	1998	1999	2000	2001
DTT		20	60	80
Digital satellite	7,200	12,500	14,000	17,900
Digital cable	1,200	5,200	9,700	15,200
Total DTV	8,400	17,720	23,760	33,180
DTV penetration	8.6%	17.9%	23.8%	33.2%

Sources: NCTA, FCC, CEA.

intervention is weak. These conditions by and large obtained in the introduction of digital TV in the United States. Similarly, in a policy-making context where judicial challenge is the norm rather than the exception, the resolution of the legal issues raised by the transition vis-à-vis cable carriage, copyrights, and other issues could be expected to last several years, if not decades. As it turned out, by the time DTT services were launched the real transition challenges began to surface.

A FALTERING PLAN

By the final days of the Clinton administration it was clear that the American transition to digital TV was faltering (Table 6.2). Only a few households were equipped to receive local DTT signals, and while digital cable and satellite subscribers grew steadily, according to the statute these households could not be counted toward the 85 percent penetration target because cable and satellite operators did not carry digital signals from all local broadcasters. The sluggish pace of penetration compromised the administration's efforts to reform spectrum management and reallocate broadcast frequencies to new users. It also created difficulties for budget planners, as the delays in the switch-off of analog stations reduced the amount that potential users were willing to bid for the encumbered frequencies outside the digital TV core band. In other words, the longer the transition was expected to take, the less would be raised through the spectrum auctions for channels 52–69 that the commission was required to conduct before September 2002. In an important policy statement released in November 1999, the commission promised to hold these auctions in conjunction with the implementation of major reforms in spectrum management policies intended to permit the deployment of new spectrum-dependent services.[23] The problem, as the statement recognized, was that there were little to no unencumbered frequencies available, and therefore new services would have to be accommodated by either sharing frequencies with incumbent users or through reallocation initiatives. The statement came only days after Congress directed the commission to anticipate the auction for channels 60–69 to plug holes in the 2000 federal budget. Now Congress required that these auction receipts be deposited in the U.S. Treasury before September 2000 – a full two years before originally planned.

The commission put the auction of the 60–69 band on a fast-track proceeding. However, given the 85 percent penetration safeguard that protected incumbents, wireless operators and other potential users demanded more certainty about when the band would be effectively cleared before bidding. The commission agreed to delay the auction for a few months and, in response to these concerns, introduced a controversial proposal to allow voluntary band-clearing arrangements between incumbent broadcasters and winning bidders.[24] In essence, analog broadcasters occupying channels 60–69 would receive monetary compensations in exchange for clearing the spectrum before the statutory date (December 31, 2006, at the earliest). The proposal ignited a heated debate. Broadcasters with significant channel assignments in channels 52–69 (notably Paxson Communications) enthusiastically supported the plan. These mostly small stations were poised to receive billions from wireless operators in return for the early shutdown of their analog operations. Compensations were expected to far exceed the actual market value of the licenses. The major broadcast organizations nonetheless opposed the proposal, arguing that it contravened the safeguards introduced by the Balanced Budget Act of 1997 in defense of analog viewers. As a matter of fact, band-clearing arrangements would create pressure to accelerate spectrum clearing and thus jeopardize the NAB's efforts to extend the transition period. Some congressional leaders reacted angrily to the idea of broadcasters receiving compensations for vacating frequencies they had not paid for. In turn, Democratic Commissioner Susan Ness and other media advocates questioned whether a proposal

---

[23] Principles for Reallocation of Spectrum to Encourage the Development of Telecommunications Technologies for the New Millennium, Policy Statement, 14 FCC Rcd 19868 (1999).

[24] Service Rules for the 746–764 and 776–794 MHz Bands, and Revisions to Part 27 of the Commission's Rules, WT Docket No. 99-168, Memorandum Opinion and Order and Further Notice of Proposed Rulemaking, 15 FCC Rcd 20845 (2000).

that reduced the number of analog TV stations to make room for new wireless services advanced the public interest in spectrum management.

The controversy prompted the commission to delay the auction once again, this time until after the November 2000 elections. The rules for voluntary band-clearing arrangements between incumbent broadcasters and winning bidders were finally published in January 2001, as Chairman Kennard stepped down following the Republican electoral triumph.[25] As expected, the commission authorized broadcasters in the 60–69 band to enter into lucrative buyout deals with winning auction bidders. A divided commission approved the rules based on the argument that the agreements advanced the public interest by accelerating spectrum recovery, despite the loss in television services as a result of the early shut-off of several analog stations operating in the 60–69 band. The vote reflected the concern about further delays in the recovery of the analog broadcast spectrum. Anticipating opposition from incumbent broadcasters, outgoing Chairman Kennard presented a letter to congressional leaders in which he candidly criticized the existing transition strategy and proposed significant reforms to speed up the migration process.[26] Kennard suggested three major changes: that the 85 percent safeguard be struck down and a fee be collected on broadcasters that continued to use their analog channels beyond 2006; the phase-in of a digital TV tuner requirement for all new TV sets; and congressional consideration of legislation addressing the issue of copyright protection in case private parties failed to reach timely agreements.

With the change in command at the commission, the hands-on approach spearheaded by Kennard, particularly during the final months of his tenure as FCC chairman, abated. A staunch market reformist, incoming Chairman Michael Powell had little interest in getting his hands dirty with what he regarded as a flawed industrial policy initiative. With the White House's consent, he was quick to postpone the auctions for channels 52–69 until a realistic picture about the timing of the switchover emerged (Congress later extended the statutory deadlines for the auctions and gave the commission increased discretion in determining when to complete the auctions).[27] However, pressure soon began mounting for

---

[25] Service Rules for the 746–764 and 776–794 MHz Bands, and Revisions to Part 27 of the Commission's Rules, WT Docket No. 99-168, Third Report and Order, 16 FCC Rcd 2703 (2001).

[26] Letter from FCC Chairman William E. Kennard to Senator Ernest Hollings, Chairman, Senate Committee on Commerce, Science, and Transportation, January 19, 2001.

[27] *Auction Reform Act of 2002*, Pub. L. No. 107-195.

the commission to remedy the faltering transition plan. With the fiscal situation deteriorating as the pace of economic growth slowed, it was all the more important to reclaim the spectrum and conduct the auctions as soon as possible. If Powell was prepared to accept the slow migration pace dictated by market forces, congressional leaders and several other parties were clearly not. Tauzin and McCain once more called for congressional hearings and threatened to draft legislation in case industry representatives failed to resolve the lingering commercial and technical disputes. During these hearings, industry leaders blamed each other for reneging on the commitments made. Broadcasters accused equipment manufacturers for failing to roll out inexpensive receivers and lambasted cable operators for refusing to accept dual carriage. Cable representatives charged broadcasters with expecting the commission to give them a free ride on their infrastructure investments. Equipment manufacturers blamed the dismal digital penetration figures on broadcasters' failure to make attractive digital programming available. Copyright holders accused equipment makers of refusing to tackle the piracy problem. As the May 1, 2002, deadline for the introduction of services by all commercial stations approached, a bleak picture of the American transition began to emerge.

In fall 2001 the NAB admitted to the FCC what most suspected all along: according to a survey conducted among its members, about a third of the stations would miss the May 1, 2002, deadline (Albiniak, 2001). Soon after, Chairman Powell announced the creation of an FCC Digital TV Task Force. While staffed exclusively by FCC officials, the task force would serve as a reference point for government and industry efforts to accelerate the pace of digital adoption and resolve outstanding standards issues. This signaled Powell's recognition that, without significant government involvement, the plan was headed for disaster. Shortly after, the commission announced significant revisions to its construction rules to allow broadcasters to take a more graduated approach in building digital facilities. The new rules relaxed the requirement to replicate the coverage of analog stations at the risk of losing interference protection, thus reducing the upfront equipment costs for the initiation of DTT services and the cost of running an analog and a digital transmitter simultaneously.[28] The commission declined to grant a blanket extension to the May 1, 2002, deadline for broadcasters in small markets as requested

[28] Review of the Commission's Rules and Policies Affecting the Conversion to Digital Television, MM Docket No. 00-39, Memorandum Opinion and Order on Reconsideration, 16 FCC Rcd 20594 (2001).

by several industry organizations, but nonetheless agreed to recognize, under certain circumstances, financial hardship as a legitimate basis for granting waivers on a case-by-case basis.

By the May 1, 2002, construction deadline, the failure of the American transition plan was vividly quantified: less than a third of the nation's 1,240 commercial broadcasters had a digital signal on the air (Table 6.1). The situation was hardly better in the perpetually underfunded non-commercial sector, despite the additional construction year granted by the FCC to public broadcasters. By April 2002, less than 20 percent of the nearly 350 public stations had converted to digital, and the system was several hundred million dollars short of its estimated $1.5 billion conversion bill (General Accounting Office, 2002). The situation presented an interesting enforcement challenge to the commission. As discussed, because of the political and judicial challenges brought against quantifiable public interest obligations, the commission generally lacked the instruments to measure the performance of its licensees. Therefore, as a practical matter, the renewal of broadcast licenses was in the vast majority of cases a mere formality. The transition, however, presented the commission with a rare opportunity to enforce a clear-cut requirement. According to its own rules, the continued failure of a licensee to meet the DTT construction timetable could eventually result in the forfeiture of the license. Nevertheless, enforcing compliance was no simple task. Neither the commission nor Congress ever introduced provisions that contemplated an en masse failure of broadcasters to meet their construction requirements. On the other hand, if the commission decided to take enforcement seriously and push for a massive license forfeiture, Congress would certainly revisit the issue. This is not only because of the historical compact between local stations and their district congressmen. As a practical matter, revoking hundreds of licenses simultaneously would leave several million households with fewer (or, in small markets, even no) TV services for a considerable period. Given the associated political costs, Congress is unlikely to endorse such a course of action. As Democrat Congressman Eliot Engel summarized it, "if on New Year's Day 2007, consumers turn on their TVs and see only snow, that could be the end of our congressional careers."[29]

---

[29] Quoted in "DTV's Political Stakes Run High," *Wired Magazine*, September 25, 2002.

PART III

The British Road to Digital TV

SEVEN

The European Context

Part III of the book begins with a short chapter discussing the European Commission's efforts to promote a harmonized transition to digital TV across the continent and to create an unified regime for the telecom and broadcasting sectors. As a member of the EU, the United Kingdom is bound by the general provisions of the EU Treaty and secondary legislation regarding regional integration and effective market competition, as well as by the more specific policies laid down in Brussels to promote and regulate digital TV. It is thus necessary to examine digital TV policies at the European Community level to understand the constraints under which British policymakers have designed and executed a transition plan. The next chapter (Chapter 8) offers a historical overview of the broadcasting sector in Britain. It discusses the origins and development of the analog television regime both in terms of the rule-based arrangements that determined market entry, funding, and competitive behavior, as well as of the ideological underpinnings that sustained the mixed system of public and commercial broadcasting. In this perspective, the transition to digital TV has been part of the profound reforms introduced in the industry since the Conservatives returned to power in 1979. However, there has also been a nontrivial dose of continuity between the old (analog) and the new (digital) regimes. As the transition unfolded in unexpected ways, it became clear that the British tradition of public service broadcasting was alive and well; and the BBC, much bedeviled by many as a symbol of the old Britain, would later became a key government ally for carrying out the transition plan.

The following three chapters narrate the efforts to introduce DTT services and complete the switch-off of analog TV. Unlike in other industrialized nations, in the United Kingdom a detailed regulatory framework preceded the launch of digital TV services. Interested parties and the government engaged in a long policymaking exercise to define the terms and conditions for the operation of digital TV before its launch in the fall of 1998. Chapter 9 discusses how this regime came about during the last period of the Major administration (1990–1997) and how different interest coalitions attempted to influence the outcome of the legislative and administrative processes. Chapter 10 turns attention to the implementation of the two key components of the government's transition strategy: the licensing of the so-called DTT multiplex operators and the transposition of European rules aimed at addressing competition problems in digital TV infrastructure. In both cases, implementation was delegated to independent regulatory authorities, allowing us to examine principal-agent relations and the functions performed by the Independent Television Commission (ITC) and the Office of Telecommunications (OFTEL). Chapter 11 closes Part III with a discussion of the efforts by the Blair administration to create a politically acceptable plan for the switch-off of analog stations and the future use of the released radio frequencies.

THE MAC INITIATIVE AND THE TWF DIRECTIVE

Television has traditionally been a difficult topic to tackle for European authorities. The reason, as Levy explains, is that "member states accorded such great political importance to broadcasting that many of them started from a position of suspicion towards any EU attempts at intervention. Each state regulated its industry differently, and such diversity, they agreed, required subsidiarity to be the rule rather than the exception in broadcasting" (1999: 163). The main EU treaties only rarely address the industry directly, the only notable exception being the Protocol on Public Service Broadcasting included in the Treaty of Amsterdam (1997), which simply established that member states can continue to fund public service broadcasters as long as such funding does not affect trade and competition in the European Community. Because of the dearth of primary legislation, the European Court of Justice (ECJ) has played a key role in establishing Community authority over broadcasting by defining it as a "tradeable service" and thus subject to European legislation (Barendt, 1995). However, European authority over questions of national politics and culture continues to be a contentious issue, and, as a major vehicle for both, television has represented an uneasy task for Community regulators.[1]

Despite the contested nature of regulatory jurisdiction over broadcasting, Community authorities have played an important role in the transition to digital TV. This role has certainly been more modest than in the case of the telecommunications sector, where the European Commission led the implementation of market reforms (Hulsink, 1999). But since the start of the transition process in the mid-1980s, EU policies have significantly affected the way member states promoted and regulated digital TV, arguably more than they have ever affected the analog broadcasting. The justification for such involvement has changed significantly over the years. The first period took place amid the high-tech trade wars of the 1980s (D'Andrea Tyson, 1992). It represents a textbook case of the failure of government policies to create advantages for local firms through standards setting (Beltz, 1991). These policies emerged in response to the Japanese attempts to force worldwide adoption of an NHK-developed system (see Chapter 4). The concern was that adoption of the system would give Japanese equipment manufacturers a competitive edge in the next generation of consumer electronics, thus weakening European competitors like Thomson (France) and Philips (Netherlands).

It is interesting to note that a similar concern for protecting national champions led to the failure of the 1966 CCIR meeting to produce agreement on color TV standards, leading to the fragmentation of world markets into three incompatible analog color TV systems (the American NTSC, the European PAL, and the French SECAM).[2] The difference was that now Western European nations were responding as a united front. After successfully blocking diffusion of the Japanese system, European nations engaged in an intergovernmental program to develop a European HDTV system under the EUREKA framework. Unlike other R&D programs funded directly by the Community (e.g., the European Strategic Program for Research and Development in Information Technology, or ESPRIT), EUREKA functioned primarily as a way to coordinate

[1] The adoption of Article 128 in the Maastricht Treaty (1992) greatly increased the Community's formal powers over issues of culture, but so far intervention based on the new article has been limited.
[2] For a discussion, see Crane (1979).

cross-national R&D.[3] In this case, however, the European Commission agreed to play a coordinating role. The initial phase of the HDTV initiative was budgeted at U.S.$400 million, funded in equal parts by the national governments involved and participating companies (among the most important were Thomson, Philips, and Bosch). The HDTV system developed was based on the MAC (multiplexed analog components) family of standards, a largely analog system initially developed by the U.K. broadcasting authority. Participating firms agreed to pool the patents from their work on the MAC program (Hart and Thomas, 1995).

The initiative was a classic industrial policy project on an intergovernmental scale: the publicly owned telecommunications operators would build the infrastructure (satellites in this case), national champions in consumer electronics would manufacture compatible TV sets, and public broadcasters would transmit programming in the new format. Community involvement was formalized in November 1986, when an EC directive mandated the use of the MAC standard in television services from high-power satellites.[4] From the very start, the initiative ran into difficulties. Several of the satellites associated with the MAC program experienced severe technical problems. Broadcasters were reluctant to use a transmission format with a small installed base of receivers, in particular the growing lot of private broadcasters who had little to gain from a forced technological migration. Community authorities made several attempts to rescue the initiative from complete failure. The European Commission designed a salvage plan based on a new directive, an action plan to subsidize MAC equipment, and a memorandum of understanding with broadcasters, satellite carriers, and equipment manufacturers to bolster credibility toward the MAC standard. The action plan failed to materialize, mainly due to stubborn British opposition to provide additional funding (Dupagne, 1998).

Ultimately, despite being heavily funded by equipment manufacturers and national governments, the ambitious MAC initiative never got off the ground.[5] With the inauguration of a new commission in 1993, and

[3] Interestingly, EUREKA was never formally brought under the Community, and thus project approval and funding rested entirely on national governments (see Sandholtz, 1992).

[4] Council Directive of 3 November 1986 on the adoption of common technical specifications of the MAC/packet family of standards for direct satellite television broadcasting (86/529/EEC). OJ L 311, November 6, 1986. At the time, only high-power satellites were suitable for direct-to-home satellite TV services.

[5] Total spending for the project has been estimated at U.S.$1.4 billion (Hart and Thomas, 1995).

the rise of Martin Bangemann at the helm of European technology policies, the initiative was finally brought to a halt. Funds earmarked for the
action plan were substantially reduced as a result of British pressure and
relocated to promote the development of widescreen (i.e., 16:9 display
format) equipment and programs, but not necessarily in MAC.[6] The
failure of the program set an important precedent not only for European
broadcasting policies but for European technology initiatives in general. The fact that an entente that included national governments, the
European Commission, public broadcasters, and the major equipment
manufacturers was unable to force a technological migration represented
a turning point in several ways. In general, it revealed the limits of industrial policy instruments on an intergovernmental scale, particularly
in rapidly evolving technology markets. More specifically, it revealed
the expansion of the number of players involved in the broadcasting
industry, as MAC advocates were unable to ignore the success of competing standards endorsed by private broadcasters. From this failure
emerged a new approach to European standards setting, an approach
that relied on the work of private standards development organizations rather than intergovernmental bargaining (David and Shurmer,
1996).

It is also important to note the involvement of the Community in the
liberalization of the market for broadcasting services. Liberalization has
effectively reduced the capacity of national regulators to control market
entry in broadcasting and thus guarantee the success of preferred operators (Servaes, 1992; Collins, 1995). In the late 1980s, the European
Commission started pushing for reforms to overcome the fragmentation
of European television markets through the harmonization of national
media legislation and the creation of a regional market in broadcasting
services. This led to the Television Without Frontiers (TWF) Directive,
the first comprehensive Community statute that translated the market
integration principles embodied in the Single European Act of 1987 to
the broadcasting sector.[7] The TWF Directive had two main goals: first,
to abolish legal restrictions to cross-border television services within the
Community; and, second, to abolish existing nontariff barriers through

---

[6] Funds were also available to support PalPlus, a backwards-compatible enhancement
to the PAL system that permitted widescreen signals to be received in existing analog
TV sets.
[7] Council Directive 89/552/EEC of 3 October 1989 on the coordination of certain provisions laid down by Law, Regulation or Administrative Action in member states concerning the pursuit of television broadcasting activities. OJ L 298, October 17, 1989.

the harmonization of national content rules relating to advertising, programming quotas, and the protection of minors.

The TWF Directive was updated in 1997 to clarify definitions and questions of jurisdiction. The update added an important provision that entitles member states to draw up a list of events that have to be broadcast unencrypted even if exclusive rights were bought by pay-TV channels. The directive reflected the European Commission's assessment of the European television market as a weak and fragmented sector, largely controlled by public quasi monopolies, and of the need to introduce changes that would allow European players to better compete on a global scale. This conflicted in several ways with concerns – often voiced by the European Parliament (EP) – about preserving cultural plurality within the Union (Schlesinger, 1997). As we shall see, this tension between the industrialist and the cultural goals associated with broadcasting would often resurface in the case of digital TV, forcing European policymakers to revisit constantly the line between member states and Community jurisdiction.

THE POST-MAC ERA

With Commissioner Martin Bangemann in charge of setting a new direction for the Community's technology policies, digital TV was subsumed within the European Information Society Action Plan (EC, 1994). The action plan chartered the course for the development of new information infrastructure and services on the continent. While the Community and its member states would play an important role in providing coordination, regulatory incentives, and targeted R&D funding, the action plan advocated a departure from traditional top-down European technology initiatives: "[T]he creation of the information society in Europe should be entrusted to the private sector and to market forces" (EC, 1994: 29). Besides market liberalization, the action plan identified harmonization of standards and network interconnection at the European level as key targets for regulatory action in the communications sector. With respect to standards setting, the new plan advocated a clear break from past approaches: "[O]pen systems standards will play an essential role in building a European information infrastructure. Standards institutes have an honorable record in producing European standards, but the standardization process as it stands today raises a number of concerns about fitness for purpose, lack of interoperability, and priority setting that is not sufficiently market driven" (p. 12).

In calling for private sector leadership, market-driven standards, and a halt to the neomercantilist high-tech rivalry of the 1980s, the action plan marked a radical turn in European policies toward digital TV. The MAC initiative debacle had proved that the times when a coalition between national governments and their national champions could effectively restructure an entire industry were past. According to the action plan, the previous focus on HDTV services was misguided. Digital TV – not HDTV – was the key development, for it allowed more efficient use of the spectrum, and accelerated the implementation of global information networks. While private market actors would take the leading role in the transition to digital TV (which the European Commission estimated would take about two decades), Community authorities had three key roles to play: first, to coordinate R&D in digital broadcasting; second, to encourage standardization; and, third, to ensure fair competition in the new services. Yet promotion and regulation activities were to be kept strictly separate.

Standardization became the initial focus of attention for Community authorities in the post-MAC era. The European Commission strongly endorsed the work of the Digital Video Broadcasting (DVB) group, an industry consortium established in the aftermath of the MAC debacle in 1993 to develop standards for the European digital TV industry. As a private standards-development organization that included equipment manufacturers, broadcasters, content producers, software developers, and representatives of national regulatory bodies, the DVB became a key player in the European transition. The involvement of many high-level Community and national regulators in the DVB effectively reduced the role of the official European standards-setting organizations (e.g., ETSI and CENELEC) to "rubber-stamping" DVB agreements (David and Shurmer, 1996). The DVB proceeded with unique speed to develop a family of standards for digital TV (cable, satellite, and terrestrial). However, this was not a particularly challenging task because industry agreement already existed around the key technologies to be used. When the DVB came to address the more controversial issue of encryption and CAS for digital TV, the divisions within the consortium, as well as the limits of its internal procedures as a standards-developing body, became evident.

At issue was whether the DVB would endorse a particular CAS system, and whether such system would be based on open or proprietary standards. Community authorities expressed strong support for a unique CAS solution that would facilitate cross-border trade in broadcasting equipment and services in the region; yet, following the new approach, they were reluctant to impose standards not fully endorsed by market players. The issue essentially pitched established pay-TV operators like BSkyB and Canal+ against public broadcasters and other independent programmers. From the outset, pay-TV operators sought to safeguard their investments in proprietary CAS technology as well as the established business model whereby pay-TV operators subsidized the cost of set-top boxes. They opposed the adoption of a common interface in digital set-top boxes that would allow the use of multiple CAS on a single decoder box (the so-called multicrypt solution) and thus reduce incentives for providing equipment subsidies. Pay-TV operators instead proposed a solution called simulcrypt, whereby different CAS "keys" were inserted in a single broadcast stream to allow reception on different set-top box populations (Kaitatzi-Whitlock, 1997). This solution was opposed by a coalition led by the BBC and German public broadcasters ARD and ZDF, which feared that pay-TV operators would discriminate in favor of affiliated programmers and impose hefty fees on third-party access to the decoder box.

To alleviate the concerns voiced by public broadcasters, simulcrypt advocates proposed a voluntary code of conduct for CAS operators that would ensure nondiscriminatory third-party access. They also stressed the drawbacks of a mandated common interface: the development of the interface would delay the roll-out of digital services; the complex circuitry and design required for a common interface would increase the costs of digital set-top boxes, thus discouraging adoption; finally, the system would be more vulnerable to piracy. The multicrypt coalition nonetheless opposed a voluntary code that lacked effective enforcement procedures (Levy, 1997). After several months of negotiations, the conflict remained unresolved. Commission representatives attempted to end the deadlock, but the differences persisted. In the end, the DVB approved both the simulcrypt and the multicrypt solutions, falling well short of the Community's goals with respect to harmonization of digital TV standards. It became apparent that legislation would be needed to address the issues that the DVB could not resolve on its own. Yet, both the European Commission and the council were reluctant to impose a solution without industry support, and the first draft of the legislation simply ignored the CAS problem. According to the council, the text of the proposed directive reflected exactly what market parties were prepared to support.[8]

---

[8] European Council (1994). Common Position No. 48/94 Adopted by the Council on 22 December 1994 (On digital broadcasting). OJ C 384/36, December 31, 1994.

The multicrypt coalition rejected the draft directive and demanded that the Community either mandate the common interface or translate into statute the access safeguards contained in the voluntary code of conduct. The coalition found sympathetic ears for its case among European legislators, typically more alert to consumer protection issues as well as more responsive to the plight of public service broadcasters. British European legislators from the Labour Party played a pivotal role in pushing for tougher regulations on CAS operators, which they considered vital to curb Rupert Murdoch's power in the British media industry. Making use of its recently acquired codecision prerogatives under the Maastricht Treaty, the European Parliament amended the directive, introducing a key provision that regulated the terms under which CAS operators could offer services to broadcasters. Initially, the British government resisted the amendment based on the argument that it overregulated an infant industry. Britain only revoked its veto after the European Council agreed to a statement that clarified that the amendment introduced by the Parliament did not entitle broadcasters to require carriage on specific digital TV platforms.[9]

The final text of the directive (henceforth Directive 95/47)[10] emerged from this bargaining between the Parliament and the Council within the context of the failure of the DVB to produce voluntary agreements and the urgency of Community authorities to establish a framework for the roll-out of digital TV. The directive covers two main areas: standardization of the transmission systems used in digital TV and the market behavior of CAS providers. With respect to the first, the directive mandates the use of approved standards in the transmission and scrambling of digital TV signals (in essence, the DVB system). On the CAS issue, the directive neither prohibits proprietary CAS technologies nor mandates a common interface for digital set-top boxes. The level of set-top box interoperability is thus left to be decided by the industry. The directive does prescribe, however, the following behavioral rules to prevent abuses by CAS operators: holders of CAS-related intellectual property are required to license it on fair, reasonable, and nondiscriminatory terms (Article 4d); CAS operators must allow cable operators full control over the encryption of satellite-delivered programming (Article 4b); finally, CAS operators must offer their service to broadcasters on fair, reasonable, and

[9] Council of Ministers Press Release, July 24, 1995.
[10] European Parliament and Council Directive 95/47/EC of 24 October 1995 on the use of standards for the transmission of television signals. OJ L 281, November 23, 1995.

nondiscriminatory terms (Article 4d). These rules represented a significant victory for public service broadcasters and independent programmers, because they translated the voluntary code of conduct proposed
by pay-TV operators into statutory access provisions. However, because
the directive lacks precise enforcement guidelines, much was left to the
transposition and implementation by member states. Not surprisingly,
this has proved quite problematic, because the directive gave national
authorities wide margins for interpretation. In fact, the European
Commission was forced to challenge the implementation in at least one
case (Spain) and to open proceedings for lack of action in several others
(EC, 1999).[11]

Crafted in the aftermath of the MAC debacle, the directive – not
surprisingly – imposed a relatively light regulatory regime for digital TV.
As the Council acknowledged, Community authorities were wary about
engaging once again in industrial planning. The directive attempted to
create a delicate balance between the demands of pay-TV operators for a
regime that provided incentives for the rapid roll-out of services based on
the existing business model and the demands of public broadcasters and
independent programmers for access safeguards. From the European
Commission's perspective, the directive established an adequate level
of regulation that produced certainty for the first phase of the transition. In a sense, tolerating proprietary technologies was the price to pay
for the massive investments in infrastructure and services required. Besides, should the market evolve in ways that required tighter rules, the
Commission could always revisit the issue. In reality, the balance left
much to be decided at the national level. As the transition evolved, the
ambiguity of the directive in terms of its scope of application and tools
would stir much debate among national stakeholders.

REGULATORY CONVERGENCE IN THE COMMUNITY

Whereas the separation between common carriers and publishers in
American law has limited the application of telecommunications policy
doctrines and instruments to the regulation of digital TV, the two areas
have come much closer together in Western Europe. The blurring of

---

[11] In July 1999, the Commission submitted to the European Court of Justice infringement
cases for nontransposition of Directive 95/47 against Austria, Belgium, France, and the
Netherlands. In the case of Spain the Commission challenged the initial transposition,
which in stark contradiction with the directive mandated a common interface for
digital decoders.

technological boundaries between telecommunications and broadcasting has led Community authorities to make increasing use of the regulatory tool set developed for the telecom sector to deal with similar problems in digital TV. These tools are essentially of two types: sector-specific legislation and general competition rules (Larouche, 1998; Ungerer, 2000). Sector-specific legislation took shape under the Open Network Provision (ONP) framework.[12] The key principle of the ONP framework was that, in network industries where dominant operators already existed, competition would only develop with the establishment of ex ante rules that prevented foreclosure of new entrants seeking access to resources under the control of incumbent operators (Nihoul, 1998). The ONP concept was implemented throughout the 1990s through a series of directives and recommendations. The key goal was to ensure that new entrants had access to the key elements (or "essential facilities") of the existing telecommunications network in transparent and nondiscriminatory terms and at reasonable cost. ONP regulations outlined basic principles for determining interconnection tariffs, usage conditions, and the availability of interface specifications, while addressing public interest goals such as a universal service and data protection in a proportionate way.

Initially, television services were explicitly excluded from the scope of application of the ONP framework.[13] Yet, as the transition progressed, it became apparent that regulatory concerns in telecom and broadcasting were increasingly similar: access to bottleneck facilities, interconnection between dominant operators and third parties, vertical integration between network operators and service providers, standardization of interfaces. These concerns cut across both sectors. European regulators thus began to gradually broaden the scope of the ONP framework in order to tackle comparable problems with a unique tool set. The European Commission's Green Paper on Convergence (EC, 1997) formally opened the debate about how to regulate the communications industry as convergence evolved. According to the Green Paper, the challenge was to adapt the existing telecom and broadcasting regimes so that regulation did not forestall but rather encouraged the convergence process: "[T]he fact that an open framework [the ONP framework] is applied to one set of infrastructure but not to others may create barriers and

---

[12] Council Directive of 28 June 1990 on the establishment of the internal market for telecommunications services through the implementation of open network provision (90/387/EEC). OJ L192, July 24, 1990 (ONP Framework Directive).
[13] See ONP Framework Directive, Article 2(4).

distort investment, particularly, if convergence of technologies extends over time to the industry and market and service levels" (1997: 23). To a large extent, the exercise implied collapsing the two regimes into a single set of rules to address similar problems across electronics networks irrespective of the underlying technology. Several member states were nonetheless wary about engaging in a grand reform exercise; they generally supported the Commission's efforts but preferred a slower reform process whereby existing rules would be modified as needed (see EC, 1998a). Some were particularly concerned about what they perceived as an attempt to transfer jurisdiction over television programming and licensing to the Community.

The Green Paper on Convergence received only lukewarm support, but the Commission nonetheless pushed forward in its efforts to extend the ONP framework beyond telecommunications. The Access Notice, adopted by the Commission in 1998, would be the first in a series of legal instruments to establish the validity of the ONP principles to the "digital communications sectors generally" (EC, 1998b: 2). The notice also opened the door for the application of ONP principles beyond physical infrastructure issues. By addressing logical interfaces, services, and even particular types of content, the notice established a broader role for ONP-type rules in digital TV. For example, the licensing of CAS-related intellectual property and control over EPG services now fall within the jurisdiction of ONP regulations (Ungerer, 2000). The next step was taken in 1999 as part of the Commission's comprehensive review of the Community communications regime launched in the wake of the Green Paper.[14] The review included a thorough report on the status of the transition to digital TV in Europe and the implementation of Directive 95/47 (EC, 1999). The report concluded that, despite several implementation problems, the directive had the important benefit of providing credible rules for the launch phase of digital TV services, balancing investment incentives with competition safeguards. It also praised the role of DVB standards in facilitating coordination in the initial roll-out of services and equipment and promoting long-term investments. Yet the report found that the transition had evolved beyond the launch phase, demanding

[14] Communication from the Commission to the European Parliament, the Council, the Economic and Social Committee, and the Committee of the Regions, Towards a New Framework for Electronic Communications Infrastructure and Associated Services (The 1999 Communications Review). COMM (1999) 539, November 10, 1999.

that the directive be updated. In particular, it reiterated the importance of set-top box interoperability and openness, important targets that had not been fully realized:

> When the Directive was adopted, it was assumed that conditional access would be the primary bottleneck. . . . There was already awareness that other elements in DTV systems could also be bottlenecks; however it was uncertain when or if they would be introduced into the market. In keeping with the decision to provide a light regulatory framework for the start of the market, these elements were not included in the Directive. Now that the market has started in most member states, it is certain that they will play an increasingly important role, with the potential to push DTV beyond its origins in broadcasting towards convergence with other forms of service provision. (EC, 1999: 21)

The report made a strong case for aligning the more specific safeguards for CAS laid down by Directive 95/47 with the general ONP framework. The European Commission's review resulted in a new regulatory package for electronic communications networks and services. The main goal of the new package was to put into practice the Commission's vision of a single regulatory regime for a converging communications sector. The package had significant implications for the regulation of digital TV services in the Community. A key principle was the separation between content and infrastructure or transport regulation. Already recognized by the Commission as the basis for Community involvement in digital broadcasting, this separation provided a useful jurisdictional demarcation between the EU and its member states. With few exceptions related to general harmonization of rules (e.g., the TWF Directive) and support initiatives for Pan-European audiovisual productions (e.g., the MEDIA program),[15] content matters were considered the province of member states. In legal terms, the separation was consistent with the restricted jurisdiction of the Community on cultural matters; in political terms, it reflected the resistance by member states to delegate much power over television to Community authorities. Historically, this separation had given national authorities the autonomy to set rules with respect to media ownership, the financing of public broadcasters, programming

---

[15] The MEDIA program is a Community fund that supports professional training and the development, distribution, and promotion of European audiovisual content.

standards, editorial pluralism, and so on. By extension, it was now being interpreted as giving member states the freedom to decide on the timetable and the licensing scheme for the introduction of digital TV. Yet, as we shall see, precise demarcation of regulatory roles would remain, in effect, problematic. In issues ranging from "must-carry" rules to the regulation of EPG services, the line between content and infrastructure regulation is less than clear and so became the separation between national and Community jurisdiction.

In the new package, Community authorities reaffirmed their commitment to market-driven standardization in digital broadcasting. Yet, they warn that mandating standards might be appropriate under certain circumstances (the growth of the mobile telephony industry after the Commission sanctioned GSM as a European standard is cited as an example of positive Community involvement in standardization). The central piece of the new package (the so-called Framework Directive) gave the Commission the authority to mandate standards when deemed necessary to ensuring interoperability and the internal market objectives.[16] Among the main candidates for compulsory standardization was the digital set-top box API, since proliferation of different proprietary technologies had erected barriers for cross-border trade in interactive TV services (Galperin and Bar, 2002). The DVB had been working for years on MHP (multimedia home platform), a standardized API that Commission officials hoped would produce full interoperability in interactive TV services, providing a smooth migration path from existing proprietary technologies toward an open set-top box architecture. However, development was hindered by quarrels within the DVB along the same lines of the earlier battle between simulcrypt and multicrypt – pitting public service broadcaster and independent programmers (who favored mandating MHP) against incumbent pay-TV operators (who opposed standardization). Community authorities ultimately took a similar approach: the Framework Directive allowed member states to extended the nondiscriminatory obligations in Directive 95/47 to interactive TV platform operators but, as in the CAS case, stopped short of mandating full API standardization. Once again, this effectively shifted the debate to the member state level.

---

[16] Directive 2002/21/EC of the European Parliament and of the Council of March 7, 2002 on a Common Regulatory Framework for Electronic Communications Networks and Services (Framework Directive). OJ L 108/33, April 24, 2002.

Of the new regulatory package, the Access Directive is the one that most directly affected digital TV.[17] This Directive represented the centerpiece of the Commission's efforts to harmonize access and interconnection obligations for all communications industries across member states. The Directive justified ex ante regulation in the broadcasting sector on two grounds: first, because of the large difference in negotiating power between dominant network operators and those who need access to such networks (i.e., the ONP argument); second, because of the need "to ensure cultural diversity and media pluralism in the area of digital television" (i.e., the cultural specificity argument).[18] The Access Directive allowed member states to impose behavioral rules on dominant providers of digital TV access services generally (not only on CAS operators as established by Directive 95/47) as well as "must-carry" obligations to ensure availability of specific programmers. Among the behavioral rules suggested are obligations to interconnect, to offer access services on nondiscriminatory terms, to keep separate accounts in the case of vertically integrated companies, to license technical interfaces on reasonable terms, and to impose controls on the pricing and the recovery of decoder subsidies.

Yet, a critical difference between the ONP framework and Directive 95/47 was left unchanged: whereas ONP obligations are imposed on dominant operators only, access rules continue to apply indiscriminately to all CAS operators. Furthermore, access obligations are predefined in the case of CAS, whereas national authorities have more leeway to choose from a toolkit of access obligations to address other problems. In light of the problematic transposition of Directive 95/47, it is not surprising that Community regulators were less willing to delegate the issue to member states. In fact, compared with Directive 95/47, the Access Directive significantly enhanced the tools for Community authorities to intervene in cases where member states fail to advance the interoperability and access goals laid down by the Community for the digital broadcasting sector.

COMPETITION CASES

Community competition regulators have also played a critical role in shaping the course of the transition in Europe through their inquiry into

---

[17] Directive 2002/19/EC of the European Parliament and of the Council of 7 March 2002 on Access to, and Interconnection of, Electronic Communications Networks and Associated Facilities (Access Directive). OJ L 108/7, April 24, 2002.

[18] Access Directive, at 8.

a number of high-profile competition cases related to the introduction of digital TV services in several member states. European competition policy has four pillars: the antitrust provisions laid down in Articles 81 (collusions between groups of companies) and 82 (abuses of dominant position) of the EC Treaty; the Merger Control Regulation, which authorizes the European Commission to review mergers above a certain revenue threshold; the provisions against state aid (e.g., subsidies) contained in Article 87 of the EC Treaty; and the provisions in Article 86 that subject public enterprises (such as public broadcasters) to general competition rules. The Commission Competition Directorate is responsible for the enforcement of these regulations, although ultimate interpretation rests with the European Court of Justice. European competition regulators have shown a noticeably uncompromising approach to the application of competition rules in digital TV, particularly in evaluating proposed mergers and joint ventures. In many cases the Commission simply refused to approve them, whereas in others it demanded significant changes to the agreements. This has raised a number of questions about the appropriate use of competition law instruments to regulate an infant industry in which significant upfront investments are required and in which technology is rapidly changing.

The strategies used by incumbent market actors to share or minimize the risk involved in digital TV ventures have often been challenged by competition authorities. For example, an important case ("MSG services") concerned a joint venture between three heavyweights in the German pay-TV market (Bertelsmann, Kirch, and Deutsche Telekom). The partnership was expected to develop digital TV access services such as CAS and subscription management. The Commission blocked the venture alleging that the creation of MSG would have strengthened the dominant position of the partners in the German pay-TV (Bertelsmann and Kirch) and cable TV (Deutsche Telekom) markets, foreclosing the likely development of competing digital TV platforms.[19] The case was later revisited when the same three firms attempted to reach a new agreement to avert a set-top box war between rival digital platforms and to join forces to develop access services for digital TV in Germany. The Commission reaffirmed its earlier position and rejected the new agreement based on concerns about the competitive effects of a combination between the premium programming rights held by Kirch and Bertelsmann, Kirch's CAS technology, and Deutsche Telekom's extensive

---

[19] M. 649 Media Services Group, OJ L364/1 (1994).

cable assets.[20] According to the Commission, the poor uptake of digital TV in Germany did not justify approving a joint venture that posed significant competitive threats in the short term. Under European competition law, there is no "efficiency defense" available to prospective digital alliances that pose a risk to competition. Such defense was omitted from the Merger Control Regulation to prevent old-style industrial policy considerations in the evaluation of cases.

In other cases, Community competition authorities have not outright rejected agreements but here extracted substantial concessions from partnering firms. These concessions often amounted to detailed requirements about the market behavior and the technologies to be supported by the new firm, through which the Commission has set policies and structured the evolution of digital TV markets. In 1999 the Commission opened a review about a proposed equity investment by BSkyB in Kirch's pay-TV business. The Commission ultimately approved the agreement, subject to a number of undertakings by the parties involved.[21] Several of these undertakings related to Kirch's entry into the digital interactive TV market. The company committed to offer digital access services to third parties on fair, reasonable, and nondiscriminatory terms; to keep separate accounts for its technical services business; and to disclose information concerning its CAS – essentially, what the new regulatory package would require a few years later. Interestingly, the Commission went beyond imposing behavioral rules and required that Kirch take the necessary steps to implement an API as standardized by the DVB (i.e., the MHP) within a year of its approval by the relevant European standards bodies. Two important cases related to the introduction of digital terrestrial (the BDB case) and interactive TV services (the BiB case) in the United Kingdom are discussed later in Chapter 10.

The approach taken by the European Commission in these competition cases has virtually amounted to digital TV policymaking through antitrust law. Not surprisingly, this has resulted in much controversy. Some have argued that the up-front costs involved in the introduction of digital TV services make large-scale operators indispensable, and this often involves agreements between leading media and telecom firms or mergers between dominant operators. Strict application of competition

---

[20] Commission Decision 1999/154/EC, Deutsche Telekom/Beta Research and Commission Decision 1999/153/EC, Bertelsmann/Kirch/Premiere (OJ L 53, February 27, 1999).
[21] Notification of 22 December 1999 Pursuant to Article 4 of Council Regulation (EEC) No 4064/89, OJ L 2985.

law has therefore slowed the roll-out of services and hindered standardization efforts in the start-up phase of the market (de Cockborne, Clements, and Watson-Brown, 1999). Others have criticized the Commission for taking a narrow perspective on the relevant markets affected in these cases, particularly before some of these markets even take shape. The argument is that, in the context of rapidly evolving, nonmature technologies, the market definitions upon which competition authorities make decisions are inherently unstable, largely based on estimations, and therefore open to future challenges (Veljanovski, 1999). As Larouche (1998) notes, in many of the cases discussed here, technological progress may have alleviated – or even eliminated – some of the competition problems identified by antitrust regulators. Adjudications thus depended on underlying assumptions about how specific markets and technologies were likely to evolve.

Underlying this debate is a more general question about the appropriate combination of generic competition law, sector-specific rules, and self-regulation in policing the communications industry (Cowie and Marsden, 1999). In the case of digital TV, there is yet another layer of complexity: the need to balance the traditional goals of broadcast regulation (pluralism, protection of minors, freedom of speech, etc.) with the goals of procompetitive infrastructure regulation. Community policies in digital TV have been based on a number of legal assumptions. First is the separation between content and infrastructure, which has provided a practical principle to carve out a legitimate realm for Community action. This formal separation of tasks has followed the historical legacy of Community involvement in new broadcasting technologies such as cable and satellite TV, in which the separation between network operator and content provider is better established; in contrast, terrestrial broadcasting by and large continues to be the territory of member states. The second assumption is the separation between regulation and promotion, established after the MAC debacle, whereby the Community assumes regulatory functions and a general coordinating role but leaves support initiatives to member states (and, in fact, becomes the watchdog of those initiatives). However, as we shall see, these assumptions have in practice proved ambiguous. The British case is particularly interesting in this respect, for policymakers have wrestled with their goal of making Britain the European hub for information society services, their embrace of the ONP principles, and their desire to maintain the historical balance between commercial and public broadcasters, a balance that often requires crossing the line between content and infrastructure regulation.

EIGHT

The Birth and Evolution of Analog TV
in the United Kingdom

The birth of the broadcasting industry in the United Kingdom is intrinsically tied to the British Broadcasting Corporation (BBC). Started in the early 1920s by a consortium of equipment manufacturers as little more than a tool to increase the sales of radio receivers, the BBC became to many in Britain and elsewhere a synonym for high-quality programming and excellence in independent news reporting. Furthermore, its institutional arrangement as a public broadcasting corporation funded by a license fee collected on all viewers and the ideological foundations of its public interest mission became the archetype – at least in statute, though often not in practice – for the establishment of broadcasting operators in many other countries. In Britain, however, the BBC was from the start a controversial institution. But for all the public debate and governmental reviews endured, the BBC has shown remarkable resilience as a dominant force in British broadcasting. In many ways, the development of digital TV in Britain has to be understood within the peculiar history of this corporation and the political efforts to redefine its role in face of the societal and technological changes in Britain since the early 1920s.

The BBC originated from the aspiration of equipment manufacturers such as the Marconi Company to exploit the commercial opportunities made possible by technological developments in radio technology. Until the end of World War I, radio was only used in point-to-point applications by the military. Manufacturers began regular broadcasts of information and entertainment in London and other cities in 1920, but the Post Office (which under the Wireless Telegraphy Act of 1904 was responsible for controlling wireless telegraphy and, by extension, radio transmissions) was reluctant to license many different services on a permanent basis for fear of overcrowding the limited radio frequencies available at the time (Briggs, 1961). Instead, the Post Office proposed that manufacturers form a broadcasting consortium to provide regular radio transmissions collectively. As a result, in 1922 the British Broadcasting Corporation was born as a de facto private broadcasting monopoly, funded by a royalty on the sale of BBC-approved receivers and a license fee from listeners collected by the Post Office. This system soon proved cumbersome and was replaced by a single fee set by the government and collected from the public. The Post Office retained the right to license more broadcasters, but there was widespread agreement that licensing broadcasters to compete against each other (as was being done in the United Kingdom) would soon result in chaos and that a cooperative arrangement could better advance the general interest in the development of broadcasting (Gibbons, 1998). As early as 1923, a government committee rejected the idea of funding the BBC with advertising for fear that it would compromise programming standards (Paulu, 1981). Nevertheless, the BBC faced severe financial shortfalls, and in 1925 a new committee chaired by Lord Crawford recommended that the BBC be reconstituted as a public corporation, yet independent from the government, and that it continue to be funded by the license fee collected on all listeners. The committee also recommended that the new company be incorporated under the Companies Act, but the postmaster general preferred to do so through a royal charter in order to give the BBC greater independence from legislators (Briggs, 1961).

On January 1, 1927, the BBC started its new life as a public corporation, supervised by a board of twelve governors appointed by the crown (in consultation with the government), who in turn appointed the director general and the corporation's other senior managers. The governors were not supposed to represent any particular party or interest group, although politics inevitably played a role in designations. The BBC was required to obtain a license from the government to conduct its broadcasting operations, essentially an agreement that specified the duties and obligations attached to the license. The corporation was thus made accountable to the government, which to date retains the prerogative, should the BBC fail to comply with its obligations, to revoke its license. Both the royal charter and the agreement that set out the BBC's general aims, internal organization, and financing have always been limited in time, effectively implying that the BBC has never been established on a permanent basis. This has allowed the government considerable discretion for periodically evaluating and reshaping the BBC. Such lack of a statutory framework has often been criticized for compromising the BBC's political independence and accountability to the public at large

(Gibbons, 1998). Despite the lack of a formal protection against political interference, however, successive governments have been restrained by a strong cross-party tradition of noninterference with the corporation's day-to-day operations and programming decisions (Verhulst, 1998). In fact, notwithstanding the heated political debate that has accompanied every charter and agreement renewal, the basic organizational principles and funding mechanism of the BBC have remained virtually unchanged since 1927.

The first director general of the BBC was the legendary John Reith, who was instrumental in imbuing the new corporation with his views about the duties of public service broadcasting. These were rooted in the argument that, as a result of the limited availability of frequency channels for radio services and of the "power over public opinion and the life of the nation" exerted by the new medium, radio should not be left to private operators but rather to a public corporation acting "as trustee for the national interest in broadcasting."[1] Reith interpreted this principle as a duty to provide programming of high-quality and educational merit to the viewing public, regardless of the heterogeneity of the public which the BBC served. In practice, the BBC's programs often reflected the moral and religious values of the British middle class to which Reith himself and many legislators belonged. As Scannell and Cardiff (1991) note, it was easy to equate the BBC with the national interest when it represented the views of a self-confident social group that permeated British politics and business. In the Reithian vision there was also a profound distrust about the private operation of broadcasting services, best represented by the American model of commercial radio and later television. Thus, when commercial operators were finally authorized, their public service obligations were specified in more detail than for the BBC, for it was thought that these operators would be more tempted to sidestep them. While the existence of a national consensus on the values that public service broadcasters were obliged to nourish would later be rejected, the belief that, as public trustees, these operators carried a responsibility to air high-quality programming – however defined – that reflected the political and cultural diversity of the nation continued to exert a major influence on thinking about broadcasting in the United Kingdom. Over the decades, public service broadcasting would prove a remarkably resilient principle, one that has critically shaped the British transition.

[1] Crawford Broadcasting Committee Report (1925), at 4.

The BBC first started experimenting with television broadcasting in 1936, although three years later the beginning of World War II halted such efforts. Television services resumed in 1946, and soon after the Labour government appointed a committee to review the renewal of the BBC charter and make recommendations about the future of the new medium. While the committee (chaired by Lord Beveridge) was not uncritical of the BBC, it recommended the extension of its broadcasting monopoly and rejected the introduction of advertising. Yet a minority report by Conservative committee member Selwyn Lloyd suggested that a private competitor to the BBC funded by advertising would provide more programming diversity and alleviate the perils associated with monopoly market power. With the Conservative victory in the 1951 elections, the Lloyd report became the blueprint for the introduction of commercial television in Britain. Opening up the television market for commercial operators was a radical step in reconfiguring the nascent television industry, a step that no other Western European nation had taken or was even seriously considering (in fact, it would take several decades for most Western European countries to license commercial broadcasters). While the Conservative Party leadership (including Prime Minister Winston Churchill) was largely indifferent to the idea of ending the BBC's monopoly, the proposal was forcefully advocated by a group of young party backbenchers, with the endorsement of a coalition of business interests that included advertising agencies and several newspapers publishers (H. Wilson, 1961; Cave and Williamson, 1995).

The Television Act of 1954 was the result of a compromise within the Conservative Party between those who wanted to break up the BBC's monopoly and those who remained anxious about the consequences of such a radical overhauling of the industry. The act thus authorized commercial television, yet under a strict set of rules and obligations that prevented real competition between the new channel and the BBC, or even among private operators. The act created the Independent Television Authority (ITA), a public body organized much like the BBC (with a board of governors appointed by the government) and that held the commercial broadcasting licenses and owned and operated the transmission network for the new channel. The ITA, in turn, allocated a number of regional monopoly franchises to private operators who provided the programming and sold advertising in each of the regions (the regional structure partly reflected the Beveridge Committee's concern about the excessive "Londonization" of the BBC).[2] The operating expenses of the ITA were financed by a levy on the revenues of its licensees. Franchises were allocated (and renewed) through a so-called beauty contest that involved qualitative comparison of bids, interviews with applicants, and public consultations. Ultimately, the ITA made its decisions behind closed doors and was not required to justify them. Because of the importance given to the financial resources of the applicant and the continuity of the service, incumbent licensees typically had an advantage, although occasionally licenses changed hands. The ITA (later renamed Independent Broadcasting Authority, or IBA) was thus not only an industry regulator: it actually held the licenses and was ultimately responsible for ensuring that the services offered by its commercial licensees complied with the public service duties and obligations set by the 1954 act.

Soon after the first regional licenses were granted, it became clear that a network system was needed to sell larger audiences to advertisers and thus support larger production budgets. What resulted was a national networking arrangement. All independent television (ITV) companies participated in the Network Program Committee of the Independent Television Association (ITVA, the trade organization for commercial broadcasters) that conducted scheduling for the entire network (Hoffmann-Riem, 1996). Under this arrangement, the five largest licensees dominated as program suppliers, selling to the smaller ones in return for a proportion of their advertising revenues. This cartel-like arrangement that prevented any competition between regional franchisees was accepted by the ITA, although the IBA would later try to modify the system (without much success) in favor of the smaller ITV companies (Paulu, 1981). In any case, the commercial broadcasting authority had little interest in promoting competition among licensees, for its income derived from a levy on the revenues of commercial TV as a whole. Without competition for a growing advertising pie, the ITV sector flourished (Cave and Williamson, 1995). A mere two years after the launch of ITV, Canadian news magnate Roy Thompson, who controlled the regional franchises for Scotland, famously defined commercial TV as "a license to

---

[2] Initially, each of the regions was also split into two different franchises for weekday and weekend programming, although this separation was later discontinued. The number of regions grew from three in 1954 to fifteen in 1962, plus a nationwide morning television license.

print your own money."[3] ITV was in essence a regulated monopoly, structured so that the effects of economic competition did not take precedence over the public service obligations imposed on commercial broadcasters.

In 1960 the Conservative government appointed a new committee to evaluate the progress of commercial TV and advise on the renewal of the BBC charter, which expired in 1964. The government also intended to authorize a third channel and sought the committee's recommendation on how to proceed. The majority of the members of the committee, chaired by Sir Harry Pilkington, shared a strong Reithian view about broadcasting (Briggs, 1985). Not surprisingly, the report of the committee criticized ITV, qualifying it as a service that "falls well short of what good public service broadcasting should be."[4] The report also criticized the ITA for its problematic lack of distance with its licensees, contending that its role was more of a defender and spokesman rather than regulator of the ITV companies. The BBC, in the meantime, made a compelling case to the committee that it needed the third channel in order to better fulfill its public service mission. The argument claimed that with the advent of ITV the BBC had been forced to schedule programming of broader appeal at the expense of more serious or experimental fare and that the availability of a second BBC channel would allow the corporation to complement its flagship service with valuable and yet less popular programming. In due course, the Pilkington Committee recommended a sweeping overhaul of the ITV structure and the award of a third channel to the BBC.

The government was nonetheless unwilling to meddle much with a highly popular service such as ITV. Thus, the new Television Act (1964) largely ignored the recommendations of the Pilkington Committee for the commercial TV sector, making only minor adjustments that empowered the ITA to monitor its licensees more closely and mandate specific types of public service programming on the ITV network. Most important, the act awarded the third channel to the BBC. The committee had also recommended that the BBC's second channel use a more advanced broadcasting system (a system using 625 lines on UHF frequencies rather than the existing system of 405 lines on VHF). In 1964 the BBC2 (as the second channel was called) started transmissions utilizing the new system. As a reference point, it is interesting to note that the transition

---

[3] Cited in Crisell (1997), p. 102.
[4] Pilkington Report on Broadcasting (1960), at 67.

from the 405-line system to the new 625-line system took two decades to complete. Because – much as in the case of digital TV – new sets were required to receive the BBC2, the new channel grew slowly. The start of regular color transmissions in 1967 created a major incentive for viewers to replace their old sets in order to receive the BBC2 service (as well as the BBC1 and ITV, which were simulcast in both formats), despite the fact that the government decided to levy a higher license fee on owners of color TV receivers in order to finance the required upgrades in studio and transmission facilities for the BBC's migration to color TV. Production of 405-line TV sets rapidly ceased, and a large rental market existed as an option to buy the new sets. By 1981 the new system had reached almost universal penetration (BIPE, 2002). Yet, 405-line transmissions were only discontinued in 1985, with just 15,000 homes (about 0.07 of total households) still dependent on the old system (Elstein, 2001). Depriving citizens – however many – of free-to-air television is by no means attractive for elected officials, and these political sensibilities remained strong in the case of digital TV.

THE CONSERVATIVE REFORMS

By 1979, when Margaret Thatcher was first elected prime minister, the United Kingdom had a mature television industry. Virtually all British households (97 percent to be exact) had a TV set, and both the BBC and ITV had grown into large corporations that produced in-house the bulk of their programming (in the case of ITV, most of it provided by the largest five licensees). The Thatcher administration thus inherited a well-established duopoly, nurtured in large part by Thatcher's own predecessors in the Conservative Party. While the existence of even limited competition between a public broadcaster and a cartel of commercial operators was unparalleled in the European context, this was clearly not enough for an administration elected on a platform of sweeping market reforms and the undoing of public utility monopolies. Furthermore, the relative stability of employment in the industry and the concentration of the 36,000-plus work force in two companies largely based in London provided fertile ground for trade unionism and a kind of professional elitism that privileged high production values over cost discipline (Goodwin, 1998). The separation of the income streams for the BBC and ITV meant that both were largely sheltered from the market pressures that result from direct competition in other industries. These were exactly the kind of inherited economic and political arrangements that the Thatcher administration was keen to take on.

Interestingly, the debate about the need to reform the broadcasting duopoly carried over from the previous Labour administration and the report of the Annan Committee. Appointed by the government to examine the future of the industry, the committee found that the existing industry structure failed to reflect the transformation of Britain into a culturally heterogeneous and politically diverse society and that the institutional arrangements failed to make broadcasters accountable to society at large (Annan Committee, 1977). The committee favored decentralization, flexibility, and diversity of services, yet it rejected the idea that market reforms would produce such results. In fact, it warned against the Americanization of the broadcasting system, for the U.S. case revealed that "unrestricted competition between three broadcasting networks narrows the range of programmes" and that "competition for the same finance lowers programming standards so as to satisfy the lowest common denominator."[5] The committee instead recommended the establishment of new broadcasting authorities accountable to Parliament, based on the concept of "regulated diversity" in broadcasting services. This essentially implied the maintenance of the key legal and economic arrangements of the existing system. This type of minor reform, however, was clearly not what the Thatcher administration had in mind for the television sector.

The first issue that the incoming Thatcher administration faced was how to set up the fourth terrestrial channel, which had been in the planning for several years. The Annan Committee had recommended that the new channel be allocated to the new broadcasting authority and funded with a mix of sponsorship, public subscription, and advertising. The administration nonetheless rejected this option and announced that the new channel would be placed under the IBA, funded mainly through advertising, and that a substantial proportion of its programming would be contracted out to independent producers (essentially, anyone but the BBC and the ITV companies). Yet the organizational details for Channel Four (as it came to be called) were left to the IBA. The authority quickly dismissed the idea of having the new channel compete directly for advertising revenues with ITV. Instead, it opted to fund it through a levy on the ITV companies, which in return sold advertising on the new channel in their own regions. After intense pressure from Welsh-language

---

[5] Report of the Annan Committee (1977), at 73.

advocates, a separate broadcasting authority (S4C) was also established in Wales to run the fourth channel.

By introducing competition in the production of television programs and opening distribution opportunities for companies not affiliated with ITV or the BBC, the creation of Channel Four in 1980 was responsible for the emergence of an entirely new industry subsector: the independent production companies. The cozy arrangement between ITV and Channel Four that prevented competition for advertising revenues hardly pleased the administration. Yet, other political priorities took precedence over reforming television, particularly during the first Thatcher administration. The government initially opted for a less politically costly strategy: instead of tackling the terrestrial duopoly directly, the state would promote new technologies such as satellite and cable TV. The idea was to confront a highly regulated terrestrial TV sector with a lightly regulated new media one. Until then, the development of new media had been stifled by restrictive rules about the types of services and programming that operators could offer, largely a result of lobbying efforts by the BBC and later the ITV companies (Negrine, 1989). Also, the Conservatives had campaigned on the need to develop a strong information technology sector in Britain. Promoting the development of broadband communications networks such as satellite and cable TV thus seemed a legitimate policy goal (Dutton and Vedel, 1992). In 1981 Thatcher appointed a minister of information technology and set up an Information Technology Advisory Panel (ITAP) to make recommendations on what steps to take. The ITAP recommended that the administration announce as soon as possible the licensing of satellite TV services and outline a plan to promote cable systems across the nation (ITAP, 1982).

In keeping with the administration's free-market leitmotiv, and in sharp contrast to cable policies in continental Europe, the ITAP proposed that the cabling of Britain rely on private financing only (Dutton and Blumler, 1988). The panel also recommended the removal of programming restrictions that confined cable to the redistribution of terrestrial channels in areas of poor reception. The government quickly followed suit by commissioning a specific report on cable to a committee chaired by Lord Hunt. The report endorsed the overall strategy outlined by ITAP and recommended that a new regulatory authority be set up to franchise and "oversee" (though not "regulate") the development of the industry. The report nevertheless proposed that the new Cable Authority be empowered to mandate minimum quotas of British programming on cable and that foreign entities be banned from controlling cable franchises. The

1984 Cable and Broadcasting Act translated the strategy outlined by ITAP and the Hunt Report into statute. It also spelled out the relation between cable policies and the drastic market reforms being introduced at the time in the telecommunications sector. Basically, cable providers could only offer local telephony services in partnership with British Telecom (the soon-to-be-privatized incumbent operator) or Mercury, the newly licensed operator. In return, the two operators were not allowed to offer entertainment services over their telecommunications networks, although they were free to apply for cable franchises.

Despite the light regulatory regime (which discharged cable programmers from most of the public service obligation imposed on the BBC and ITV), private financing was slow to develop. This lack of interest by financial investors was partly explained by the tax policies implemented by the Thatcher administration that essentially discouraged long-term capital investment of the type required by cable (Dutton and Blumler, 1988). In addition, the restrictions placed on foreign entities limited the interest of American cable operators who better understood the economics and marketing of the cable business. The Thatcher administration nevertheless stood firmly behind its belief that cable development should be privately funded and refused to commit any public funds. Engaging in a sort of grand public project to cable Britain similar to France's Plan Câble (in which funds and coordination came mainly from the public telecommunications operator) was squarely against what the government stood for. By 1988 only twenty-three franchises had been awarded reaching less than 12 percent of British households, and of those only ten were operational (Goodwin, 1998). The pace of investment picked up slightly at the end of the 1980s, fueled by the expectation that the government would lift the restrictions on foreign investment and permit cable operators to offer local telephony services in direct competition with telecommunications operators (which it did in 1991). But for the most part the development of cable fell well short of expectations both as a way to introduce competition in the broadcasting market and as the foundation for a revolution in information technology in Britain. By no small measure, this failure was due to the success of a rival platform: satellite TV.

The impetus for the development of satellite TV in Britain also came from a two-pronged interest by the Thatcher administration in having a head start in what promised to be a large market with substantial high-technology spillovers and in gradually freeing the television industry from the existing duopoly. A study commissioned by the government endorsed this strategy, adding that, should Britain fail to move rapidly in licensing domestic satellite TV, services licensed in other European countries but still capable of being received in Britain would preempt the market and render locally licensed services unviable (Collins, 1994). Thus, in light of the need to speed up the process, the government approached the IBA and the BBC to ascertain their interest in satellite TV. At the time, the IBA was occupied with the introduction of Channel Four and expressed little interest. The BBC, on the other hand, accepted the challenge and proposed an initial service with two channels (one of them subscription-based) that would later be expanded to include commercial programmers. Yet, again, the government made clear that the venture would not receive public funding. Unable to find private financing for the venture, the BBC appealed to the government, which in turn attempted – unsuccessfully – to entice the IBA and the ITV companies into the venture. Ultimately, the BBC-led partnership failed, and the government, having lost the momentum for an early start, decided to advertise the satellite TV franchise through the IBA. In December 1986 the franchise was awarded to British Satellite Broadcasting (BSB), a consortium that included newspaper publisher Pearson (publisher of the *Financial Times*) and ITV licensees Granada and Anglia TV.

BSB was still Europe's first licensed satellite-to-home TV service. It planned to broadcast a three-channel service of news and entertainment in the MAC format, following required technical specifications from the IBA and European legislation related to high-power satellites. As noted, the deployment of the technology associated with MAC services suffered several setbacks, forcing BSB to delay the start of services until 1990. By then Sky TV, a rival satellite TV service controlled by Murdoch, was already beaming from a medium-power satellite using the conventional PAL technology. Because Sky TV was transmitted through the Luxembourg-based Astra satellite, it did not require a broadcast license from the IBA and essentially fell outside the control of British authorities. Furthermore, the TWF Directive prevented British authorities from blocking the reception of Sky in British soil. Having launched fourteen months after Sky and incurring higher costs due to the use of an unproven transmission standard, BSB, the "official" satellite TV licensee, was headed for disaster.[6] Yet the government was unwilling to come to the rescue. As a cabinet minister explained before Parliament, "BSB is a

---

[6] By the time BSB launched, Sky had already sold over 600,000 dishes and locked long-term movie contracts with Hollywood content distributors.

commercial venture, they knew when they took on the contracts of the risks – and I respect them for that – and there could be no guarantees of success from the government or elsewhere."[7] On the verge of collapse a the end of 1990, BSB agreed on the terms of a merger proposed by Sky, with Murdoch retaining control of the newly formed company, BSkyB.

The BSB-Sky merger illustrated how problematic it had become for British regulators to control market entry in the face of new communication technologies that ignored national borders and the European integration process (Collins and Murroni, 1996). The IBA considered the merger a serious breach of BSB's contract and opened proceedings to revoke its license (a move that ultimately had no effect as BSB customers transitioned into BSkyB). News reports about Murdoch having warned Prime Minister Thatcher of the merger in advance, and the fact that she failed to take any action, have often been cited as evidence of an exchange of favors between the Australian media magnate and the Conservative government (e.g., Smith, 1999). The administration, argue its critics, had several policy instruments to scrutinize and possibly to block the merger but instead cleared it without even referring it to the Monopolies and Mergers Commission (MMC), the competition watchdog. Prime Minister Thatcher and her cabinet certainly had no particular interest in preventing Murdoch – whose newspapers were generally supportive of the administration – from controlling what was seen as a highly risky business venture. Furthermore, any action against Sky was certain to raise issues of market integration in Brussels, where the European Commission had just completed the passage of the first directive liberalizing the European television market (the TWF Directive).

In the meantime, a new agenda had been brewing within the Thatcher administration. After the failure of its cable policies and the delays in the launch of satellite TV, government officials became increasingly convinced that, if significant reforms were to be introduced in the television sector, the terrestrial duopoly had to be tackled. This became particularly evident during Thatcher's second term after the 1983 elections. The primary target of reforms was the BBC. After a series of incidents related to the BBC's coverage of the Falklands War and the conflict in Northern Ireland (which were deemed "too neutral" by the administration), a growing majority in the cabinet supported the introduction of serious reforms to the corporation. Furthermore, the BBC's request for

---

[7] Cited in Goodwin (1998), p. 50.

a substantial increase (41 percent) in its license fee prompted calls to rethink its funding scheme and reconsider the introduction of advertising. Free-market advocates were now winning the argument within the Conservative Party about the distortions introduced by a broadcaster funded through a blanket tax on all viewers. As a first step in this direction, the administration set up a committee to advise the government on the financing of the BBC. Alan Peacock, a well-known free-market academic, was appointed chair.

Not surprisingly, the report of the Peacock Committee was highly critical of the existing industry structure (which it described as a "comfortable duopoly"), proposing that "British broadcasting should move toward a sophisticated market based on consumer sovereignty" (Peacock Committee, 1986: 135). Yet, contrary to what most expected, the committee rejected the introduction of advertising on the BBC, at least in the short term. Instead, it recommended that the license fee be maintained until the technology to implement a full-fledged subscription system for the BBC was deployed. The committee also recommended that the license fee be linked to the retail price index (RPI), which typically rose slower than programming costs, in order to create cost-efficiency pressures on the corporation. Peacock went beyond its narrow mandate to analyze the funding of the BBC and suggested other reforms to the sector, such as the allocation of ITV franchises through competitive bidding, the introduction of a minimum quota of independent productions for the BBC and ITV, and the end of the funding arrangement between Channel Four and ITV.

The Peacock Report became the blueprint for the reforms pioneered by the Thatcher administration in the terrestrial sector, despite the report's disappointing rejection of advertising for the BBC that Prime Minister Thatcher personally favored. Its recommendations were translated into legislation in the Broadcasting Act of 1990, which radically reshaped the structure of the commercial TV sector. Labour and most incumbent ITV operators opposed the reforms, but more importantly, so did a number of Conservative front benchers in Parliament, who managed to introduce a number of Reithian safeguards to the broadly deregulatory bill. The act replaced the IBA with a new, "lighter touch" regulator, the Independent Television Commission (ITC). The new body would still license commercial TV operators and enforce their contracts but would not hold broadcast licenses or run the transmission network for ITV (the act mandated the privatization of the ITV transmission network). Also, among the new agency's duties was to ensure fair and effective competition in the provision of broadcasting services (Prosser, 1997). Cable and satellite also came under the ITC's jurisdiction (thus the short-lived Cable Authority was abolished), although radio broadcasting fell under the new Radio Authority.

The act introduced competitive bidding in the allocation of ITV licenses, though qualified by a number of "quality" safeguards (heavily lobbied by a coalition that included Labour and the ITV incumbents) that still allowed for some regulatory discretion in the licensing process.[8] Real competition for advertising revenues was introduced with the separation of Channel Four from ITV and the authorization of a new advertising-funded channel (Channel Five). The act transformed Channel Four into a public trust and allowed it to sell its own advertising, although the government agreed to a safety net scheme whereby Channel Four was guaranteed 14 percent of total terrestrial advertising revenues.[9] Finally, following Peacock, the act introduced a minimum 25 percent quota of independent productions on all terrestrial broadcasters, including the BBC.[10] The Broadcasting Act of 1990 also transformed the structure of ownership in the commercial TV sector by unleashing a wave of consolidation among ITV companies. Using the powers delegated by the act, the government proceeded to relax the restrictions on the holding of ITV licenses, a trend that continued through the next Conservative administration. By the time the party left power in 1997, ITV was essentially controlled by the "big three" licensees: Granada, Carlton, and United News and Media (later absorbed by Granada).

The final text of the Broadcasting Act of 1990 did not go as far in the liberalization of the terrestrial TV market as the Thatcher cabinet had hoped. Several compromises had to be made within the Conservative Party to make the reforms acceptable to a number of cultural conservatives concerned about the lowering of programming standards that market reforms could trigger. Nevertheless, the "comfortable duopoly" was formally terminated. Ironically, the main result of the compromises

[8] Essentially, the act required that applicants pass a "quality threshold" and granted the ITC authority (under "exceptional circumstances") to award a license to an applicant that has not submitted the highest bid.
[9] As it turned out, Channel Four ad revenues largely exceeded the 14 percent threshold, which under the act translated into payments from Channel Four to the ITV companies (this scheme was ended in 1996).
[10] In the case of the BBC, the Office of Fair Trading (OFT) – a nonministerial department established by the 1973 Fair Trading Act to enforce competition and consumer protection legislation – was made responsible for monitoring compliance with the independent productions quota.

struck by the government aimed at preserving a quality threshold for British TV was that the ITC was hardly the light regulator originally intended. This became evident in the first test of the new ITV franchise auction system in 1991: of the forty bids made for the sixteen licenses available, thirteen failed to pass the quality threshold, while of the thirteen licenses contested (for three licenses only one bid was received) only six went to the highest bidder (Cave and Williamson, 1995). Similarly, in the case of Channel Five the first invitation to apply (issued in 1992) produced only one bid, but the ITC was not satisfied with the plans presented and declined to award the license (the license was finally awarded in a second round of bids in 1995). The ITC also retains a high level of discretion in deciding whether licensees have complied with the programming obligations stipulated in their licenses. The lack of precise procedural obligations on the ITC in the adjudication of licenses or license-related cases has severely limited the role of the British courts in limiting the agency's discretion.[11]

Overall, the BBC endured surprisingly well the wave of market reforms introduced by the Thatcher administration in the broadcasting and telecommunications sector. It could still count on a secure stream of income through the license fee – reduced, however, by the inflation peg proposed by Peacock – and managed to escape the jurisdiction of the newly created broadcasting authority. With the change of leadership in the Conservative Party in 1990, it was widely believed that the new cabinet led by John Major would continue the reforms in the sector by refocusing attention on the BBC. As it turned out, the new administration had no intention to change the funding scheme of the BBC, break up the corporation, or implement any of the draconian reforms floated during the Thatcher years. There was in fact a much more benevolent tone toward the BBC than before, well reflected in the rather innocuous Green Paper on the Future of the BBC released by the government in 1992 (DNH, 1992). For the BBC, the market reforms introduced by the 1990 act had complicated the legitimacy problem of keeping high enough ratings to justify the blanket license fee, but at least the political climate had changed in its favor.

Several factors explain this change. First, staunch free-market reformers were now a minority in the cabinet. Second, the public controversy generated by the ITV franchise auctions of 1991 had somewhat reduced the political appeal of reforms in the sector (ironically, Mrs. Thatcher

---

[11] For further discussion, see Gibbons (1998) and Prosser (1997).

herself criticized the outcome). Third, in the years between the Peacock Report and the change of party leadership, the BBC had, under the leadership of Deputy Director General (and, after 1993, Director General) John Birt, undergone substantial internal reorganization aimed at making better use of its resources and enhancing the "professionalism" of its news reporting. In a manifesto outlining a vision for its future, the BBC acknowledged the need for making improvements both in terms of internal efficiency and accountability to the public (BBC, 1992). In a sense, the BBC was internalizing the concerns raised by its critics. The senior management knew that, were major changes not adopted, the very existence of the corporation would be up for debate during the review of the royal charter, which expired in 1996. By accepting funding cuts and implementing cost-saving reforms, the BBC was implicitly accepting a more modest role in post-Thatcher Britain.

The Major administration's proposals for the renewal of the BBC charter, released in 1994, presented few surprises. Following the new consensus on a reduced, more efficient BBC, the government proposed the continuation of the license fee (until at least 2002), the maintenance of its current services (BBC1, BBC2, and five national radio channels), and retention of the current governance structure (DNH, 1994). The new royal charter and agreement, announced in late 1995 (and approved by Parliament in February 1996), clearly reflected the new tone toward the corporation: "[T]he BBC is a national jewel," affirmed Virginia Bottomley, who as national heritage secretary was responsible for broadcasting policy in the Major cabinet (DNH Press Release, November 27, 1995).

Overall, there were only two issues in which the administration's proposals for the BBC parted with the status quo. The first was in endorsing the privatization of the BBC's transmission network, an issue originally raised by the Thatcher administration in 1988 but later shelved until the charter renewal. According to the government, the separation of transmission services could reduce barriers to entry in the industry as well as provide the BBC with an injection of capital for its new undertakings, including digital TV. The second was in recommending the expansion of the BBC's commercial activities. These activities, according to the government, could supplement the license fee and help establish a British presence in international media markets, although the government strongly warned that "commercial activities must be clearly separated from services in the United Kingdom funded from the license fee" (DNH, 1994: 23).[12] In order to encourage these activities, the government proposed to repeal the provisions in the 1990 act that prevented the ITC from licensing commercial services to the BBC. Although the government suggested that international markets should be the main target of the BBC's commercial efforts, these changes also opened the door for the corporation to participate in digital TV commercial ventures in Britain, which, as we shall see, came to be critically important for the British transition almost a decade later.

---

[12] For this purpose, a wholly owned commercial subsidiary, BBC Worldwide, was formed in May 1994.

NINE

Being First: The Digital TV Race

The shift in the Conservative Party's attitude toward the BBC in the 1990s hardly represented the abandonment of its program to expand choice and introduce market reforms in the broadcasting sector. While the Major cabinet was certainly more sympathetic to the principles of public broadcasting and the Reithian tradition, market liberalization was still very much in the agenda. By the mid-1990s, however, the term had acquired a new meaning. After the reforms introduced by the 1990 act, competition – however imperfect – now existed in the terrestrial market, and though more liberalization was without doubt possible, Tory leaders were confident that the industry was headed in the right direction. The problem was now in the pay-TV sector. BSkyB had become successful to a degree that few could have imagined only a few years before. After two years of heavy losses in the aftermath of the Sky-BSB merger, the new company was now well into profitability and completely dominated the pay-TV sector. By 1994 BSkyB had almost 3 million subscribers, had secured contracts with the Premier League for exclusive rights to live football coverage, and was the major content supplier for the struggling cable industry. In addition, it controlled the dominant CAS and subscriber management operator that provided access services to other programmers (a subsidiary called Sky Subscribers Services Limited, or SSSL). BSkyB was increasingly perceived as a monopolist in the pay-TV sector, a perception only reinforced when the competition watchdog opened an investigation about BSkyB's practices in the supply of premium programming to cable operators. The Major cabinet was not particularly sympathetic to Murdoch. Staunchly Conservative throughout the Thatcher years, the Murdoch-controlled newspapers (in particular the respected *Times* and the widely read tabloid *Sun*) had turned critical of the Major administration since the 1992 elections (Butler and

Kavanagh, 1997). Gradually, introducing reforms in the television sector became synonymous with challenging BSkyB's dominance in the pay-TV sector.

Another theme of the Thatcher era that the Major administration had hardly abandoned was the promotion of information technology through the early deployment of new communications infrastructure. Moved onto the backburner for a number of years following the debacle of the cable and satellite initiatives of the 1980s, this theme returned in the beginning of the 1990s, fueled by new technological breakthroughs and ambitious technology policy initiatives in the United States and other industrialized nations. The groundwork for the development of such initiatives in the United Kingdom had been laid down during the first Thatcher period through the work of the ITAP and Kenneth Baker, who was then minister for information technology. Baker himself was now home secretary, and the link between broadcasting and telecom policy-making seemed stronger than ever. In 1991 the government ended the telecommunications duopoly created in 1983, allowing cable companies to offer local telephony service in their own right. At the same time, a report that British Telecom (BT) – barred from offering entertainment services under its telecommunications licenses – was planning to start a video-on-demand service sparked wide controversy about regulatory asymmetries between telecommunication and broadcasting operators (Hills and Michalis, 1997). The commercial and jurisdictional bound-aries between the two industries seemed in flux, and the government, criticized by many for not doing enough to encourage the development of advanced communication services in Britain, was caught in a frenzy to develop "new opportunities for United Kingdom businesses in providing multi-media services in an expanding global market" (DNH, 1994: 1).

The combination of these two policy goals – challenging BSkyB's dominance of the pay-TV industry and promoting Britain's lead in in-formation technologies – persuaded the Major cabinet of the need to move rapidly in the introduction of digital terrestrial television (DTT). The cabinet believed that a successful launch of DTT ahead of other na-tions could advance both goals. First, a terrestrial pay-TV service would provide competition to BSkyB in a way that cable had been incapable of, essentially because of the lower start-up costs involved in the deployment of the transmission infrastructure, the nationwide character of the ser-vices (cable operators were still fragmented in local franchises, although a wave of industry consolidation was under way), and the "plug and play" character of the reception equipment. Second, launching DTT in advance of other nations would give equipment manufacturers (such as Pace Microelectronics, which manufactured decoders for BSkyB) an edge in what promised to be a large worldwide market. Moreover, the eventual shutdown of analog channels would release valuable radio frequencies that, according to government estimates, could generate as much as £5 billion in new business per year (DNH, 1994). As Ian Taylor, then science and technology minister, acknowledged, the government's support of digital TV was part of a long-term spectrum strategy to release the "huge wealth creating value . . . into the UK economy when the analogue spectrum is reinvested in new broadcasting and telecommunications services" (DTI Press Release, December 15, 1995). The early introduction of DTT would also create opportunities for new information services and give British companies a first-mover advantage in their development. There was thus a perceived opportunity to advance two important goals of the administration, but timing was of critical importance. While DTT trials were well under way in the United States, BSkyB was widely believed to announce soon the launch of its digital satellite services, which many feared would make terrestrial competitors unviable. There was therefore a short window of opportunity for strategic policy action. For the DTT project to succeed, an early launch was essential.

But why DTT? In other words, why not pursue the same goals through the development of other digital platforms such as a broadband wireline network as proposed by BT or even an alternative satellite operator? The answer is twofold. First, the DTT platform was more amenable to national regulatory controls than satellite, and the instruments for such control could well be adapted from the existing analog regime. As Collins argues, the failure of BSB was a crucial turning point: "[F]or the first time an officially sponsored monopoly failed in competition with an unplanned, and officially unwelcome, new entrant to the market" (1997: 387). It was thus important to promote the emergence of a digital platform that, unlike satellite TV, would be squarely under the jurisdiction of British authorities. The fact that DTT allowed more regulatory maneuvering in defense of specific types of programming also struck a chord with public service broadcasting advocates and cultural conservatives across parties. In contrast with cable, increasingly controlled by U.S. investors since the lifting of investment restrictions in the 1990s, and satellite TV, wholly in the hands of Murdoch through a service based outside the United Kingdom's borders, DTT would better allow policymakers to exercise authority over the structure and output of digital TV services and, in particular, to defend the British tradition of public service broadcasting. Moreover, public service broadcasters could best compete in a platform with limited carriage capacity than among the hundreds of channels that digital cable or satellite would offer. While not guaranteed, DTT at least gave the BBC a good chance of success in the digital age. The BBC's senior managers understood this well and pressured the government for a rapid introduction of DTT services.

The launch of digital TV services had been in the agenda since the early 1990s. In 1991 the ITC commissioned a frequency-planning study to identify the channels available for the eventual launch of DTT. The study, undertaken by NTL Incorporated (the privatized transmission arm of the former IBA that provided transmission services for ITV and Channel Four), predicted that four frequency channels (each covering at least 74 percent of the population) would be available for DTT services (NTL, 1991). A follow-up document by the ITC outlined the main strategic choices that the government faced in the implementation of DTT and the switch-off of analog TV. In this discussion document, the ITC estimated that the transition would demand at the very least ten years from the introduction of digital TV services (ITC, 1993). This transition period was considered necessary due to the investments made by consumers in analog TV equipment (TV sets and video casette recorders essentially), the need to develop economies of scale in the production of digital equipment, and the need for European-wide agreement about digital broadcasting standards. In addition, the ITC stressed the need to provide incentives for both broadcasters and consumers to take up DTT ahead of a ten-year deadline. Based on the premises established by the NTL study (four national DTT networks interleaved within the analog broadcast spectrum), the ITC document suggested three possible introduction strategies.

The first was a simulcasting strategy whereby an additional frequency channel is loaned to the existing operators (the BBC, ITV, Channel Four, S4C, and the new Channel Five) for a finite period in which they are expected to broadcast their services in both analog and digital format. According to the ITC, this could be done by amending the existing licenses (except for the BBC, which would require a change to its charter and agreement). At the end of the simulcasting phase analog transmissions are phased out and the operators return the analog frequencies to the government. This was essentially the model for the introduction of DTT in the United States. Yet, the proposal parted ways with the American model in one significant issue: HDTV. While recognizing that in order to stimulate DTT adoption the new services would have to be offered in an enhanced format, the ITC wrote off HDTV as the main driver of DTT penetration. Instead, it suggested the introduction of less challenging improvements such as the 16:9 picture aspect ratio (a widescreen format closer to what cinema offers), the benefits of which according to the ITC were "almost indistinguishable from that of HDTV using current display technology and under normal viewing conditions" (ITC, 1993: 6). Such skepticism about the benefits of HDTV would in fact permeate the ITC's policies for years to come. The document recalls that this strategy was successfully used in the transition from the old 405-line black-and-white system to the existing 625-line color system. Yet, it also points out that, because of the need to interleave DTT channels within the analog broadcasting spectrum, power levels for digital transmissions would have to be kept low during the simulcasting period to prevent interference, a provision that would severely compromise DTT coverage in the initial phase (with four channels and the existing network configuration the document estimated a coverage of about 80 percent, significantly lower than the 99 percent of analog TV).

The second possible strategy for the introduction of DTT was based on the premise that any new digital channels should be made available to any prospective users, with none being set aside for simulcasting. Under this strategy, called the "new services" model, DTT frequencies would be awarded to the highest bidder under the auction scheme laid down by the 1990 act, and existing broadcasters would be forced to bid "like anyone else" for the right to offer DTT services. According to the ITC, the main benefit of this strategy was that the availability of new services would provide a greater incentive for the adoption of DTT than the provision of an improved signal (e.g., widescreen) of the existing channels. On the other hand, this model posed questions as to when the analog frequencies could be recovered. The commission also expressed concerns about the ultimate benefits of a strategy that simply offered yet another digital platform: "[S]ince satellite receivers are already in the market, providing the opportunity for an increasing number of new services to be introduced, the need to bring in a new technology terrestrially purely to open up some further new channels may not seem great" (ITC, 1993: 8). In other words, pitching DTT directly against digital cable or satellite TV was not the way to go.

A third strategy – that the ITC seemed to favor – was a combination of the previous two in what the document calls the "simulcast-plus-new-services model." This model presupposes that, with the more efficient use of the radio frequencies offered by digital TV, enough frequencies could be available to license a number of new services alongside the simulcasting of the existing analog channels. While simulcasting would guarantee that the transition does not disrupt the current offering, the new services could provide the additional incentive for viewers to take up DTT.

The ITC document also suggested that the frequencies initially allocated to Channel Five (channels 35 and 37) could be used instead for DTT. This sparked a fresh round of controversy about the introduction of the new commercial channel authorized by the 1990 act but that the ITC declined to award after the first round of bids in 1992. The discussion centered around whether it was wise to go ahead with a new analog terrestrial channel expected to cover only about 75 percent of the population when these frequencies could be used to launch the new generation of broadcasting services. Furthermore, the launch of Channel Five on those frequencies required the retuning of millions of VCRs to avoid interference at an estimated cost that ranged from as little as £5 million to as much as £350 million.

The different interest groups lined up on the issue as expected. The majority of the ITV licensees favored the use of the frequencies to launch DTT in order to avoid the entry of another competitor in the terrestrial market. With the support of the British Radio and Electronic Equipment Manufacturers Association (BREMA, the trade organization for the equipment manufacturers), this group mounted an extensive public campaign around the claim that the new analog channel would delay the launch of DTT for many years. On the other hand, advertisers and prospective market entrants such as Time Warner and Pearson opposed the new proposal and defended the original frequency allocation plan. Meanwhile the BBC, always loath to cede more spectrum to the commercial TV sector, came in favor of the digital scheme. The corporation was in fact already working on a technical plan in which the two frequency channels were awarded to the BBC to launch – as early as 1997 – a national DTT service that would offer the existing terrestrial channels plus some additional services, some of them subscription-based. Besides keeping a new entrant off the market, the plan was meant to demonstrate the BBC's willingness to collaborate with a pet government project in light of the upcoming charter review. The terrestrial incumbents found an unexpected ally in Michael Heseltine, the influential cabinet member that headed the Department of Trade and Industry (DTI), then responsible for the allocation of radio frequencies. Heseltine, a Conservative with a surprising penchant for grand government projects, was eager to snap jurisdiction over Channel Five away from the Department of National Heritage (DNH) and champion the development of digital TV under his wing.

The government praised the BBC's enthusiasm about DTT. Also, the plan to provide subscription channels that would complement the income stream from the license fee was in line with the government's goal of increasing the BBC's commercial activities. In July 1994 the administration released the White Paper on the Future of the BBC, which outlined its proposals for a new BBC charter and agreement (DNH, 1994). This document provided the first decisive statement by the Major administration in support of the transition and the first indication of the strategy favored by the cabinet. According to the White Paper, the government was committed to a transition that would enlarge the choice and quality of services for viewers while also opening opportunities for British technology companies. The BBC was expected to play an important role in the early introduction of DTT, although the White Paper makes it clear that no license fee funds should be allocated to finance the new services. Instead, it suggests that the BBC use the proceeds from the privatization of the BBC transmission network – one of the key proposals of the White Paper – to fund the launch of digital services, or else seek private sector financing. This was described by DTI officials as "a carrot on a stick" approach: the government supported the BBC's enthusiasm about DTT and wanted the corporation on board for the introduction of services but, in return, wanted the privatization of its transmission network, which was expected to raise about £200 million. According to the document, the ultimate goal was to "combine the early introduction of digital broadcasting services by the BBC with the benefits of privatisation of the transmission network, which would stimulate competition and reduce the barriers to entry for new operators, without increasing the costs to the BBC" (DNH, 1994: 28).

In the end Heseltine failed to convince his colleagues in the cabinet that the tender for Channel Five should be postponed indefinitely to make room for DTT. A compromise was reached whereby the ITC would readvertise the license for Channel Five, but the new broadcaster would utilize only one of the two frequency channels originally allocated (this effectively reduced coverage from 75 to about 50 percent of the U.K. population). The other frequency channel, it was decided, would for the moment be reserved for the introduction of DTT services. This was nonetheless a victory for Heseltine and other Channel

Five opponents who had conveniently become DTT enthusiasts. More important, it signaled to market actors that the introduction of DTT services had become a real priority for the administration, as resources previously allocated to other initiatives were being diverted to promote the transition. The announcement set off a rush among incumbent broadcasters and prospective entrants to develop commercial and technical plans for DTT. Shortly after, the BBC announced that it would start experimenting with digital broadcasting in early 1995 and that it was budgeting large investments in new studio equipment to provide DTT services in widescreen format. NTL announced that it would invest tens of millions of pounds to provide transmission services for DTT broadcasters. Yet, some key questions about the introduction of DTT remain unresolved. Which frequencies would be made available for DTT and how would they be allocated? Would the government auction off the new licenses? What ownership restrictions and programming requirements would apply for the new services? What role would the BBC and other existing broadcasters be called to play? Before committing to DTT, market actors wanted the government to present a full-fledged transition plan.

In anticipation of the government's release of its DTT proposals, the ITV companies spelled out their own vision of the transition. These companies had a lot at stake as the introduction of new services could dilute the value of their licenses, acquired in some cases at a high cost in the 1991 licenses tender. According to press reports, the government was considering a plan in which the terrestrial incumbents were only allocated enough capacity to simulcast their signals in digital format, a plan that the ITV licensees believed would diminish the appeal of their services in an increasingly crowded marketplace. In a document submitted to the DNH in the spring of 1995, ITV supported the "carrot and stick" approach laid out by the government. The carrot, however, must be to award each of the existing analog broadcasters (the BBC, ITV, Channel Four, and the new Channel Five) an additional frequency channel in order to simulcast the existing analog programming *and* develop new digital channels. Should any incumbent fail to utilize its second frequency channel within a specified time period, the channel would be withdrawn and made available to other operators. Once the transition was completed (in no less than ten to fifteen years according to ITV), the analog frequencies would be returned to the government. Given that the ITC had identified only four frequency channels available for nationwide DTT services, the ITV plan basically prevented any new market entry during the simulcasting phase. Awarding incumbent broadcasters a full frequency channel to simulcast in digital format and introduce new services was nonetheless a fair bargain, argued the ITV companies, in light of the costs that would have to be borne in launching and promoting DTT. It would also speed the transition process because only incumbent operators had the capacity to create the kind of programming needed to spur take-up.

The ITV companies also argued that privileging incumbent broadcasters would stimulate the local programming industry and increase the supply of content for export, for incumbents with "spare production capacity" would not rely on imported content as new operators probably would. This argument was intended to resonate with independent producers and the industry unions, which have heavily lobbied for the imposition of restrictions on imported programming in the United Kingdom and at the European level. According to the ITV proposals, there were few British companies – apart from those in ITV – equipped to undertake the effective commercial development of digital, and, unlike the ITV companies, few of those were committed to local production. This was also meant as a surreptitious attack against BSkyB, for this company was often charged with not complying with the European content quotas mandated by the TWF Directive.

In March 1995 BSkyB formally announced that it expected to launch a digital satellite service by the end of 1996, with capacity for more than one hundred channels. The announcement sent shock waves throughout the industry, leading to increased pressure by established broadcasters – and, in particular, the BBC – on the administration to press ahead with the legislative framework for the introduction of DTT. This came at a time of great turmoil in the Major administration and the Conservative Party leadership. John Major had won the 1992 elections by a razor-thin margin that gave the incoming administration a slim Parliament majority of twenty-one seats. Yet, by 1995, the deep divisions on the issue of European integration within the Conservative Party and the perceived weakness of the government had decimated the majority to only a few votes (Butler and Kavanagh, 1997). In June 1995, in an effort to regain party control and shore up favorable public opinion, Major called for a vote of confidence. Despite the internal turmoil Major managed to win reelection as party leader and proceeded to reorganize his administration. Heseltine, for whom the introduction of DTT had become a pet project, was promoted to deputy prime minister with wide oversight powers over all government policies. Virginia

Bottomley, a Conservative of strong Reithian views, was moved to the DNH and placed in charge of pushing the administration's broadcasting policy agenda. As she recalls, the cabinet had a keen interest in DTT, but the introduction of a legislative framework for the services was greatly accelerated as a result of pressure from incumbent operators and, in particular, the BBC: "[D]igital broadcasting was critical to their plans for the future. The BBC appreciated that legislation was necessary to create a level playing field for commercial enterprises" (Bottomley, 2000: 121).

THE WHITE PAPER ON DTT

The government's DTT proposals were finally released in August 1995 (DNH, 1995a). Together with the proposals for the future of the BBC (DNH, 1994) and for the relaxation of media ownership restrictions (DNH, 1995b), they formed the core of the new broadcasting legislation that the administration planned to introduce. The proposals were released amid grand statements by administration officials about the dawn of "a new television era." In the words of National Heritage Secretary Bottomley:

> Britain stands on the edge of a broadcasting revolution, led by the new digital technology. Like the transformation from black-and-white to colour or from the valve to the transistor, a new era of television and radio is opening. . . . For the viewer and listener, the digital revolution will create a huge increase in variety and choice. There will be more channels, better pictures and sound and a whole new range of services. The digital format will underpin the convergence of broadcasting, telecommunications and computer technologies, speeding the arrival of the information superhighway. Digital broadcasting will offer many people their first experience of the new information society. It will help develop interactive services like home shopping, home banking, information and education services. Meeting this demand will lead to significant investment opportunities and new jobs in programme-making, new information services, transmission facilities and the manufacture of digital television and radio sets. The consumer, the industry and the economy will all benefit.[1]

[1] Letter to the *Times*, August 11, 1995.

As the White Paper on DTT explains, a new legislative framework was needed to allow terrestrial broadcasters to compete in digital services with cable and satellite operators, so that the values embodied by the British broadcasting system ("the envy of the world," according to the white paper) could be preserved in the digital era. Nonetheless, the government also warned that it was committed to help develop a "fair and effective" digital broadcasting market, not privileging any particular platform. In practice, a difficult balance would have to be struck between promoting DTT and creating a level playing field between the three digital platforms (DTT, cable, and satellite). The government also clarified that the legislation being introduced only provided market players the opportunity to launch services and compete, but success was far from guaranteed by government diktat: "[T]here is strong consensus in the industry that the costs of digital broadcasting have fallen to the point where it is commercially viable. The government is not in a position to second guess this judgment, which is a matter for commercial decision" (DNH, 1995a: 1).

The release of the White Paper was supposed to build support for the government's transition strategy among the key industry players. In reality, however, the plan hardly catered to the demands of the incumbents. The key government proposal was to divide the licensing of DTT services into two types of companies: those operating the transmission platform (the so-called digital multiplex operators) and those offering programming and other services such as EPGs and interactive TV. Much like satellite and cable companies, the operators of DTT multiplexes would select and bundle channels or services through contracts with licensed programmers and service providers. Licenses for programming and other services would be awarded to any qualified applicant subject only to the normal requirements applying to satellite channels (taste and decency standards, advertising rules, and so on). Licenses for multiplex operators, on the other hand, were limited by the availability of frequency channels allocated to DTT. Control of the DTT platform thus effectively rested on the multiplex operators, who would be responsible for selecting channels, promoting the service, and interacting with subscribers.

The available multiplex licenses would be awarded by the ITC through competitive tender, based on three general criteria: the level of infrastructure investment proposed by the bidder in order to launch services "as quickly and as widely as possible across the UK"; the level of additional investment proposed to promote the early adoption of receivers by the public (i.e., equipment subsidies); and the variety of the programming proposed. According to the White Paper, the government expected six frequency channels (with coverage ranging from 60 to 90 percent of the U.K. population) to be available for DTT, each able to carry at least three television channels of "excellent picture quality." This represented an increase of 50 percent from the four multiplexes originally planned in the SPECTRE study. The proposals left the door open for the ITC to offer the available multiplexes separately or in packages but established a cap of two multiplexes per operator. The cap was justified on the need to promote competition in DTT services, though packages of two were allowed to attract bidders given the large investments involved. To address concerns that direct payments to the treasury would prevent multiplex operators from investing more heavily in infrastructure and equipment subsidies, the government proposed that the tender for the DTT multiplex licenses did not involve a cash bid for the initial licensing period (twelve years). The allocation process for DTT multiplexes would thus be a traditional beauty contest.

Recognizing the need to engage established operators in the introduction of DTT, the government's proposals included "guaranteed places" for public service broadcasters on the available multiplexes. Essentially, the BBC, ITV, Channel Four/S4C, and Channel Five would each be automatically awarded control of a third of the capacity of a multiplex (two-thirds in the case of the BBC because of its two channels). In return, the proposals required the simulcasting of 80 percent of their analog programming in the digital channel. Should any eligible broadcaster decide not to take its guaranteed capacity, this would be made available to new entrants. A special provision stated that, should the BBC decide to take its guaranteed capacity, the ITC would ensure carriage on the multiplex with the largest geographical coverage. The proposals forbade the development of subscription services over this guaranteed capacity but left the door open for public service broadcasters to apply for additional multiplex capacity on the same terms as other applicants, subject to the general ownership restrictions. Besides the two-license cap, programmers were limited to control of up to 25 percent of the capacity available on the multiplexes (excluding the capacity reserved for incumbents). Applicants would also be subject to the general ownership restrictions proposed in the government's White Paper on Media Ownership released earlier that year. The proposals also established a limit of 10 percent of the multiplex capacity that could be used to offer services other than programming, whether operated by the multiplex licensee, a channel programmer, or a third party.

The government's proposals aimed to achieve a balance between introducing competition in broadcasting services and enticing existing broadcasters, without the cooperation of whom the transition was unlikely to succeed. In an address to the Royal Television Society shortly after the release of the White Paper on DTT, Bottomley described the balance as follows: "[W]hilst existing broadcasters will have an inside track for the provision of public service broadcasting, they will have to compete on an equal footing with the new broadcasters for the opportunity to provide additional new services" (DNH Press Release, September 14, 1995). Aside from the guaranteed places, the lack of a cash bid component in the allocation of multiplex licenses was certainly meant to please the incumbents. In a traditional beauty contest with substantial regulatory discretion to judge quality, the reputation of the established programmers made their proposals more credible than those of the new entrants. This represented a marked policy reversal for the party that had fought hard in the 1980s to introduce market reforms in the licensing of commercial TV, ultimately codified in the Broadcasting Act of 1990. However, the government considered that auctioning the multiplex licenses would compromise the financial viability of DTT operators and, in particular, its capacity to stimulate take-up by subsidizing the cost of set-top boxes (estimated at between £200–300 apiece). These subsidies were deemed critical, in particular if operators had to wage a head-to-head fight for customers with BSkyB, which was widely expected to launch digital services before the start of DTT. As Bottomley explained, despite the government's general support for levying fees on spectrum users, "any requirement to make payments during the first licence period is unrealistic, given the levels of up-front investment involved" (DNH Press Release, September 14, 1995).

The separation between multiplex operators and programmers effectively represented a loss to established broadcasters by unbundling control of the service from the supply of programming. This was not the level playing field that the BBC, ITV, and the other incumbents had hoped for to compete in digital services with BSkyB and the cable companies. The guaranteed places offered by the government to the incumbents – a third of a multiplex – was just about the necessary space to transmit one channel in a resolution equivalent or slightly superior to the existing analog service. In total, the guaranteed capacity amounted to less than 30 percent of the estimated capacity of the DTT platform. According to the plan, the remaining 70 percent would be up for grabs. In the White Paper on DTT, the government had in fact explicitly rejected the plan proposed by the ITV companies whereby each incumbent received an entire frequency channel for DTT:

> If a frequency channel for digital broadcasting were allocated to a single broadcaster, that would mean allocating each broadcaster the equivalent of at least three television channels and potentially many more. The spectrum would effectively be in the control of perhaps only six broadcasters, so limiting opportunities for new broadcasters and for competition, and constraining the variety of programmes on offer to the viewer. (DNH, 1995a: 8)

THE BROADCASTING ACT OF 1996

As expected, the broadcasting establishment gave a lukewarm response to the government's proposals. BSkyB predictably criticized the entire DTT plan, deeming it an "unnecessary detour on the road to the digital future" and questioning the viability of DTT in the face of competition from soon-to-be-launched digital satellite services that boasted far more channel capacity (Frean, 1995). Greg Dyke, chairman of Pearson TV and a well-known Labour supporter, bluntly asserted that "the government proposals as put forward don't have a prayer" and that "no-one will invest" based on the proposals (Snoddy, 1995: 5). Other incumbents shared this assessment. The key concern was the separation between multiplex operators and programmers. According to the ITV companies, this made programmers "junior partners" in the launch of DTT. Incumbents also criticized the multiplex licensing process, arguing the selection criteria put too much emphasis on the willingness to invest in infrastructure and subsidies rather than on programming. As an alternative, they proposed that other companies that would ultimately benefit from the switch-off of analog transmissions (e.g., mobile telephony operators) be made to contribute to pay the transition bill.

In their formal response to the government, the ITV companies had few words of support for the transition strategy outlined in the White Paper. They praised the administration's commitment for an early launch of DTT and the attempt to engage the established terrestrial broadcasters to guarantee a programming quality threshold in DTT. Yet, the response raised "significant concerns" about the proposals (ITVA, 1995). As a general matter, the ITV companies argued that the government should not only provide a legislative framework for the launch of services but enact "some positive policies" to ensure a successful migration of terrestrial services to digital: "[U]nless the government believes that all programme services can, within a reasonable period, be delivered down telecom cables to every household in the UK – or that it would be acceptable for all broadcast services to be delivered from a Luxembourg satellite – DTT would seem to merit special attention" (ITVA, 1995: 3). Again, the main concern was the separation of multiplex operators and programmers: "[T]he ITV companies can see no public policy justification for such a profound change" in the structure of the sector (1995: 9).

The response called inadequate the guaranteed capacity allocated to existing operators and reiterated the demand that a full multiplex be granted to each incumbent. Interestingly, the ITV companies now resorted to the argument used by U.S. incumbents: terrestrial broadcasters needed a second frequency channel to develop HDTV services. This was a bold move given the ITC's pessimistic assessment of HDTV and the fact that the government proposals made no reference whatsoever to high-definition services. As an "absolute minimum" the ITV companies demanded 9Mbits/s, or 50 percent more capacity than proposed by the White Paper. The response also urged the government to set a definite date for the switch-off of all analog channels and to reconsider the prohibition to offer subscription services over the guaranteed capacity. As for the licensing of multiplexes, the ITV companies accused the government of replacing the traditional selection criteria based on the quality and diversity of the programming with an industrial policy criterion based on the willingness to subsidize the deployment of decoders: "[M]aking subsidies part of the bidding process elevates what ought to be a secondary objective into a primary one, with potentially serious consequences" (ITVA, 1995: 8). The ITV companies called the proposal "fundamentally misconceived" and suggested that if rapid take up of DTT was a primary public policy goal, then the subsidies should come directly from the government.

Interestingly, the ITC echoed the issues raised by its licensees. In its response to the government's proposals, it raised several questions about the implementation complexity of the two-tier licensing system proposed and the effectiveness of subsequent regulation of such system (ITC, 1995). In addition, the commission argued it may prove difficult to secure the commitment of existing broadcasters to DTT given that the system relegates them to subcontractors of the multiplex operator. The ITC's defense of the existing licensing system came as no surprise, for the proposals challenged the commission's regulatory jurisdiction because multiplex operators would in effect have more in common with telecommunications operators than traditional broadcasters. The ITC urged the government to award licenses that covered both multiplex operation and programming, subject to overall limits on the control over digital by incumbents. It also supported the demand for a target switch-off date for analog channels, which according to the ITC could be achieved over a period of fifteen years. As for the criteria for the award of DTT multiplexes, the ITC criticized the proposals for being too narrowly focused on financial investments and instead suggested a broader criterion that would judge the applicant's overall commitment to the development of DTT – criteria that would preserve its discretion to select commercial TV applicants as prescribed in the 1990 Broadcasting Act.

The BBC responded to the government's proposals on the same critical note. To begin with, the corporation made it clear that it was not prepared to spearhead alone the development of digital TV channels, as it had in the case of digital radio: "[I]t would not be practical – or an appropriate use of the license fee – for the BBC to attempt, single-handedly, to kick-start the much more expensive DTT market. While the BBC is in a position to act as a catalyst, it can only do so if the commercial environment is attractive to a number of major players in the market" (BBC, 1995: 4). In fact, the BBC saw its role as a provider of free, high-quality British programming for the various digital platforms. The corporation called on the government to revise the dual licensing scheme, to establish a firm timetable for switch-off of analog channels, to extend the duration of the multiplex licenses (from twelve to fifteen years), and to tighten enforcement of EU Directive 95/47 to prevent abuses of dominant position in the pay-TV market and the potential proliferation of different DTT standards.

The Labour opposition was quick to capitalize on the discontent generated by the White Paper on DTT and joined the incumbents in criticizing the government's proposals. Labour spokesman Graham Allen described the approach as "fundamentally flawed" for two main reasons: the lack of a time frame for the switch-off of analog channels, which broadcasters and equipment manufacturers demanded before committing investments; and the timid transposition of EU Directive 95/47, which according to Allen (echoing the BBC's arguments) would allow BSkyB to act as a gatekeeper for digital programmers and opened the door for the deployment of incompatible set-top boxes. That Labour would side with the industry incumbents was not only a tactical maneuver to weaken the Major administration further in the run-up to the 1997 general elections. It also reflected the new direction in which Tony Blair was taking the party since taking command in July 1994. Under the New Labour banner, Blair was trying to overcome four consecutive election losses with a modernized platform that included a less confrontational approach toward business interests and the support for many of the market reforms introduced during the Thatcher era (Norris, 1997; Butler and Kavanagh, 1997). New Labour leaders had no plans to reverse the liberalization of the communications sector; in fact, in many ways they intended to continue these reforms. But the release of the White Paper on DTT gathered little attention from Labour media policymakers, who were absorbed with the more controversial government proposals on media ownership released earlier that year. As a former DNH official argues, there was probably little understanding at the time about the implications of digital TV, and so the more tangible issues of media concentration and cross-ownership took prominence in legislative debates about the government's package of media reforms.[2]

Despite sustained criticism from both incumbents and Labour, the government remained committed to its original plan. In December 1995 the first draft of the new Broadcasting Act containing the government's transition plan was introduced in Parliament. In the four months between the release of the White Paper on DTT and the first draft of the new legislation, incumbents had fiercely lobbied the government for changes that would give them a more prominent role in the transition. Yet, in the bill submitted to Parliament, the government made only token concessions. The much-criticized foundation of the plan – the separation between multiplex operators and programmers – was left intact. In terms of the guaranteed capacity allocated to incumbents, the bill was nonetheless more generous than the White Paper. The BBC emerged as the biggest beneficiary of the changes as the new scheme conceded to one of the corporation's key demands: full control of its own multiplex, and the one with the largest geographical coverage (so-called Multiplex 1). The other incumbents also received an increase in their guaranteed capacity but not an entire multiplex as demanded by the ITV companies. According to the bill, existing operators would share capacity on two other multiplexes, as follows: ITV and Channel Four would share control of the multiplex with the second-highest coverage (Multiplex 2) – except in Wales where Channel Four would share its half with S4C – while Channel 5 would control half the multiplex with the third largest

2. Interview with Paul Bolt, former head of broadcasting at the DNH (July 2002).

coverage (Multiplex A). In return, the new bill raised the simulcasting requirement from 80 to 100 percent. The other half of Multiplex A and the remaining three multiplexes (B, C, and D) were to be offered on competitive tender administered by the ITC. Although applicants would bid for each of these available multiplexes separately, the government agreed to raise the ownership cap from two to three multiplex licenses. The bill reiterated that the bidding process would not include upfront payments. Rather, licensees would be selected by the ITC in a traditional beauty contest according to the three criteria set in the original plan (infrastructure investment, programming diversity, and decoder subsidies).

The government, though not meeting their key demands, was trying to entice existing broadcasters to participate in DTT. After four months of unrelenting criticism from the industry establishment, the cabinet felt that changes were needed to create a more attractive proposition for would-be applicants. The increase in capacity allowed the development of new digital channels, particularly for the BBC. By raising the ownership cap to three multiplex licenses, the government left open the possibility of a single company controlling the majority of the capacity not already assigned to incumbents. Administration officials privately admitted that a single DTT operator would create stronger competition to BSkyB in the pay-TV market – a key government goal in the early launch of DTT. Despite the pressure, the administration decided against setting a final date for the switch-off of analog services. Yet it made a minor concession by including in the new bill a provision that called for a review of the transition timetable after five years of the start of licenses, or when 50 percent of viewers were equipped with digital receivers. Overall, these were not major concessions, but, given the tone of the responses received, the cabinet felt it prudent to show a willingness to negotiate with the media establishment, particularly as the government's slim majority presaged a bumpy ride through Parliament for the new broadcasting bill.

The new broadcasting bill raised more debate than usual in Parliament. If television issues typically raised passionate ideological arguments among legislators, the fact that the government could barely count on a majority created a fertile ground for debate. Much of the controversy, however, focused on two issues not directly related to the government's transition plan. The first was the selling of sports rights to pay-TV channels. Following the TWF Directive, the Broadcasting Act of 1990 had established a list of sports events for which the rights could not be sold exclusively to pay-per-view channels. The ban nonetheless excluded subscription channels such as News Corp.'s Sky Sports, which since the passage of the 1990 act had successfully outbid free-to-air broadcasters for the rights to several popular events. When the bill reached the House of Lords, the BBC and ITV relentlessly lobbied for an amendment that would close this loophole. These companies knew that their chances were best among the peers than in the Commons, because in the run-up to the general elections legislators from both parties would be unwilling to endorse an amendment against Murdoch's interests. After a humiliating vote in the Lords in which many Tory peers joined Labour and the Liberal Democrats in support of the amendment, the government agreed to close the loophole.

The second and far more controversial issue related to cross-ownership restrictions between newspapers and commercial TV licenses. The Broadcasting Act of 1990 has codified into law a limit on cross-ownership between national newspaper publishers and commercial TV licensees, setting a 20 percent cap on the equity control of licenses by the publishers. The new bill proposed to replace this equity cap with a share of voice criterion that allowed newspaper groups with less than 20 percent of the national newspaper circulation to control commercial TV licenses, with a cap of 15 percent of the total television audience. The 20 percent clause essentially affected only the two largest newspaper publishers, News Corp. and the Mirror Group (publisher of the *Daily Mirror*, a Labour-leaning newspaper). When the bill reached the Commons, Labour attempted to force the introduction of an amendment to raise the 20 percent ceiling on the grounds that such limit presented an unjustified regulatory obstacle to the formation of stronger British media companies. In an apparent reversal of roles, the Labour opposition found itself arguing for a more deregulatory bill than that proposed by the Conservative government. This was not only an attempt to favor a traditional party supporter but also a clear sign of the economic pragmatism introduced by the New Labour leadership. The administration nevertheless clung to its feeble majority in the Commons, and the amendment was ultimately defeated.

Overall, during the passage of the bill through Parliament, the government's plan for the introduction of DTT suffered only minor alterations. One of the most significant relates to the criteria to be used by the ITC in the awarding of multiplexes. The government agreed to introduce an overall criterion that empowered the commission to judge applicants based on whether they would "promote the development of digital television broadcasting in the United Kingdom otherwise than by satellite."[3] The new criterion not only enhanced the regulator's discretion in the licensing process but also gave a clear indication of the administration's goal to pit DTT against satellite TV: creating competition to BSkyB was now a statutory requirement in the selection of applicants (Collins, 1997). A second important amendment – heavily lobbied by incumbents – was the introduction of a backstop power for the ITC to set transmission standards in order to ensure compliance with EU Directive 95/47 and promote compatibility between multiplex operators. Both government and the incumbents wanted to avert a set-top box war between multiplex operators that could result in the proliferation of incompatible decoders. Given the constraints imposed by Directive 95/47, the amendment nonetheless left to the industry the decision of how decoder interoperability would be achieved. As the government explained, "the legislative framework does all that is practicable to encourage the production of set-top boxes or digital television sets capable of receiving all digital channels, whether transmitted by satellite, cable, or terrestrial means" (DNH, 1996: 13). There were also minor amendments such as the introduction of a "must-carry" rule that requires digital cable systems to provide carriage to the existing public service broadcasters (but not to their new digital channels), an increase in the amount of capacity granted to Channel Four and S4C in Wales (S4C now shared Multiplex A with Channel Five in that region), and a new requirement on the operator of Multiplex A to provide a minimum amount of Gaelic programming during prime time in Scotland.

The passage of the new Broadcasting Act on July 24, 1996, sealed into law, almost intact, the government's proposals for the introduction of DTT released less than a year before. It was a plan that initiated a significant transformation in the structure of the terrestrial sector with the separation of multiplex operators and programmers and opened the market to potential new entrants. There was little doubt that a bold experiment in industry restructuring had begun. The government had certainly toned down some of the reforms in order to make DTT a more competitive platform against other pay-TV operators and to attract the interest of incumbent broadcasters. After all, without takers for the almost 60 percent of the capacity up for grabs (three and a half multiplexes out of six), the objectives associated with DTT would not be accomplished. But the bargaining had more to do with the small letter

---

[3] Broadcasting Act 1996, Section 8(1).

than the larger thrust of the plan. While strongly dissatisfied with the strategy outlined by the administration, incumbents found few vehicles to block the proposals or force substantial changes.

Perhaps the only incumbent to benefit from these changes was the BBC, due to its solid cross-party backing in Parliament and the strong support of several cabinet ministers, including DNH Secretary Virginia Bottomley.[4] But while the act granted the BBC a full digital multiplex, it also imposed the privatization of its transmission network, the proceedings of which were earmarked to fund new digital services.[5] But the BBC still cautioned against betting on the success of the new terrestrial platform: "[T]he BBC has to plan for a future in which it cannot rely on a single distribution system going into every home in the country. It follows that in order to reach the whole audience, we will have to ensure that our core licence fee funded services are available through each of the main delivery outlets" (BBC, 1996: 53). As the transition strategy for which it had heavily lobbied turned out much less in its favor than expected, the BBC did not want its hands tied to the administration's DTT experiment.

At the same time, the other incumbents were also preparing plans to utilize their guaranteed capacity and in some cases bid for the available DTT licenses. Negotiations to form bidding consortia for the DTT multiplexes had started even before the final passage of the 1996 act. On the technical front, the incumbents (along with BT and several equipment makers) were key participants in the Digital Television Group (DTG), an industry forum aimed at coordinating efforts to develop technical standards for digital TV. This mostly technical body had effectively lobbied the DVB against the introduction of a specification in the European DTT standard that would have delayed the launch of services in the United Kingdom and increased the cost of receivers in the short term.[6] The need to introduce DTT as early as possible – essentially before or at least

---

[4] This support was reflected in a somewhat generous license fee increase, based on the retail price index (RPI), set as follows: 1997–1998: RPI; 1998–1999: RPI + 3 percent; 1999–2000: RPI + 0.5 percent; 2000–2001: RPI – 1 percent; 2001–2002: RPI – 2.5 percent (DNH Press Release, December 18, 1996).

[5] The BBC's plans included a widescreen version of its staple channels (BBC1 and BBC2), a new twenty-four-hour news channel, additional themed channels funded by subscriptions (through its BBC Worldwide subsidiary), a range of educational services, and extended news coverage of regional and local issues (BBC, 1996).

[6] At issue was whether the DVB would require the use of the more advanced 8K carrier system or allow an implementation of DTT based on the readily available 2K carrier system. Interview with Peter Marshall, technical director, Digital TV Group (July 2002).

shortly after the launch of BSkyB's digital service – was a key point of agreement between industry and the government. Now that the legislative framework and the technical details were in place, the ball was in the ITC's court to expedite the licensing of DTT multiplexes as directed by the new Broadcasting Act.

TEN

Murdoch Phobia?

Among the innovations introduced by the Broadcasting Act of 1996 was the division of tasks in the implementation of the transition strategy between the ITC and the OFTEL. While the ITC would allocate and enforce the two types of DTT licenses (programmer and multiplex operator), the act delegated the sensitive issue of set-top box standards and interoperability to OFTEL. The telecom regulator already had jurisdiction over certain aspects of analog TV (e.g., the provision of transmission services to commercial broadcasters), but it was now being called to play a much greater – and politically sensitive – role. Of course, the broadcasting regulator reacted angrily to such territorial invasion. The ITC began working on the licensing of DTT even before the final approval of the 1996 act. In May 1996 it launched an industry consultation on how to proceed with the licensing process, which included a first draft of both types of DTT licenses. This was mostly a technical document but nonetheless signaled that the ITC was ready to put the licensing of DTT on a fast track as required by government and incumbents. The Major administration supported an accelerated timetable and expressed its goal that licenses be awarded by early 1997. In order for the government to make a credible claim about having launched the first DTT platform in the world, it was important that the licenses be awarded before the 1997 general elections.

In October 1996 the ITC formally launched the invitation to apply for the multiplex licenses. At stake were the three and a half commercial multiplexes (Multiplexes B, C, and D, plus half of Multiplex A). The invitation clarified several points left open by the 1996 act. First, expected coverage varied widely between the different multiplexes – from 90 percent for Multiplex A to only 69 percent for Multiplex D. This assumed a recommended implementation with a digital capacity of approximately 24Mbit/s, an implementation that favored data carriage capacity (i.e., more channels) over geographical coverage. Applicants were expected to indicate the timetable for achieving maximum coverage within the first four years of the duration of the license. The ITC expected services to start no later than July 1, 1998, or a year after the award of the licenses, whichever was later. At the request of the industry, the commission decided against offering the licenses in packages of two or more multiplexes. Still, applicants could apply for up to three licenses as established by the 1996 act, although the ITC required that separate applications be filed for each license. Applicants were expected to submit specific plans about the roll-out of receiving equipment (including subsidies) as well as evidence of substantial financial backing. According to the invitation, "there would be considerable room for doubt about this support if the applicant has not been able to attract named and substantial investors who would subscribe for the great majority of the equity investment" (ITC, 1996: 29). Clearly, the commission wanted to avoid a repeat of the failed licensing of analog satellite services in the late 1980s.

As soon as the licenses were advertised, the "big three" ITV companies (Carlton, Granada, and United News and Media) announced their plans to participate. Potential new entrants also manifested interest, in particular International CableTel, an entrepreneurial cable operator based in the United States that controlled sixteen cable franchises across the country and had recently expanded into transmission with the purchase of NTL. The key question was whether the two industry heavyweights, the BBC and BSkyB, would enter the fray, and how. Most believed that BSkyB would not be interested in providing its programming and technology to a rival digital platform. In the eleventh hour, however, the company announced it would join British Digital Broadcasting (BDB), a bidding consortium formed by Carlton and Granada. This gave BDB a clear advantage against its rivals in terms of programming, since it was assumed that DTT would need to carry some of the premium content controlled by BSkyB to succeed.

While the last-minute announcement by BSkyB surprised many, the revelation (also by the January 31, 1997, application deadline) that the BBC had granted first option on its new digital channels to the BDB consortium sent shock waves across the industry. Having pleaded to maintain a strategy of neutrality with respect to the competing digital distribution platforms, and already in control of a full multiplex by government fiat, the BBC was now joining two of the largest ITV companies and its satellite archrival in the bid for the multiplex licenses.

The combination of programming, technical, and financial resources that the BDB partners brought together raised many eyebrows. Yet, as one journalist described it, this was a "coup" that certainly reinvigorated the prospects for DTT (Culf, 1997: 3). BDB planned to launch a pay-TV service (twelve basic plus three premium channels) that relied heavily on the existing programming assets controlled by its partners. According to the bidding documents, it was ready to spend up to £300 million, the bulk of which would go into the digital set-top boxes subsidy. The only rival bid for the operation of Multiplexes B, C, and D came from Digital Television Network (DTN), a wholly owned subsidiary of the NTL/CableTel group. Lacking the programming assets of its rival, the DTN offered a more innovative range of new channels and interactive TV services. For the available half of Multiplex A the only bid came from S4C Digital Networks, a wholly owned subsidiary of Welsh broadcaster S4C.

The government welcomed the rival bids and the involvement of the established market actors as an endorsement of its much-bashed transition strategy:

> The real commercial interest now evident in digital terrestrial gives the lie to all the jeremiahs and the prophets of doom who said that DTT would be of no commercial interest and that digital would be monopolised by one company and one platform. The major players are now at the table; the commitments they are offering promise to make a reality of the government's vision for the new digital age. (DTI Press Release, January 31, 1997)

Upon receiving the applications, the ITC opened a six-week period of public consultation. While under the terms of the invitation each of the multiplexes could be awarded to different bidders, the assumption was that the ITC would avoid splitting the licenses in order to create a stronger proposition and avoid coordination problems in the launch of services. Besides, both BDB and DTN had indicated their strong preference for a package of three multiplexes.

From the outset, the BDB consortium emerged as the frontrunner. The alliance between four of the largest industry players legitimized the new platform in the eyes of financial backers as well as the public in general. Not surprisingly, the proposal submitted was heavy on the staple programming of British television, including new BBC science and history channels (in partnership with Flextech, a programmer controlled by U.S. cable giant TCI), a diet of entertainment and films based on the Carlton library, and sports channels based on the rights for soccer and other popular sports controlled by Granada and BSkyB. Another selling point of the BDB proposal was that BSkyB's participation could preempt the proliferation of incompatible decoders for DTT and digital satellite TV services. The DTN proposal, on the other hand, stressed innovation. It included the launch of twenty data services linked to new sports, business, science, and travel channels. These new on-screen services would be linked to a return path (either a cable or a telephone line) that would offer viewers interactive TV services such as home banking and shopping. The main question raised was whether DTN would be able to assemble the funding needed for this costly venture. The allegations that two potential DTN backers, United News and Media (UN&M) and French pay-TV operator Canal+, had pulled out of the deal at the last minute only fueled these doubts (although UN&M was reportedly ready to invest in DTN should it win the licenses).

It soon became clear that the licensing tender would also be fought in public. Editorial pages began to fill with articles and letters supporting or opposing either of the bidders, seemingly reviving the public drama that surrounded the allocation of the ITV franchises in 1991. The main argument against BDB was that, by linking three of the biggest players in the British media industry plus the BBC, the consortium would effectively preclude the emergence of competition in digital TV. As the chairman of DTN explained it, "the ITC, in awarding the licenses, has a unique opportunity to ensure that there is real competition in the UK pay-TV market. Only one bid – DTN's – will pit genuine competitors against each other in the bid to develop digital television in the UK."[1] A prominent media scholar even argued that "if the ITC does not award the licence to DTN, it will be an act of willful cowardice unprecedented in the history of British television regulation" (Barnett, 1997). Michael Green, chairman of Carlton and of the BDB consortium, responded to the accusations: "I find it hard to understand how a business that starts life with no customers and no revenues can be branded a monopoly. And I find it even harder to see how ploughing millions of pounds into building a digital terrestrial network, promoting set-top boxes and establishing a new platform for running services can be called anti-competitive."[2] After the May 1997 general elections, there was speculation that the Labour victory would sway the balance one way or another. Some argued that Blair

[1] Letter by James Gatward to the *Guardian*, March 27, 1997, p. 20.
[2] Letter by Michael Green to the *Guardian*, February 24, 1997, p. T11.

189

needed to repay the support received from the Murdoch newspapers; others pointed to the close friendship between the Labour leader and UN&M boss Lord Horlick. Yet, in practice, the new government could do little to influence the ITC's decision.

Shortly after the elections, the licensing process took another turn with the announcement by the EU competition authorities that an investigation had been launched about the BDB consortium. "There is a problem so far as the pay-TV business is concerned because there could be an enhancement of an already dominant position" declared competition commissioner Karel Van Miert.[3] As noted, European Community authorities had rejected several high-profile ventures related to digital TV in Germany and the Nordic countries. The outcome of these cases made clear that Van Miert was unwilling to approve joint ventures that advanced long-term industrial policy goals at the expense of competition. It was later revealed that OFTEL and the Office of Fair Trading (OFT) had also expressed to the ITC similar concerns about the BDB bid. In response to these concerns, the ITC informed the BDB consortium that BSkyB had to abandon its equity stake in the joint venture due to the competition problems raised by the alliance. Yet the ITC demanded that BSkyB remain a programming partner to BDB; otherwise, the programming proposals submitted would have to be completely revised. In short, the ITC was prepared to award the multiplex licenses to the BDB consortium as long as it undertook measures to alleviate the issues raised by competition authorities in London and Brussels. Only a few days later, BSkyB announced that it had reached an agreement with Carlton and Granada to pull out of BDB and that the remaining partners had agreed to assume BSkyB's funding commitments. In compensation, BSkyB received £75 million (payable only if BDB's bid succeeded) and a seven-year programming supply contract with BDB. The agreement clearly satisfied the ITC. It addressed the concerns raised by BSkyB's participation in DTT and yet did not weaken the appeal of the new services.

AND THE LICENSES GO TO . . .

On June 24, 1997, the ITC announced that the licenses to operate Multiplexes B, C, and D would be awarded to the BDB consortium. The financial resources and the programming rights that the BDB partners brought to the new platform had clearly tilted the balance in their

---

[3] *Financial Times*, June 4, 1997, p. 11.

favor. According to the ITC, BDB's application offered "a greater degree of assurance than that of DTN that the proposed services could be established and maintained throughout the period of the licenses" (ITC Press Release, June 24, 1997: 3). A key selling point was that funding for the BDB consortium would come from the internal resources of its two equity partners, both of which ranked among Britain's top hundred companies (by contrast, DTN's plan depended on the ability of International CableTel to raise additional capital, and the company's debt was already at £2 billion). Interestingly, the commission acknowledged that DTN's programming proposal was more innovative. However, unwilling to take risks, the ITC ultimately favored the tried-and-true content package assembled by BDB. With respect to the concerns raised by competition authorities, the ITC explained that it was satisfied with the measures undertaken by the consortium (the withdrawal of BSkyB as an equity partner), and that an additional safeguard would be added to the BDB license to prevent Granada from acquiring full control of the consortium as long as it held a significant equity in BSkyB (at the time, Granada held a 10 percent stake in the satellite operator).

The ITC decision raised heated controversy. Much of the debate revolved around whether the conditions imposed by the commission would effectively block BSkyB from exercising control over DTT services and therefore prevent real competition in the distribution of pay-TV and in the acquisition of content rights. BSkyB's practices in the pay-TV market were already under investigation by the OFT. Cable operators complained that, under the current contracts for the supply of premium programming, encryption, and subscriber management services offered by BSkyB, they could neither compete with nor differentiate themselves from the satellite operator (Hills and Michalis, 1997). OFT released the results of the investigation shortly after the ITC award announcement (OFT, 1996). The competition watchdog concluded that BSkyB did hold "a powerful position in the wholesale pay TV market" and that this created barriers to entry that raised concerns, because, although BSkyB was not acting anticompetitively, "the competitive process is being impaired" (OFT Press Release, July 24, 1996: 1). However, the agency ultimately demanded only minor alterations in the contracting practices between BSkyB and its cable customers. According to OFT Director General John Bridgeman, the anticipated positive impact of the digital transition on competition in the pay-TV market significantly factored into the decision not to impose stronger restrictions on BSkyB's market behavior. In other words, given the government's commitment to promote DTT as an alternative to BSkyB's digital service, there was no need for draconian action. Yet, by awarding the DTT licenses to BDB, the ITC was, in the eyes of many, taking the competitive process a step back.

The public release of a study that OFTEL had submitted to the ITC during the award process concerning the implications of the DTT license tender for competition in the television market fueled even more controversy about the BDB award (OFTEL, 1997). The starting point of the analysis, already outlined in previous OFTEL documents (e.g., OFTEL, 1995), was that digital technologies heralded the end to the distribution bottlenecks that characterized analog TV. In the future, vigorous competition for viewers and programming rights between the different digital platform operators (terrestrial, cable, and satellite) will greatly reduce the need for detailed programming rules designed to ensure that operators behave in the public interest. In other words, market forces are likely to align viewers' preferences with content supply without the need for regulatory intervention: "[I]n future, there is an opportunity to let commercial competition do much of the work which has necessarily had to be done in the past by regulation. . . . This is possible because there is enough spectrum across the terrestrial, cable, and satellite platforms to allow vigorous competition in the supply of programming at both the wholesale and retail level" (OFTEL, 1997: 3). However, OFTEL warned that these benefits would only be realized if true competition existed across digital platforms and in the supply of premium programming. The new task for regulators, according to OFTEL, was to nurture such competition and prevent dominant firms from leveraging market power across the supply chain.

The study identified three distinct markets that would be affected by the multiplex tender: the market for premium content rights, the market for distribution of digital TV services, and the market for services to pay TV operators (e.g., CAS and subscription management services). According to OFTEL, there was significant risk that BSkyB's dominance in the premium programming market would be reinforced by its participation in DTT, because the company would be placed in an even stronger position to negotiate with rights holders and at the same time stifle the emergence of rival bidders for those rights. This in turn weakened competition between transmission platforms as the DTT operator would effectively depend on the terms dictated by BSkyB for access to premium programming (essentially the same conclusion that the OFT investigation had drawn with respect to cable). Furthermore, DTT operators would also need to contract access services (e.g., CAS) from BSkyB. Therefore, the result of BSkyB's participation in DTT would be the foreclosure of competition in an industry already dominated by the BDB partners. OFTEL's final conclusion is blunt: "[I]f the BDB consortium is granted licenses to operate DTT multiplexes B, C, and D, one of the effects could well be to foreclose competition in UK premium programming across all platforms and to significantly weaken competition between transmission networks.... The net effect would be less, not more, competition in digital television" (OFTEL, 1997: 2).

The release of OFTEL's study infuriated Sir Robin Biggam, chairman of the ITC. This was not only another round in the ongoing turf war between OFTEL and the ITC about jurisdiction over DTT. The OFTEL study presented a fundamentally different regulatory paradigm, one based not on the imposition of sector-specific rules aimed at securing desired behavior from the regulated firms (the traditional ITC approach) but rather on general competition principles. From this resulted a different conclusion about the award of the multiplex licenses. Don Cruickshank, the director general of OFTEL since 1993, was a respected regulator who firmly believed in the need to introduce market reforms in the broadcasting sector. The revelation of his endorsement of the DTN bid undermined the ITC's decision and fueled speculation about possible legal challenges. Forced to respond, the ITC chairman claimed that every member of the commission had read OFTEL's submission and that the issues had been addressed with BSkyB's withdrawal from the winning consortium. The controversy intensified when BSkyB revealed that in fact it did not hold the broadcast rights for Premier League soccer on DTT, although it did have the first right of negotiations. DTN executives reportedly considered seeking judicial review of the ITC's decision. However, the track record was hardly encouraging: the courts had previously dismissed complaints from unsuccessful bidders in the franchise tenders for ITV licenses in 1991, and for Channel 5 in 1995. In both cases, the courts noted that the Broadcasting Act gave broad powers to the ITC to exercise expert judgment about programming and financial matters in the allocation of commercial TV licenses.[4]

DTN nevertheless decided to take its case to Brussels and filed a formal complaint with the EU competition authorities. This delayed the award of the licenses that the ITC had hoped to make within twelve weeks of the June 24 announcement. The EU investigation focused on two issues: the

---

[4] For a discussion of these cases, see Gibbons (1998).

crossover of directorships between BDB and BSkyB (BDB's director, Gerry Robinson, was chairman of both Granada and BSkyB), and the duration of the programming supply contract between the two companies. At the end of 1997 the European Commission notified the ITC that it would give clearance to the BDB joint venture subject to the following conditions: a reduction in the duration of the programming supply contract between BSkyB and BDB from seven to five years; the deletion of clauses from the contract that created disincentives for BDB to compete for film and sports rights against BSkyB; and certain changes to the joint-venture agreement to ensure that Granada would not prevent BDB from competing with BSkyB. According to commission officials, the creation of BDB, provided that the foregoing changes were undertaken, was in principle procompetitive, since it brought a new competitor to a market – pay-TV – dominated by a single firm. On December 19, 1997, the ITC announced that the conditions imposed by the commission would be written in the BDB license and proceeded to award the consortium the operation of the three multiplexes. DTN's complaint was formally rejected by the EU competition authorities a few months later.

The allocation of broadcasting licenses through beauty contests is inherently controversial as regulators have to make contestable judgments about future programming quality and business plans based on the limited evidence available. The challenge was even greater in the case of the DTT tender, for the technology as well as the commercial opportunities presented by the new platform were largely unproved. In delegating the allocation of multiplex licenses to the ITC, the administration found that the regulator favored a cautious approach to the transition. This is reflected not only in the granting of the DTT licenses to a group of well-established analog TV operators but in the very decision to award the licenses in a single package, even when the legislation made it possible – and the administration initially favored – splitting the licenses between different market entrants. Staffed largely by veterans from the IBA, the commission was risk-averse, haunted by the ghost of the BSB failure. In its analysis, rival multiplex operators with limited channel capacity would have little chance against BSkyB, casting a shadow on the future of the DTT platform and the eventual switch-off of analog channels. Only a strong new pay-TV entrant licensed on rather favorable terms would stand a chance against BSkyB and the cable companies, particularly given the initial coverage restrictions of DTT. ITC officials essentially favored gradual rather than radical change in the introduction of DTT, but this contrasted with OFTEL's vision of the transition. The clash between the two regulators and their different regulatory paradigms would become even more evident in the implementation of the EU Directive 95/47 discussed in the next section.

THE GATEKEEPERS OF DIGITAL TV

The second major part of the administration's transition strategy was the development of the regulatory framework for digital TV services. This encompassed a number of issues, but without doubt the most prominent was the transposition of EU Directive 95/47 and the creation of rules for digital TV access services, including CAS. Surprisingly, the rather technical issue of CAS and related services gathered as much, if not more, attention than the licensing process. The BBC and, to a lesser extent, the ITV companies certainly deserve much of the credit. An intense public relations campaign accompanied their lobbying efforts to impose tight rules on operators of CAS and related services. Both organizations had been key participants in the decision-making process within the DVB group and in the European debates that resulted in Directive 95/47. As noted, the issue pitted the established pay-TV operators – above all BSkyB and French operator Canal+ – against terrestrial broadcasters and, in particular, public service broadcasters. At stake was how to prevent pay-TV companies that also controlled the dominant CAS operators from discriminating against independent channels and favoring affiliated broadcasters in the provision of set-top box access services. Following the failure of self-regulatory efforts within the DVB group and the ambiguous wording of the nondiscriminatory requirements introduced by Directive 95/47, the issue moved from the European arena to the member states, where the directive needed to be transposed into national legislation.

The issue took a higher profile in the United Kingdom than in other member states because of the controversial role of News Corp. in the British media industry (Levy, 1997). As discussed, BSkyB controlled the dominant CAS and subscription management service operators for analog TV. Preventing BSkyB from leveraging this position onto the digital TV programming market was at the top of the regulatory agenda for the BBC, particularly as it undertook new commercial ventures. A study commissioned by the BBC and released in the aftermath of the DVB code-of-conduct fiasco warned that "analogue subscription television providers, well positioned with their skills to move into the digital market, can establish de facto monopoly positions by controlling access to consumers through their ownership of conditional access companies. Regulatory intervention will be necessary to prevent the development of this anticompetitive scenario and ensure consumers benefit fully from competition and choice in digital television" (Arthur D. Little, 1994: 1). According to the BBC, this situation was nowhere more apparent than in the United Kingdom, as BSkyB prepared to start its digital satellite services and deploy its proprietary CAS technology before the launch of DTT. At issue was also the attempt to prevent digital TV from becoming synonymous with pay-TV. In the event that DTT failed, the corporation wanted to ensure that license fee payers would have access to the BBC services without a pay-TV subscription:

> DTT is likely to follow rather than precede the digital satellite and, probably, digital cable television in the marketplace. Not only will it be late, but it will also be more limited in its range of services. . . . Notwithstanding its long-term potential to transform the UK's national broadcasting system, there is no guarantee that DTT will establish itself as economically viable alongside these alternative delivery systems. If commercial operators are unwilling or unable to take on the risks involved, DTT could fail – casting real doubts on the long-term viability of public service broadcasting in the UK. (BBC, 1995: 10)

For the BBC, the transposition of Directive 95/47 was another round in the battle for its future.

The first indications about how the government intended to proceed with the transposition of the directive were contained in the White Paper on DTT of August 1995. In this document the government acknowledged that despite the possibility that broadcasters make use of different CAS and even deploy separate set-top boxes, such an arrangement would be "very expensive, unpopular with consumers and also inefficient" (DNH, 1995a: 23). In accepting this argument, the Major administration implicitly established the basis for the regulation of CAS services as a gateway facility. Yet the White Paper went little beyond a literal transposition of the rules established in Article 4c of the directive: "[A]ny provider of encryption or subscription management for digital terrestrial broadcasting should not discriminate in favour of or against any particular multiplex provider or broadcaster" (ibid.). This did not satisfy the BBC and ITV, both of which demanded more specific rules to prevent discrimination. In its response to the White Paper, the BBC argued that CAS and subscriber management services needed to be "tightly regulated" and favored a government-mandated CAS standard for DTT (BBC, 1995). Both urged the government to also address the issue of discrimination in navigation systems (i.e., EPGs), an issue not explicitly tackled by Directive 95/47. According to BBC Director General John Birt, regulation was needed to ensure that "the Gateway controller cannot relegate BBC1 or ITV to Channel 249."[5]

The White Paper proposed that the providers of CAS and related services be licensed by the DTI under the Telecommunications Act and thus be regulated by OFTEL, which would write the appropriate nondiscriminatory obligations in the licenses. This sparked an angry reaction from ITC officials. Peter Rogers, deputy chief executive of the ITC, vehemently opposed the government's proposal. He observed that the existing legislation empowered the television regulator to ensure "fair and effective" competition in broadcasting services and to regulate the services provided by its licensees in connection with broadcasting, although the legislation excluded the services provided by companies not licensed by the ITC (which was the case of SSSL, the dominant CAS operator). According to Rogers, the government could simply close this loophole: CAS and related services, argued Rogers, "are broadcasting issues within the normal and accepted scope of broadcasting legislation" and thus "responsibility for them would rest more logically with the Commission [the ITC]" (Rogers, 1995: 174).

OFTEL, on the other hand, welcomed the proposal. This was an important step in the direction of a common regulatory framework for broadcasting and telecommunications that the agency strongly favored. Besides, it already regulated several aspects of broadcasting, and its expertise in addressing similar access and interconnection issues in the telecom sector could be applied to the case of digital TV (OFTEL, 1995). In a document released shortly before the government's White Paper on DTT, the agency had already laid out its vision of how to regulate CAS and related services. According to OFTEL, digital TV fell under the general category of BSM (broadband switched mass-market) services, which also included telecommunication services such as Internet access. To facilitate investments and secure the benefits of market competition in BSM services, OFTEL suggested two key regulatory principles: "any-to-any connectivity" and "open access for service providers." The first promoted interconnection between users, whereas the second embraced

---

[5] "A Glorious Future: Quality Broadcasting in the Digital Age," Remarks to the Edinburgh International Television Festival, August 1996.

open access obligations to secure competition in the provision of services running over a common infrastructure. This clearly applied to the case of CAS: "[I]f conditional access systems prove expensive to duplicate and if the issue of conditional access is not sufficiently addressed in the regulatory regime, it might then be possible for one company to dominate the delivery of broadband channels by satellite and by extension, by an expanded terrestrial system as well" (OFTEL, 1995: 37).

OFTEL's vision went beyond the more limited scope of Directive 95/47. What the agency proposed was a detailed regime for access and interconnection in digital TV infrastructure based on general competition law and sector-specific rules borrowed from telecommunications regulation. It implied the imposition of nondiscriminatory obligations and the use of procompetitive regulatory tools to a degree previously unknown to the broadcasting sector. As expected, BSkyB raised serious concerns about entrusting regulation of CAS to OFTEL. But the Major administration stood behind its proposal, and in January 1996, just as the new broadcasting bill was being introduced in the Parliament, the DTI published its first consultation on the implementation of Directive 95/47 and the new CAS licenses. The consultation document revealed the government's endorsement of OFTEL's vision: "[T]hose who control conditional access systems are important potential gatekeepers in this part of the communications market – just as those who control the transmission systems are in a similar position, and are regulated under the Telecommunications Act" (DTI, 1996: 12). According to the DTI, regulatory safeguards were particularly important when the dominant provider of CAS and related services was also involved in the provision of pay-TV programming – which was precisely the case of BSkyB – because this vertical integration "provided an incentive for the operator to use its market power in conditional access to improve its position elsewhere in the market, especially by favouring its own connected business and discriminating against competitors" (1996: 9). These had much in common with the arguments presented by public service broadcasters in the context of the DVB debates about CAS. The administration thus seemed prepared to take the issue far beyond the strict letter of Directive 95/47.

The DTI proposed that the directive be implemented through a CAS license that would carry the following obligations: to provide services to all relevant broadcasters on nondiscriminatory terms, to provide services on "fair and reasonable" terms, to provide services on an unbundled basis, to furnish all relevant information about the services, and to keep separate accounts for CAS and subscription management services in the case of vertically integrated operators. OFTEL would be empowered to review and modify the terms under which services were offered, to require licensees to contract under terms dictated by the director general, and to require disclosure of technical information. This closely resembled, in principles and instruments, the regime utilized for the introduction of competition in the British telecommunications industry: close scrutiny of interconnection contracts between network operators and service providers, near compulsory licensing of technical information, and broad powers for OFTEL to impose obligations and define the terms (including price) of services provided by dominant networks operators. It represented a much tighter regulatory environment than in analog TV, where CAS and subscription management operators were only bound by general fair trade rules.

The DTI proposals nonetheless stopped short of imposing an open interface for digital set-top boxes as demanded by terrestrial incumbents. DTI officials cited several concerns.[6] First, a common interface would lower investment incentives (since operators will be less willing to subsidize an open box) and possibly stifle innovation. Second, such implementation would certainly raise eyebrows in Brussels, since the council had explicitly refused to endorse a common interface in Directive 95/47. Moreover, this would also require clearance under single-market procedures because of its impact on internal trade in consumer electronics. Third, a common interface would increase the cost of decoders, thus discouraging adoption.

With the DTI's release of the first draft of the CAS license in June 1996, the battle over the implementation of Directive 95/47 not only intensified but also moved to the public arena. For the BBC-led coalition, the issue had to be framed not as a technical question but as one of preventing the creation of a digital empire by News Corp. They found amicable allies among the left-leaning press, traditionally opposed to Murdoch and more recently disillusioned with the rapprochement between Labour and the "digital dictator," as one newspaper editorial described the Australian media magnate. The recent removal of the BBC from News Corp.'s satellite service in Asia at the request of Chinese authorities was repeatedly cited as evidence of the threat that Murdoch posed to public service broadcasters and media democracy in general. In October 1996 the stakes of the transposition debate increased dramatically with the revelation that BSkyB had placed an initial order of digital

---

[6] Interviews with DTI officials (July 2002).

set-top boxes embedded with its proprietary CAS technology. This represented a blow to the government's plan for an integrated decoder capable of receiving different digital services (satellite, DTT, and possibly cable). The stable cast of Murdoch critics was now joined by consumer interest associations such as the National Consumer Council and the Consumers' Association, which claimed the set-top boxes ordered by BSkyB would lock viewers into a particular digital TV platform and prevent effective competition in digital broadcasting services. Nevertheless, in the run-up to the May 1997 elections, many doubted whether either party would be willing to confront Murdoch. "When will the Conservatives or the Labour party be able to beg or borrow the guts to stand up to Rupert Murdoch?" wondered a newspaper editorial.[7]

Both parties responded to the accusations by giving assurances that the issues were being addressed in primary legislation as well as in the CAS license. The government pointed to the recent transposition into national law of Article 4(d) of Directive 95/47. This required holders of CAS-related intellectual property rights to grant licenses to equipment manufacturers on fair, reasonable, and nondiscriminatory terms. More important, it also prevented holders of such rights from discouraging manufacturers to include in the same product a common interface or competing CAS technology.[8] According to the government, this adequately addressed the concerns related to BSkyB's initial order of proprietary decoders. The Labour opposition also reacted against the accusations that it had agreed to abandon support for tight regulatory controls on CAS operators in exchange for the endorsement of the Murdoch-controlled newspapers. Critics were particularly infuriated by the party's lack of support for an amendment to the broadcasting bill – introduced at the committee stage by two Tory backbenchers – that mandated the CAS common interface. MP Lewis Moonie, a Labour spokesman on broadcasting affairs, reminded critics that the party had instead forced the introduction of a backstop power for the ITC to set transmission standards in the new broadcasting bill. According to Moonie, the amendment was "over-prescriptive."[9] Once again, the Labour block found itself in the uncomfortable position of justifying a more deregulatory position than several Conservative MPs.

---

[7] "Murdoch: The Digital Dictator," *Guardian*, October 29, 1996, p. 16.
[8] The Advanced Television Services (Industrial Property Rights) Regulations S.I. No. 2185 (1996).
[9] Letter by Lewis Moonie to the *Daily Telegraph*, November 2, 1996, p. 19.

As the DTI consultation on the implementation of Directive 95/47 reached its final stages at the end of 1996, the BBC-led coalition insisted on toughening the nondiscrimination obligations to be written in the CAS licenses. In particular, broadcasters demanded two amendments: the introduction of a common interface mandate for digital set-top boxes, and the extension of the regulatory principles of the directive to other set-top box components such as the API and the EPG. At a minimum, the coalition demanded a code of conduct for EPG providers that prohibited discrimination in relation to the amount and quality of the information displayed for each channel and ensured "due prominence" to public service broadcasters. These demands reflect a profound distrust about the effectiveness of competition-based regulation to address the concerns raised by BSkyB's position in the pay-TV market. Having flourished under a regime based on ex ante rules designed to ration competition and produce specific market outputs, analog terrestrial operators were reluctant to delegate implementation of Directive 95/47 to a regulator with a well-known distaste for picking market winners or serving political masters.

Despite intense pressure from the BBC-led coalition and the threat by several Labour backbenchers to force a debate, the government refused to change course. When the final rules were submitted to Parliament at the end of 1996, it became clear that the government had only agreed to make a minor concession: to force CAS operators to provide technical information to broadcasters. The CAS class license would empower OFTEL to force licensees to make any relevant intellectual property available to broadcasters if the regulator considered that withholding such information prevented the provision of CAS services on reasonable terms. The amendment nonetheless stopped short of compulsory licensing as demanded by the BBC. Appearing before Parliament, Science and Technology Minister Ian Taylor described such a demand as "an extreme step which the United Kingdom would contemplate only if no other action to tackle anti-competitive behaviour was available."[10] Labour backbenchers were ultimately unable to force a debate that the party leadership feared would spark more controversy about the new direction of its media policies and jeopardize its newfound camaraderie with Murdoch. Parliament thus rubber-stamped the government's proposals, and the implementation of EC Directive 95/47 became law in early 1997.[11] Yet the battle

---

[10] *Parliamentary Debates*, Commons, December 12, 1996.
[11] The Advanced Television Services Regulation S.I. No. 3151 (1996).

was far from over. With the matter in OFTEL's hands, stakeholders now shifted their attention to the regulator's interpretation of the directive.

UNLOCKING COMPETITION: OFTEL's APPROACH

The first step taken by OFTEL was the publication of a consultation document. According to OFTEL, there were five main goals in the implementation of CAS regulation: to ensure that control of CAS was not used to distort or prevent competition in digital TV services, to ensure that such control was also not used to restrict choice in consumer equipment, to minimize "as far as possible" switching costs between digital platforms, to facilitate consumers' access to information about the range of digital TV services available, and to ensure that the pricing of CAS services was not used anticompetitively (OFTEL, 1996: 2–3). The document specified the implementation guidelines for each of the obligations contained in the CAS license (fair trading, nondiscrimination, unbundling of services, intellectual property licensing, separate accounting, data confidentiality, and publication of charges). In OFTEL's view, the market was unlikely to support competing CAS operators in the short term, as households tended to resist acquiring more than one set-top box. Thus, the more the decoder deployed by the first mover included proprietary technology, the greater the need to regulate CAS and related services as an essential facility. Many of the guidelines clearly addressed BSkyB's early roll-out of proprietary decoders.

OFTEL also warned that, should the decoder deployed by the first mover support a single EPG, there will be a need to regulate the way the information is presented to the viewer, with rules addressing the ordering of the channels and services available and the ease of access to them. This represented another step beyond the original directive, because the European statute did not tackle EPG regulation. OFTEL's implementation guidelines also addressed in great detail the question of whether platform operators could recover set-top box subsidies through CAS service charges to third-party broadcasters. This represented a delicate issue because the 1996 act explicitly favored the awarding of multiplex licenses to those willing to provide subsidies to accelerate the roll-out of DTT. It was also widely expected that BSkyB would offer its boxes well below cost, a strategy that had proved successful during the battle for the analog satellite market in the early 1990s. According to OFTEL, the goal was to ensure that subsidies were recovered in a competitively neutral manner and did not fall disproportionately on third-party broadcasters accessing the subsidized decoder. The guidelines thus stipulate that charges made to third-party broadcasters for CAS services can include a component related to the recovery of subsidy but that such a component must be proportional to the use the broadcaster makes of the set-top box capabilities. In other words, the more BSkyB required viewers to subscribe to its own channels in order to qualify for the subsidy, the less it could recover the subsidy from CAS charges to third parties. In addition, OFTEL determined that costs for the promotion of services (i.e., marketing costs) would not be considered as part of the subsidy and thus were not to be recovered through CAS charges.

Overall, OFTEL's implementation proposals went far beyond the directive in creating a procompetitive regime for digital TV. As expected, the BBC-led coalition strongly endorsed OFTEL's approach. As the winds turned in their favor, the coalition saw an opportunity to press its case even further. The BBC demanded tighter rules for EPGs. It asked OFTEL to establish a "common standard" for EPG front pages that included each broadcasters' icon, and to set rules to ensure that EPG operators do not discriminate between broadcasters in terms of ordering, ease of access, or pricing. The corporation also demanded that public service broadcasters, given their universal service obligations, be exempted from contributing towards common CAS costs.[12]

BSkyB, on the contrary, expressed grave concerns about OFTEL's implementation guidelines, which would severely constrain the operation of its CAS subsidiary (SSSL). The company criticized OFTEL's overall approach for applying the principles and doctrines developed for a mature market (i.e., telecommunications) to an infant market (i.e., digital TV) where no monopolist existed. According to BSkyB, OFTEL overstepped its authority to regulate CAS operators. The regime for CAS operators needed to reflect the European directive, not OFTEL's own vision of the digital TV market. BSkyB in particular criticized the provisions for the recovery of decoder subsidies, for they affected the company's plans to combine digital satellite TV with a new interactive TV service developed in partnership with BT, Midland Bank, and the Japanese electronics giant Matsushita. Called British interactive Broadcasting (BiB), the joint venture planned to offer a range of interactive TV services via the BSkyB digital decoder box using two satellite transponders and a wireline return channel provided by BT. In return, BiB would bear the cost of

---

[12] Because of the way in which broadcast rights are sold, free-to-air broadcasters often require the use of CAS when carried on cable or satellite to ensure that the signal only reaches the audience for which the broadcaster has purchased the content rights.

subsidizing the set-top boxes deployed by BSkyB. OFTEL's guidelines severely restricted the options for the recovery of the BiB subsidy.

OFTEL released the final version of the CAS guidelines in the spring of 1997. The regulator remained committed to its approach to the regulation of CAS as a problem of essential facilities. It not only rejected the arguments presented by BSkyB but in many cases strengthened the safeguards imposed. As requested by the BBC-led coalition, OFTEL extended the compulsory licensing obligations to the API specifications and reinforced the EPG rules. In another blow to BSkyB, the final guidelines forbade exclusivity agreements between dominant CAS operators and interactive TV service providers to which the CAS operator is a partner (according to press reports, BSkyB hoped to sign an exclusivity agreement with BiB to provide interactive TV services through its set-top box in return for the subsidy payment). The guidelines were later complemented by a series of OFTEL documents that both extended and expanded the CAS regime. In June 1997 DTI and OFTEL announced the intention to extend the regime applied to CAS operators to other types of services. The key proposal was to extend the CAS regime to what the administration called digital interactive services (e.g., point-to-point information services, interactive TV, data broadcasting), which were provided under different OFTEL licenses. OFTEL wanted to replace these different licenses with a single access control class license based on the regime established for CAS operators. Despite objections from BSkyB and BT, the DTI began issuing the new access control class licenses in August 1999. A few months later, OFTEL determined that SSSL held a dominant position (within the meaning of Article 82 of the EC Treaty) in the market for access control services in the digital satellite platform, thus triggering the access obligations established by the new license.

OFTEL also gave considerable attention to the pricing of CAS and related services. In late 1997 OFTEL released its pricing proposals, which were based on two basic principles: that comparable customers receive comparable terms and conditions, so that the pricing scheme allowed differentiation between different types of broadcasters; and that prices lie somewhere between the stand-alone and the incremental cost of providing the service. Price differentiation would be allowed between four types of broadcasters: free-to-air, pay-TV channels, pay-per-view services, and interactive TV. OFTEL would initially give guidance to and monitor commercial agreements between CAS operators and broadcasters rather than establish direct price controls. However, the regulator warned that "should the proposed approach be unsuccessful in delivering fair, reasonable, and non-discriminatory prices without the need for on-going intervention by OFTEL, then it might be necessary to adopt an RPI-X approach, or even to determine individual prices" (OFTEL, 1998: 14). The proposals again sparked an angry reaction from BSkyB. The company argued that OFTEL's pricing guidelines imposed "excessively onerous burdens" on CAS operators and lowered investment incentives. Several of the issues raised by BSkyB were now echoed by BDB.[13] Despite the criticism, the final pricing guidelines released by OFTEL in May 1999 deviated little from the original proposals. OFTEL maintained the reference band for pricing (between stand-alone and incremental costs), imposed strict limits on the recovery of set-top box subsidies through access charges, and strengthened the provisions related to vertically integrated CAS suppliers (OFTEL, 1998). In general, the guidelines stopped just short of the kind of price controls imposed on BT for interconnection charges.

It may seem paradoxical for the United Kingdom to extend the access obligations contained in Directive 95/47 far beyond the original intent of the statute. After all, Britain only reluctantly accepted the European Parliament amendments to the directive that enshrined these obligations into law. Yet, in the period between the passing of the directive and its implementation by OFTEL, several changes had taken place in terms of the key policy actors involved in the process and the profile of the issue.[14] The DTI officials involved in the negotiation of the directive during the 1994–1995 period, under Michael Heseltine's lead, were concerned about what they considered an overly interventionist European bill that imposed significant losses on BSkyB – a company with substantial investments in the United Kingdom and headed by a longtime supporter of the Conservative Party. They thus resisted the amendments introduced by the EP (which strengthened the access obligations imposed on CAS operators) and instead favored a toned-down directive complemented by self-regulation (the voluntary code of conduct drafted by the DVB). Much had changed by the time the DTI and OFTEL transposed the directive in 1996–1997. The BBC-led coalition had successfully built a case, through the different DNH/DTI consultations as well as a sympathetic press, about the need to curb Murdoch's grip over British media.

---

[13] The BDB license in fact contained a provision that mandated the inclusion of a common interface in BDB's set-top boxes. This was possible under Directive 95/47 because the mandate was not implemented through primary legislation but rather a license agreement (see EC, 1999).

[14] Thanks to David Levy (BBC) for his insight on this issue.

Moreover, with the introduction of the government's proposal for a new broadcasting bill in the spring of 1995, the issue was now being discussed in cabinet meetings rather than at the level of DTI senior staff. Having turned his press against the Major administration, Murdoch was unlikely to receive continued favorable treatment.

The new Labour government also supported OFTEL's effort to extend, both in depth and scope, the obligations contained in Directive 95/47. The Labour Party had in fact campaigned about the need to rationalize the institutional structure of communications regulation and to apply consistent rules across sectors. Much of the intellectual basis of the New Labour media policies stemmed from the work of the Institute for Public Policy Research (IPPR), a Labour-leaning think tank closely associated with key members of the Blair administration. After the elections, OFTEL found enthusiastic political support for creating a procompetitive regime for digital TV. This left incumbents unable to block or even force significant changes to OFTEL's guidelines. Despite the various public consultations held, OFTEL's closed administrative procedures provided few opportunities for interest-group pressure. With the courts rarely challenging OFTEL on procedural grounds, the only possible recourse was an appeal to Community authorities alleging improper transposition of Directive 95/47. Some European Commission officials shared the concern about OFTEL's overzealous interpretation of the directive. In clear reference to OFTEL, they wrote: "[T]elecom regulators used to transposing the heavy telecom regulation intended to control dominant telecoms operators have not brought a light touch to what is an entirely different situation, a new market starting up" (de Cockborne, Clements, and Watson-Brown, 1999: 8). However, because the directive had given a great deal of latitude for implementation to member states, there was little room for Community action.

THE BiB CASE

The British implementation of Directive 95/47 was finally put to test in Brussels in the context of the investigation conducted by European competition authorities about BiB. With the official announcement of the joint venture shortly after the May 1997 general elections, British regulators took notice. After all, this partnership involved two of the most powerful players in the communications sector at large – BT and BSkyB. OFTEL Director General Don Cruickshank publicly remarked that he would be looking "very closely" at how the joint venture intended to operate (OFTEL Press Release, May 7, 1997). In private, he admitted that his initial reaction was that "two great, ugly monopolists were getting together."[15] Two main concerns emerged: first, the terms under which service providers and broadcasters would be allowed to reach customers of the proposed interactive TV platform; second, how BiB planned to recover the expected subsidy of around £300 per set-top box deployed by BSkyB. The kind of hybrid services that BiB proposed to deliver boosted the government's case for moving toward a unified regulatory regime under a single authority, but for the moment the issue had to be dealt with the instruments at hand. Incumbent analog broadcasters also took notice, because BiB proposed a "walled garden" service in which only a carefully selected group of broadcasters and interactive TV providers would participate. For the BBC, BiB represented another front in its battle for privileged access to new communication platforms. Being left out of BiB could relegate the corporation to secondary status in the next generation of broadcasting services.

When the BiB case came before OFTEL and the OFT, there was little doubt that the final word would have to come from Brussels. Both agencies thus gave preliminary approval to the venture while EU competition authorities worked on the case. EU competition tsar Van Miert quickly stated that BiB raised several concerns, among them the foreclosing of competition in the pay-TV market and the enhancement of BT's dominant position in the telecommunications sector. According to Van Miert, BiB combined two companies that were potential competitors in the market for interactive TV services. In addition, commission authorities worried that BiB would discriminate against third parties with respect to the terms of access to the subsidized boxes and that competing interactive TV platforms would not develop because of the first-mover advantages and the subsidy provided by BiB (McCallum, 1999). There was wide speculation that the BiB deal would be opposed in Brussels based on the precedent of the twin MSG cases.

After several months, the commission announced that it would approve the formation of BiB subject to several undertakings by the parties involved: the legal separation of BiB's subsidy payment from its digital TV services, the removal of all exclusive access rights to the subsidized set-top box, the obligation to license proprietary set-top box specifications to third parties, the obligation to provide access control services to

---

[15] "OFTEL Clears Way for BiB to Move into Digital Venture," *Independent*, October 30, 1997, p. 25.

third-party interactive TV providers, the removal of the requirement to subscribe to BSkyB's digital pay-TV service as a condition for receiving the BiB subsidy, and BT's commitment to not expand its cable interests and divest from its current cable franchises in the United Kingdom.[16] The result of the investigation revealed that European authorities, much like OFTEL's, were ready to extend the principles and tools used to open the European telecommunications market to other communications infrastructure sectors, irrespective of their maturity.[17] The strict conditions imposed on the joint venture did more than address the concerns raised by OFTEL and OFT about BiB; in a sense, they validated OFTEL's entire approach to the regulation of CAS and its implementation of Directive 95/47.

---

[16] Notice published pursuant to Article 19(3) of Regulation 17, OJ C 322 of October 21, 1998. For a discussion, see Galperin and Bar (2002).
[17] This point is further elaborated by Ungerer (2000).

ELEVEN

Digital TV and the New Labour

If the architects of the British transition strategy belonged to the Major administration, the task of carrying along the plan fell to the Labour government elected in May 1997. On the one hand, the new administration had the unenviable task of pushing forward a plan created by the previous administration that many considered unviable. On the other, the transition fit nicely with several of New Labour's goals for the communications sector. In general terms, the elections did not represent a fundamental turn in Britain's transition path. Tony Blair was elected on a platform that by and large emphasized continuity with the regulatory reforms introduced during the Conservative years, and there was little support to reverse course on the issue of digital TV. The new administration, however, did bring a new emphasis on the development of the information society in the United Kingdom that digital TV policies had to accommodate. This theme would pervade Labour's media policies for much of the first Blair period (1997–2001). The new administration also brought to bear a more skeptical attitude about the capacity for communication markets to work effectively in the absence of procompetitive regulation. For the Tories, ex ante rules were necessary only in the initial stages of reforms as traditionally closed markets evolved toward self-sustaining competition; for Labour officials, many of these rules were not temporary remedies but rather essential pillars of competition in markets that would otherwise tend toward monopolization (see DTI, 1998; 2000). This combination of fresh policy goals and a less fervent belief in the ability of market forces to deliver social benefits provided a fertile ground for a more hands-on approach to digital TV, particularly as it became apparent that, without the very visible government hand, completing the migration process would take several decades.

In September 1997, Chris Smith, the new secretary of state for culture, media, and sport (the new department that replaced the DNH), outlined the new administration's approach to digital TV. In a speech before the Royal Television Society, Smith reassured industry leaders that the government essentially intended to advance the transition within the framework established by the previous administration. However, this did not preclude a more proactive approach:

> To a large extent, it will be for viewers – or, if you prefer to use the phrase, the market – to decide which digital services succeed, on which platforms. But it would be idle, or indeed disingenuous, for the Government simply to leave it at that. In broadcasting, we are talking about an industry which plays a crucial role in determining individuals' sense of their own identity, moulding their tastes, interests and consumer preferences. . . . We are also, crucially if more prosaically, talking about an industry which has always been very heavily regulated. The transition from that regulated past to a more abundant and unconstrained future is a process which itself needs to be carefully managed. (DCMS Press Release, September 18, 1997: 4)

According to Smith, the government would not replace the operation of market forces but rather was prepared to use the available policy instruments to expedite this market-driven process. As the debates about OFTEL's implementation of Directive 95/47 subsided, attention turned to how to speed up the roll-out of services and equipment in order to accelerate the switch-off of analog stations and release spectrum for new broadcasting and telecommunications services. Shortly after its inauguration, the administration introduced legislation aimed at creating flexibility and introducing market incentives in the allocation of radio frequencies.[1] Chris Smith believed that the government needed to give a strong signal as to when it was prepared to start the switch-off of analog TV. In the absence of clear switch-off criteria (recall the Major administration refused to introduce them in the 1996 act), the industry could fall into a classic chicken-and-egg paralysis because market actors lacked a time frame for investments.

The new administration thus began by commissioning a study to evaluate the costs involved in the migration, the expected duration of the transition, and the most effective instruments for the government

---

[1] These proposals became the Wireless Telegraphy Act of 1998.

to expedite the process. The study endorsed Smith's approach: it concluded that there would be significant benefits from the announcement of a switch-off date resulting from a more rapid decrease in the price of reception equipment and better coordination in the investment decisions of market actors (NERA/Smith, 1998). Without an announcement, even in the most optimistic scenario it would take no less than fifteen years for digital services to replicate the penetration of analog TV. On the contrary, if the government announced a switch-off date, the transition period could be reduced by as much as five years, with little additional costs to households. The study also rejected a government mandate banning the sale of analog TV equipment, suggesting instead that direct financial assistance or tax privileges be used to encourage take-up, particularly with the most obstinate analog viewers in the final stages of the transition (the so-called granny factor). The cost of these subsidies, the study suggested, could be offset with proceeds from spectrum auctions for the frequencies eventually released by the switch-off.

The administration welcomed the study's broad conclusion that justified government intervention as a means to expedite the switch-off process but declined to take any immediate action. While committed to the transition, Blair felt apprehensive about policies that could be construed as favoring the take-up of DTT to the detriment of other digital platforms, in particular satellite services. Therefore, when ITV Digital (the commercial name taken by BDB) launched in the fall of 1998, there was little indication as to when or under what conditions analog TV would go dark. BSkyB had launched its digital satellite service only a few weeks before, abating its much-anticipated first-mover advantages over DTT. As expected, the two operators were deploying incompatible set-top boxes: BSkyB's boxes used a CAS developed by BSkyB subsidiary NDS and a proprietary API; ITV Digital instead opted for a CAS developed by Canal+'s subsidiary SECA and a simpler, nonproprietary API called MHEG-5 endorsed by the DTG consortium. Locking in subscribers as early as possible was thus critical to the success of the platforms. In spring 1999 BSkyB announced that it would offer its set-top boxes to viewers free of charge, with the only condition being that the box remained connected to a phone line in order to receive BiB's services (BiB committed to spend up to £500 million on decoder subsidies). This left ITV Digital with few options but to match the free decoder offer, which began draining the company's financial resources. In the corridors of the DTI and the ITC, this costly battle was worryingly reminiscent of the events leading to the fall of BSB.

Table 11.1. *BBC Share of Industry Revenues and Audience,*
1993–1998 (%)

	1993	1994	1995	1996	1997	1998
Share of industry revenues	42	39	36	34	32	31
Audience share	43	43	43	45	42	41

Source: DCMS (1999).

At the same time digital TV services started, Chris Smith announced the formation of a committee to advise the government on setting the license fee for the BBC after 2002 (the previous administration had set it up to that year). The license fee review came at a challenging time for the BBC. While its share of audience remained stable at around 40 percent, its share of industry revenues had declined from 42 to 31 percent in the past five years (Table 11.1), and the corporation faced substantial costs related to the launch of its new digital channels. The committee's remit was limited to recommending the future level of the license fee, which the government had established would remain the main source of funding for the BBC over the duration of its existing charter (until 2006). However, advocates of public service broadcasting feared that the review would spark a larger debate about the BBC's funding scheme along the lines of the Peacock Committee. Much to the BBC's relief, Gavyn Davies, a prestigious City economist and an old friend of John Birt, was named to chair the committee. Unlike Peacock, Davies was well known for his Reithian views about public service broadcasting (Graham and Davies, 1997). For many senior BBC officials, this was a unique opportunity to press their case for a substantial revenue increase to fund the BBC's digital expansion.

In its submission to the Davies Committee, the BBC presented a powerful argument about the need to collect an additional £650 million per year through 2006. The transition to digital TV was central to the argument. As the transition evolved, more market players would compete for a finite number of eyeballs, and such a ratings war could compromise quality standards. As a result, digital TV, even more so than analog TV, demanded a well-funded public broadcaster that would set quality benchmarks. Moreover, original British programming was the kind of content that would drive digital TV take-up, and the BBC, as the largest content producer in the United Kingdom, was uniquely positioned to provide it. The corporation expected to spend an additional

£1,250 million on content through 2006 (in both existing and new services), of which about £600 million would come from internal savings and its own commercial activities ("self-help," as it was called); new license fee funds would provide the rest. Without a substantial increase to the license fee, the BBC warned, the British broadcasting system would increasingly resemble that of the United States:

> The UK stands at a crossroads; it can opt for a US style environment, in which a minority-interest public service broadcaster has no real significance in the market – no market power – and therefore a negligible impact on the ecology of the US broadcasting, or it can elect to sustain the ability of the BBC to influence the UK broadcasting market by ensuring – through its strength and presence – the BBC has an impact on quality, range and diversity in the digital world as in the analogue world. (BBC, 1999: 5)

The submission was complemented by a study that examined the impact which levying a "digital license fee" (DLF) – payable on top of the regular license by those who received digital services – would have on the take-up of digital TV. The corporation considered the DLF one of the most politically acceptable proposals to increase its level of funding, because it resembled the scheme introduced in 1968 to finance the BBC's conversion to color TV. The study recognized that, all things being equal, levying the extra tax on digital TV viewers would evidently slow take-up (London Economics, 1999). Yet, if the additional funds sufficiently increased the number and quality of the digital services offered by the BBC, this would compensate, or even more than compensate, the disincentive created by the DLF. By examining the introduction of related communication technologies such as the VCR and satellite TV, the study concluded that the effect of the DLF on take-up, if the additional funds were properly utilized, would be negligible.

Not surprisingly, the conclusions of the Davies Committee, released in July 1999, generally echoed the BBC's claims. The committee agreed that the BBC required additional funding to participate fully in what it termed the "digital TV revolution" (DCMS, 1999: 11). According to the Davies Report, the full potential of this revolution was yet to be unleashed, and a well-funded BBC had a key role to play in unleashing this potential through the development of new digital programming and online content. The committee found that the BBC had been put on a "strict financial diet" for many years and that continuing this diet "would effectively freeze the BBC out of the digital world" (1999: 32).

Table 11.2. *U.K. Digital TV Penetration by Platform*
(000s of households)

	1998	1999	2000	2001
DTT	36	527	970	1,350
Digital satellite	225	2,065	4,520	5,920
Digital cable	0	155	820	2,020
Total DTV	261	2,747	6,310	9,290
DTV penetration	1.1%	11.5%	26.0%	38.3%

Source: European Commission.

This diet had a negative impact on analog services, as funding (at least 10 percent of licensee fee revenues according to the report) was being diverted to finance the BBC's new digital services at the expense of the core analog channels. While internal efficiencies and commercial activities had helped offset the problem, the committee argued that additional license fee funds were necessary to finance the BBC's new digital services. The key recommendation of the Davies Committee was the introduction of a DLF to be collected over a period of ten years, after which it would essentially disappear with the switch-off of analog TV. Preferred over a blanket increase in the license fee, this solution would be consistent with the "British tradition" of having those who enjoyed the benefits of new services pay for them; otherwise, new digital channels would be funded by all and yet accessible only by those who had acquired digital reception equipment. At the time, only about 10 percent of British households had migrated to digital (Table 11.2).

However, the level of the DLF proposed by the Davies Committee (about £24 a year through 2006) fell significantly short of the BBC's demand. The committee was not convinced about the BBC's case for an additional £650 million in funding through 2006. In particular, the committee noted that the BBC had only vaguely described many of the proposed services on which the additional funds would be spent. In addition, granting the full amount requested would lower the incentives for the BBC to seek for even further internal savings and develop its commercial activities: "[W]e would like the BBC to be reassured by the Government that every penny they can squeeze from these resources in the future will be permanently available for spending on improved services. But at the same time it is advisable to keep a strong funding discipline so that the BBC is not tempted to relax in these areas in the future"

(DCMS, 1999: 57). The level of the DLF proposed by the committee would generate an additional £150–200 million per year through 2006, only about a third of the original BBC request. Yet, this still represented a 2–2.5 percent per annum revenue growth in real terms, a much better settlement than the BBC had gotten throughout the Conservative period.

The Davies Report triggered an outcry from commercial broadcasters and digital platform operators. They claimed that the DLF represented a tax on innovation that penalized companies and viewers who had already invested in digital TV equipment and, contrary to government policies, would postpone for years the completion of the transition. Interestingly, rival market players such as ITV Digital and BSkyB allied against the DLF and, more generally, the BBC's planned digital expansion. The BBC submission was the target of much criticism. According to Carlton CEO Clive Jones, it was simply false that the negative effect of the DLF on penetration could be offset by higher-quality BBC programming because the corporation's digital services accounted for only 1 in 200 viewing hours and a tiny fraction of overall programming spending. A tax on digital TV would simply kill the struggling DTT platform, argued Jones. After nearly a year, ITV Digital had managed to attract about half a million customers, far less than BSkyB's 2 million (see Table 11.2). Of course, the task was far more challenging for ITV Digital, since BSkyB was essentially migrating its analog customer to the digital service. BSkyB and the cable operators also joined in to protest against what they called a "digital poll tax," in reference to the infamous local tax introduced by the Thatcher administration in the late 1980s that led to widespread civil disobedience. Opposition to the DLF was backed by a study commissioned by commercial broadcasters. The study predicted that the introduction of the DLF would have a significant adverse impact on the take-up of services, slowing penetration by as much as 20 percent by 2008 and retarding the analog switch-off by approximately three years (NERA, 1999). Such a delay would also go against the grain of government policies aimed at introducing market mechanisms in the allocation of spectrum. According to the study, a delay of three years could cost the treasury about £680 million in forgone revenues from spectrum fees.

The cabinet was reportedly split on the DLF question. Some ministers felt concerned about imposing a new tax just weeks before the 2000 local elections, as polls showed a substantial drop in support for the Labour administration in general and overwhelming opposition to the DLF.[2] The

[2] *Guardian*/ICM Polls.

picture that emerged from the assortment of economic studies about the effect of the DLF on the transition was one of great uncertainty. While the additional fee would clearly reduce take-up incentives, the extent to which higher-quality BBC services could offset such effect was simply unknown. A new study commissioned by the DCMS to provide a "balanced assessment" endorsed the BBC's case that the impact of the DLF on digital TV penetration would be minimal – retarding the switch-off by as little as six months (Creigh-Tyte, 2000). Yet several Cabinet members – including Smith and DTI Secretary Stephen Byers – were more sympathetic to the second-best option suggested by the Davies Committee: a blanket £5 increase to the general license fee over the next two years (2000–2001). Prime Minister Blair was concerned about policies that would seem to favor DTT over satellite, which would immediately turn the Murdoch press against the administration. On the other hand, if the BBC study was right about the natural plateau of pay-TV, promoting DTT was inevitable to achieve switch-off.

THE TRANSITION TESTS AND THE REJECTION OF THE DLF

Meanwhile, the cabinet decided it was time to give the market a signal about when the government expected the analog switch-off process to begin. Chris Smith made the announcement in a September 1999 speech before the industry establishment, which since 1995 had been demanding that the government set a clear switch-off time frame. The announcement was timed to coincide with the initial stages of the auction for 3G wireless licenses. While frequencies for 3G services had already been identified, it was important to provide potential bidders information about the future release of spectrum that could potentially be used for competing services. The administration established that the switch-off process would begin once two tests were met: availability and affordability of digital TV. The availability test would be achieved once the digital signal of the existing terrestrial broadcasters replicated the coverage of their analog signal, namely, 99.4 percent of the U.K. population.[3] Given the estimation of initial coverage for the DTT multiplexes at no more than 90 percent (for BBC's Multiplex 1), this was a challenging target. Smith recognized that reaching the remaining 10 percent of the population not covered by DTT would be "no easy task," and that some form of subsidy

---

[3] Except for Channel Five, which as noted reached only about 75 percent of the population.

might be needed to convert the last analog holdouts as suggested by the NERA/Smith (1998) study. The second test – affordability – called for digital TV receiving equipment to be "an affordable option for the vast majority of the people." This task seemed much easier given that since the spring of 1999 both ITV Digital and BSkyB were essentially giving away decoder boxes. Smith, however, clarified that the administration would consider the affordability test met once digital TV equipment reached 95 percent penetration – again, a very tall order given the estimated 60 percent plateau of pay-TV and the poor availability and prohibitive cost of alternative reception equipment (i.e., not provided by a pay-TV operator) such as integrated digital sets.[4] How quickly could these tests be met? According to Smith, the administration expected the transition to be completed sometime between 2006 and 2010, and he challenged industry leaders to work toward this goal.

The announcement did not meet broadcasters' demand for a credible commitment to a clear switch-off date. The two tests put forth by Chris Smith were certainly better than nothing, but that still left the United Kingdom without a transition schedule comparable with that of the United States. Appearing before Parliament, Smith acknowledged that the 2006–2010 target had to be taken cautiously, and that the tests, not the target dates, were paramount.[5] Furthermore, the announcement hardly represented a statutory mandate; the next government could easily decide to rethink the tests completely. Why did the Blair administration avoid setting a firm switch-off date, much like the Major government did in the 1996 act? The answer lies in the political costs associated with such a commitment. Given the difficulties in forecasting digital TV penetration, the cabinet wanted at all costs to avoid a situation whereby, should actual penetration fall behind projections, the government would be forced to choose between extending the switch-off date (at the expense of credibility) or cutting off service to millions of late adopters. Leaving the poor and elderly (the likely late adopters) as well as teenagers (who relied on older second and third TV sets in the household) without television was hardly an attractive option, particularly for a Labour administration. As noted, when the 405-line system was shut down in 1985, only about 15,000 households relied on the service. Until then, the Thatcher administration had been reluctant to shut down the system, even when redeploying the spectrum would have generated large

---

[4] According to BREMA, only 30,000 integrated digital TVs were sold in 1999, compared with 5.5 million analog sets.

[5] *Parliamentary Debates*, Commons, October 29, 1999, col. 1209.

economic benefits (the spectrum used by 405-line services was eventually allocated to mobile radio services). Likewise, the Blair cabinet did not want to commit to a target date that could later turn into a political fiasco for the administration.

In December 1999 the Parliament weighed in on the DLF debate with the release of an opinion report by the House of Commons Culture, Media and Sport Committee (Culture, Media, and Sport Committee, 1999). The report dealt an important blow to the DLF. Although the decision rested entirely with the cabinet, the strong tone of the document emanating from this Commons committee fully controlled by Labour MPs shattered what little support the DLF had among ministers. The report started by recalling that the BBC had already been granted additional funds for the launch of digital TV services by the previous administration – a license fee settlement above inflation for a period of three years and the £244 million generated by the privatization of its transmission network in early 1997. The committee strongly criticized the BBC's senior management for failing to give a detailed account of how and when the additional funds requested would be spent (even though several BBC senior managers had testified before the committee, including John Birt, his designated successor Greg Dyke, and Board of Governors Chairman Sir Christopher Bland). "There is nothing resembling an overall corporate plan setting out the division of costs on particular services as a basis for public consideration of the price tag for the BBC's new vision," wrote the committee (1999: 8). Another concern raised was the lack of a clear distinction in the BBC's digital strategy between its public service and its commercial activities, such as the BBC Online and News 24, which competed head-on with private services without a clear justification. The committee also rejected the claim that a well-funded BBC would drive digital TV penetration: "[T]he notion that the BBC is uniquely positioned to attract a new mass audience to digital television is a hunch and a hunch which flies in the face of the evidence of the development of the digital market so far" (1999: 12). On the question of funding, the report strongly criticized the DLF proposal:

> The digital license fee supplement would slow take-up of digital television and delay analogue switch-off. It would hamper the possibility of marginally free digital television being available to consumers and would accordingly bear most heavily on the most disadvantaged in society. In short, it would run directly counter to the objectives of public policy. Regardless of any decision on the

funding requirements of the BBC, we recommend that the proposal of the Davies Review for a digital license supplement should
be rejected. (1999: 23)

A number of implementation concerns were also raised about the
DLF. The administration acknowledged that new legislation would be
required to compel digital platform operators to release subscribers'
information, which was essential for the implementation of the DLF.
BSkyB and ITV Digital strongly opposed the release of subscriber data
and threatened to take the issue to the courts in London and Brussels.
They were joined by the Conservative opposition in arguing that the DLF
not only violated the EU Treaty's provisions against state aid but that re-
leasing the names and addresses of pay-TV subscribers conflicted with
existing data protection legislation. In February 2000 the government
finally announced its rejection of the DLF. Though sharing the Davies
Committee's assessment of the need to increase funding for the BBC as
the transition progressed, the administration favored the second-best
option: a modest increase in the general license fee (1.5 percent above
inflation through 2006). This would generate approximately £200 million per year in additional funds, an amount roughly equivalent to the
projections for the DLF. According to the government, the rest of the
funding requested by the BBC for its digital expansion (about £450 million) would have to come from "self-help." In announcing the new license
fee settlement, Chris Smith echoed many of the concerns raised by the
Commons Committee. He warned the BBC against developing new services that replicated those of commercial operators and announced the
appointment of an independent panel to carry out periodic reviews of
the BBC's fair trading commitment.[6]

The license fee settlement reflected the Blair administration's vision
about the role of public service broadcasting in a post-transition media
environment. The government rejected the argument advanced by many
(e.g., Elstein, 2001) that the spectrum abundance and the personaliza-
tion of TV schedules made possible by the transition rendered the role
of public service broadcasters – along with much of the existing broadcasting regime – superfluous. The majority of the cabinet believed that
the BBC had an important role to play even after the analog switch-off –
hence the decision to end what the Davies Committee called the BBC's
"financial diet." Yet this role would necessarily be more restricted than
in the analog era: "[T]he government does not however believe that the

---

[6] *Parliamentary Debates*, Commons, February 21, 2000, cols. 1239–1243.

BBC should do everything. Specifically, it does not expect the license fee to fund strands of the market, such as dedicated film and sport channels, to which the distinctive role of public service broadcasting has little extra to offer" (DCMS, 2000: 1). What was taking shape was a new, post-Reithian justification for the existence of a tax-funded BBC, something incipiently articulated but not fully developed during the Major administration. According to the new vision, a strong BBC was desirable in the digital era to deliver the kinds of programming that market players would not and to provide a "quality benchmark" for commercial operators (DTI, 2000). In this respect, the administration fully endorsed the Davies Committee's findings; however, strict safeguards were necessary to keep the corporation – still a dominant force in the British media industry as shown in Table 11.1 – confined to its new role.

One of the key instruments developed by the government to monitor the BBC's digital expansion was the enactment of a new set of procedures for the approval of new BBC digital services. The procedures established that proposals for new BBC digital services would be subject to a period of public consultation in which the government would request opinions from industry representatives, the ITC, the Radio Authority, and consumer groups. If approved, services would still be subject to periodic reviews by the DCMS to ensure the BBC was acting in accordance with the terms of the approval. In considering the proposals, the DCMS would assess whether the new services were compatible with the BBC's core public service role, and whether the value to the public was proportionate to the likely impact on the market, particularly when commercial operators offered similar services. In other words, the new procedures were designed to ensure that the corporation did not use license fee funds to overstep its newly reduced public service mandate.

Shortly after, the exhaustive scrutiny of the BBC proposals to revamp its digital services proved that the government was serious about enforcing the new vision. After a nine-month review, the DCMS gave conditional approval to three new BBC digital channels (two of those aimed at children plus a new culture channel) but rejected a new service (called BBC3) targeted at sixteen to thirty-four year olds, on the grounds that the channel would offer little beyond what commercial operators already offered and that its contribution to digital TV take-up would be minimal (DCMS Press Release, September 13, 2001). Nonetheless, as the transition lost steam, the government would find it increasingly difficult to implement its new vision for the BBC. With the main commercial operators in the red as a result of an advertising market downturn and a draining free decoder war, the BBC would emerge as the only player capable of rescuing the government from the collapse of its transition strategy.

THE DEMISE OF ITV DIGITAL

Since the start of services in the fall of 1998, the poor performance of DTT was a source of concern for the administration. The key problem was coverage. The DTT network had been engineered to compete head-to-head with digital satellite; several technical compromises had been made in favor of a rapid roll-out of services and greater channel capacity, essentially at the expense of signal strength and geographical reach. In terrestrial transmission a fundamental trade-off exists between carriage capacity and signal robustness. The DTT network was originally planned for only four multiplexes (e.g., ITC, 1993); the two additional ones thus came at the expense of better geographical coverage. For the ITV Digital service, actual coverage was estimated at below 60 percent (DTG, 2000). By definition, then, almost half of the households could not be serviced. In addition, actual reception was further reduced by the fact that many old rooftop antennas could not pick up the DTT signals, and neither could most portable (set-top) antennas. The coverage problems presaged a transition that, according to the government's availability test, would extend far beyond 2006–2010. The ITC took the initiative by commissioning a series of studies aimed at identifying the technical barriers for analog switch-off within the parameters laid out by the administration (the availability and affordability tests). The studies agreed on the urgent need to improve coverage in order for DTT to approach the 99.4 percent availability of analog TV (DTG, 2000; ITC, 2000). But improving coverage would be difficult during the simulcasting period. Because frequency channels for DTT were interleaved within the analog TV spectrum, the power of DTT signals had to be limited to prevent interference with analog broadcasts. Terrestrial incumbents argued that coverage could also be improved by converting some or all of the frequencies used for analog TV to boost existing DTT services – which not incidentally would reduce the threat of future market entry.[7] The problem was that this solution required the switch-off of analog channels before the government tests had been met. In a sense, the

---

[7] One study estimated that universal coverage for at least two DTT multiplexes (enough to carry the existing terrestrial operators) could be achieved by converting two of the existing analog networks to digital (ITC, 2000).

administration faced a classic chicken-and-egg problem: coverage would only improve after the switch-off of analog TV, but the government had rejected switch-off before substantial digital coverage existed (the availability test).

The proposal also conflicted with the government's goal to make more spectrum available for new telecommunications applications. Reusing analog channels for DTT would sharply reduce the frequencies released by the transition. The £22.5 billion netted by the auction of the 3G wireless licenses in March 2000 had revealed a strong demand for radio frequencies, and the government was committed to putting more spectrum on the market. In December 2000 the administration released its proposals for an overhaul of the communications regulatory framework (DTI, 2000). In the White Paper, the government stated its intention to "value the spectrum used by broadcasters and introduce new mechanisms to enable communications companies to trade spectrum" (DTI, 2000: 15). Shortly after, the government announced a comprehensive review of spectrum management policies. The review aimed at improving efficiency in the use of radio frequencies through market tools such as spectrum valuation, trading, and pricing (Cave, 2002). The problem was that the introduction of market reforms in the management of radio spectrum was not easy to reconcile with the administration's commitment to DTT. Making DTT work would demand more rather than less spectrum.

Despite the rather favorable terms in which the commercial licenses had been granted, DTT continued to struggle. In fall 2001 rumors about the possible collapse of the ITV Digital service started to circulate in the City. Besides the coverage problems and the powerful competition from BSkyB's digital satellite service, a slump in the advertising market (down 12.5 percent in 2001) severely damaged the finances of the company's main shareholders, Carlton and Granada. Having already spent £750 million, ITV Digital reportedly needed a capital injection of £500 million to improve services and continue the free set-top box battle with BSkyB. Pressure began to mount from the financial backers of Carlton and Granada to close the costly DTT venture, and the government braced for a possible collapse of ITV Digital. Senior ITV managers lobbied for a helping hand from the administration; at the very least, they demanded the relaxation of ownership rules for commercial TV to allow a Carlton-Granada merger. Administration officials nonetheless thoroughly dismissed any possible bailout. The times in which the government picked up the tab for its national champions were long gone, said the officials (besides, British authorities were never inclined to that in the first place). In early 2001 the administration had already given Carlton and Granada a steep rebate in their ITV license payments to the ITC (the so-called digital dividend, estimated at about £100 million per year), and that was as far as the cabinet was prepared to go.[8]

A collapse of ITV Digital would require a major rethinking of the transition strategy. Within the administration, advocates of a more hands-on approach to the transition were invigorated. In October 2001 the administration released a so-called Digital TV Action Plan. It was a clear indication that the government was preparing for the worst. The plan did not directly address the ITV Digital question. In fact, the government adamantly characterized it as platform-independent. The Action Plan was essentially a broad road map of the essential tasks to promote digital take-up and complete the analog switch-off. Arguably more important than the list of tasks was the setting up of a mechanism for the different government departments involved in the transition to coordinate their efforts and resolve jurisdictional conflicts. Coordinated by senior DTI and DCMS officials, the plan also included a so-called Stakeholders Group that would allow key market players to participate directly in the policymaking process (the group was headed by Barry Cox, chairman of Channel Four and a close friend of Prime Minister Blair). Among the first initiatives within the framework of the Action Plan was the implementation of a digital TV public awareness campaign and a pilot project (named "Go Digital") to provide free reception equipment to a limited number of households. Ultimately, the Action Plan did not propose any fundamental changes to the existing transition strategy. Yet, as administration officials recognized, the plan did represent a significant change in the way the administration was prepared to implement it.[9] By bringing key policymakers and market players to the same table and establishing a schedule for the completion of specific actions, the government was flexing its muscles in support of a strategy that the imminent collapse of ITV Digital had sent back to the drawing board.

ITV Digital finally went under in spring 2002. Its much anticipated bankruptcy was catalyzed by the inability to renegotiate its contract with the Football League. The collapse prompted wide speculation about how the government would react. A House of Commons committee stacked

---

[8] The rebate came from a reduction in the percentage of advertising revenues payable by ITV companies to the ITC for every home that received ITV in digital format.
[9] Interview with DCMS officials (July 2002).

with Labour MPs called the failure of ITV Digital a "body blow to the progress towards digital switch-over" and suggested the use of more interventionist tools, such as providing free digital decoders on a wider scale and banning the sale of analog TV equipment (Culture, Media, and Sport Committee, 2002: 60). Nevertheless, administration officials were quick to characterize the bankruptcy of ITV Digital as the failure of a private company resulting from unwise commercial decisions; the government's switch-off plan was still on track (DCMS Press Release, April 26, 2002). In reality, the collapse had already been factored in the Action Plan. Following the surrender of its digital multiplex licenses by ITV Digital, the government instructed the ITC to conduct an accelerated licensing process to be completed in less than six weeks. The new DTT beauty contest, much like its predecessor, resulted in several unexpected alliances.

The most controversial alliance was Free-to-View, a consortium formed by the BBC, BSkyB, and Crown Castle (the privatized transmission arm of the BBC) that championed a mostly free DTT service with programming provided by its partners. Surprisingly, Carlton and Granada were again bidding for the DTT multiplex licenses through a consortium called Digital Terrestrial Alliance (formed between ITV and Channel Four), proposing a service that combined an assortment of free channels with a so-called pay-lite component. Two additional bids were submitted under a platform operator model with no programming specified (i.e., the multiplex operator would simply run the network and resell capacity to unaffiliated programmers). The ITC quickly dismissed these bids; according to ITC officials, these were not times for more policy experiments with DTT.[10] Ultimately, the ITC had the unenviable task of choosing between handing over DTT to two of the most powerful players in the industry (the BBC and BSkyB) or else giving back the licenses to its previous owners.

On July 4, 2002, almost exactly five years after the original award of the DTT multiplex licenses, the ITC announced that it would award the licenses to the Free-to-View consortium. According to the commission, the decision was based on the need to give DTT "a fresh start" (ITC Press Release, July 4, 2002). This fresh start meant not only that the licenses would in fact change hands but also that the commission was endorsing a different commercial proposition for DTT. ITV Digital had failed not only because of technical problems related to its premature launch

---

[10] Interviews with ITC officials (July 2002).

but also because of false assumptions about consumer demand in the pay-TV market. The BBC-led bid was based on the old model of terrestrial TV – free services supported by advertising and the license fee – rather than on head-to-head competition with BSkyB and the cable companies. The BBC and BSkyB represented a safe pair of hands to help push the transition forward, unlike the unproven platform-operator model proposed by the two underdog bidders. Besides, handing back the licenses to Carlton and Granada would have been politically unacceptable.

The decision pleased the government. With the BBC in the driver's seat of DTT, the administration could better steer the transition toward the 2006–2010 switch-off target. After all, the government had the last word on the BBC's finances and services, and with the BBC charter up for renewal in 2006, it could certainly persuade the corporation to put its weight behind this effort. For the BBC, controlling the DTT platform was a way to rebuff the critics of public service broadcasting and the license-fee scheme. If the transition succeeded, much credit would go to its operation and promotion of the DTT platform and the corporation could once more claim to have spearheaded the roll-out of new broadcasting technologies in the United Kingdom. The administration rewarded the BBC for rescuing its DTT plan. As ITV Digital faltered, the government showed increased signs of easing its stance toward the corporation. A few weeks before the ITC announced the new license award, Tessa Jowell – who replaced Chris Smith after Blair's landslide reelection in June 2001 – announced that the government did not intend to introduce significant changes to the BBC's funding scheme in the next charter. Shortly after the ITC award, the government finally approved the BBC's new youth-oriented digital channel, BBC3 (DCMS Press Release, September 17, 2002).

Did the Blair administration backpedal on its vision of a slimmed-down BBC in the digital age? To a certain extent, yes. Faced with a major blow to its transition strategy, the administration adopted a pragmatic response. DTT was from the start a political project, designed by the Major administration to achieve a number of policy goals. It thus seemed logical that the analog switch-off would have to be directly promoted and carefully managed by the state. One of the original justifications for DTT – creating competition to BSkyB in the pay-TV market – disappeared without a trace from the policy agenda, but this hardly concerned the government. In fact, many senior DTI and DCMS officials believed this goal ran against a smooth transition. The participation of BSkyB in the original DTT beauty contest had stirred much controversy; now, it ruffled few feathers. Was the BBC's control of DTT a case of industrial policy through other means? Perhaps, but of all the available tools for the government to speed up the transition (e.g., direct set-top box subsidies, a ban on the sale of analog TV equipment), this was arguably among the most subtle. For many, having the BBC run the DTT network and promote take-up was certainly preferable to overt government spending or intrusive rules on digital TV equipment and services. Moreover, if the DTT experiment continued to fail, the government could again shift the blame onto others. Committed to fostering the transition, the Blair administration accepted the BBC's new role as the more politically acceptable strategy for doing so.

PART IV

New Television, Old Politics

TWELVE

One Goal, Many Paths

In the two preceding parts of the book we discussed the introduction and evolutionary path of digital TV in the United States and the United Kingdom. We observed how in response to common challenges related to spectrum management, industrial competitiveness, macroeconomic stability, and a new international agenda for the communications sector, governments engaged in programmatic efforts to reshape the broadcasting sector centered around the migration from analog to digital TV. In the final part of the book, I seek to explicate the remarkable differences in the transition strategies implemented in both countries, and reflect on what they tell us about government regulation of broadcasting at times when the capacity and the appropriateness of state control over the industry are under challenge.

The first step to accomplish this task is to identify the main patterns of the transition strategy adopted in each nation (Table 12.1). These patterns permeate the choices made about how to promote digital TV and tackle the coordination problems and regulatory issues that emerged throughout the migration process. Transition policies combined traditional concerns in media regulation with the new fiscal and industrial challenges that industrialized nations confronted in the late 1980s and early 1990s. They thus bear a triple imprint: first, the imprint of international forces that raised the stakes associated with the development and implementation of new broadcasting technologies (discussed in Chapter 2); second, the imprint of domestic institutions that mediated these forces and defined the constraints and capabilities for policy response at the national level; and, third, the imprint of the organization and normative models peculiar to the broadcasting sector of each nation. To accomplish our explanatory task we therefore need to operate within three levels of analysis: the international context in which transition

229

Table 12.1. *Comparing the Patterns of Digital TV Policies in the United States and the United Kingdom*

United Kingdom	United States
Aggressive promotion of competition	Reinforcement of local oligopolies
Extensive reforms to existing regime	Minimal reforms to existing regime
Confrontational, rapid implementation	Fragmented implementation, policy gridlock
Defense of public service broadcasting	Defense of commercial incumbents

policies originated, the domestic configuration of interests and institutions, and the legacy of analog broadcasting regimes.

By analyzing these patterns, we are also in a position to evaluate results. Because of the long-evolving nature of the transition, this exercise is necessarily preliminary. Nevertheless, the events of the past two decades offer ample material with which to attempt a comparative assessment of digital TV policies in the United States and Britain. In conducting this evaluation, one should notice the shortage of objective criteria against which these policies can be judged. As the previous chapters revealed, the transition involved difficult policy choices between somewhat incompatible goals, many of which are not easily measured. Do the spectrum efficiency gains that would result from an early switchover to digital outweigh the social costs of temporary losses in analog TV services? Do the coordination benefits from government-mandated standards outweigh the likely stifling of innovation? The answers to these and other questions largely depend on how one defines the public interest in broadcasting. Although scholars may argue endlessly about it, the reality is that this definition is a political one and has varied continually since the birth of the industry following changes in the technology and the political-economic context for television. Not surprisingly, the struggle between different interpretations of the public interest in broadcasting and the role of government in managing changes in the information and communications technology sector has been at the heart of digital TV debates. In evaluating policies, I do not seek to put these debates to rest. Rather, the goal is to map out the implications of the regulatory choices made in each case for the different stakeholders and the overall architecture of the industry. Such exercise, I suggest, indicates best-practice instruments and principles for governing this rapidly changing sector.

THE BRITISH WAY: COMPETITION AND CHANGE

The key pattern of the British digital TV strategy has been the aggressive promotion of market competition in broadcasting and related services. The transition was perceived as a unique window of opportunity to introduce procompetitive reforms, particularly in pay-TV and the acquisition of programming rights. Policies were often designed to tilt the market in favor of new entrants, but the government did not control entry or exit (though in a sense the industry regulator did). Implementation rested on two pillars: primary legislation and administrative law. The government delegated strategically to independent agencies, fragmenting jurisdiction to prevent the emergence of a single regulator capable of administering the pace and the direction of the transition, thus retaining control. Where delegation occurred, it was carefully designed to minimize deviations from its preferred strategy.

In perspective, British digital TV policies must be analyzed within the larger context of the reforms initiated by Thatcher and continued during the Major administration. As discussed in Chapter 8, these reforms significantly reshaped the British terrestrial TV sector by separating operation from regulation, introducing competitive bidding in the allocation of commercial licenses, and unleashing competition for advertising revenues between operators. The pay-TV sector, by contrast, evolved in the opposite direction. Following the failure of Thatcher's cable TV policies and the merger of the two existing satellite operators (BSB and Sky), BSkyB took control of the pay-TV market and leveraged this position to become the major supplier of programming for its own competitor (the cable companies). The lack of competition in this fast-growing sector frustrated the Major cabinet, particularly after Murdoch, despite his well-known Conservative inclinations, turned his press against the administration. The BBC and the ITV companies effectively seized on the conflict between Murdoch and the administration to lobby in favor of rules that limited BSkyB's expansion. They persuaded the Major cabinet and key legislators that, in the absence of regulatory checks, Murdoch would eventually extend his domination of analog pay-TV to other media, including digital TV, thus threatening the balance between public and commercial operators that characterizes British television. Rather than defending the national pay-TV champion, the Major administration in fact set out to confront it by creating a competing pay-TV platform and rigging the market in favor of rival programmers.

The separation between multiplex operators and programmers in the licensing of DTT services represented a major restructuring of the existing arrangements in the sector. This dual licensing scheme effectively cut the cord of direct control of the airwaves by terrestrial broadcasters. As noted, the ITV companies and other incumbents forcefully resisted the plan and instead proposed a scheme similar to that in the United States whereby each analog licensee received a second frequency channel to launch digital services. The Major government explicitly rejected their proposal, noting that this would increase the transmission capacity allocated to incumbents to the detriment of potential new entrants (DNH, 1995a). In other words, why use the transition to reinforce the position of existing operators when digital TV could nurture competition in broadcasting services? It is worth recalling that the initial scheme proposed by the Major administration reserved only about 30 percent of the total DTT capacity for the incumbents (the so-called guaranteed capacity). The government later agreed to increase this to about 50 percent of the total DTT capacity in order to secure cooperation from the incumbents. Still, the dual licensing scheme represented a bold experiment in reorganizing terrestrial TV. Direct access to viewers could no longer be taken for granted in DTT, as broadcasters would no longer "own" their frequency channels.

The favorable terms under which the DTT multiplex licenses were awarded revealed the government's commitment to the success of the new platform. The government insisted that no upfront payments be made in the initial licensing period because of concerns about the ability of potential DTT operators to challenge BSkyB. Head-on competition with the satellite operator would certainly involve heavy subsidies for reception equipment as well as bidding wars for the most attractive programming. Taxing operators during the initial period could jeopardize their financial position. As noted, this represented a major policy reversal for the Conservative Party. Just a few years before, Thatcher had overcome considerable resistance within the party's own ranks to introduce competitive bidding in the allocation of ITV licenses. As the value of spectrum soared, the opportunity costs of these foregone payments escalated. The Major cabinet was nonetheless persuaded that this was necessary to ensure the success of DTT. The Blair administration was initially more cautious about favoring DTT. Yet, it agreed to reduce significantly the license payments made by the ITV companies as the transition progressed, notably favoring Carlton and Granada (the main ITV Digital shareholders). Although such favorable treatment did not prevent the ultimate collapse of ITV Digital, several regulatory cards were stacked in favor of DTT.

The licensing of DTT operators posed an interesting dilemma for British policymakers. Initially, the Major cabinet hoped that several operators would be licensed to compete against BSkyB and the cable companies. The initial proposals in fact included a cap of two licenses per operator to ensure diverse control of the new platform. Nevertheless, when potential investors resisted the idea of several small operators fighting against the satellite giant, the government agreed to relax the cap. A single DTT operator would certainly be in a stronger position to challenge BSkyB. The model was the liberalization of the basic telecommunications services market, where an initial period of duopoly was considered necessary to nurture competition against BT (Thatcher, 1999). The government, however, declined to establish the number of new market entrants and left the decisions in the hands of the licensing authority, the ITC. It was clear from the start that ITC officials had a more cautious approach to DTT than the administration. Staffed largely by veterans of the IBA – an agency that had operated (as well as regulated) commercial TV in close cooperation with its own licensees – the ITC favored a transition strategy that did not challenge the existing industry arrangements and relied on the expertise and the resources of incumbent operators.

To prevent agency shirking, the Major administration included in the Broadcasting Act of 1996 a detailed list of criteria upon which the ITC was to select the new DTT operators. Quantitative criteria such as the expected amount of set-top box subsidies and the service coverage targets were particularly important, because the absence of a cash bid component effectively enhanced the discretion of the ITC (and hence possible deviation from the government's preferred outcome) in the selection process. In awarding the three commercial DTT licenses in a single package to the BDB consortium, the ITC somewhat mitigated the procompetitive character of the British plan. Did the Major cabinet have in mind a different outcome, perhaps with licenses split between different operators and less control in the hands of existing players? Possibly, although in retrospect the idea of several small DTT operators competing against BSkyB and the cable companies was probably unrealistic.[1] Did the collapse of ITV Digital reveal fundamental flaws in the British

---

[1] Notwithstanding the numerous technical faux-pas in the configuration of the ITV Digital network, the failure of DTT operators in other European countries such as Spain suggests that DTT is generally ill-suited to compete against satellite and cable in the pay-TV market (see BIPE, 2002).

transition strategy? Hardly so. There is evidence that competition between ITV Digital and BSkyB has been the key driving force behind Britain's worldwide leadership in digital TV adoption. The rapid licensing of DTT forced the satellite giant to accelerate the introduction of digital services and the conversion of analog customers. Heavy spending on decoder subsidies by both operators offered unique opportunities for viewers to experiment with digital TV in very favorable terms. Innovative services (e.g., BiB) were developed to attract customers.

In a sense, competition did its dirty work, reducing costs, promoting innovation, and punishing the less viable firms. While promoting DTT, the government's strategy was not rigged in favor of any specific company. Despite sustained pressure from Carlton and Granada, the Blair government flatly refused to rescue ITV Digital from bankruptcy, even when its collapse represented a major blow to the government's analog switch-off target in 2006–2010. Such disruptions were a natural part of the competitive process that the Labour administration now advocated for the media sector as fervently as its Conservative predecessors.

Scholars have long noted that legislators tend to delegate regulatory tasks when faced with issues of considerable technical complexity (McCubbins, 1985). This was without doubt the case of Directive 95/47. By delegating implementation of the directive to OFTEL rather than the ITC, the Major cabinet had several goals in mind. The first was to fragment authority in order to retain control over the transition. Most important, however, the administration delegated the task to the agency most likely to create rules in consonance with the administration's goals for digital TV. By the mid-1990s OFTEL had established an impressive track record of aggressive market reforms to promote competitive entry into BT's businesses. Its intent to extend this regime to other industry sectors, including digital TV, was a matter of public record (e.g., OFTEL, 1995). Had the government decided in favor of implementation by the ITC, the regime for CAS and related services would have resembled the analog TV regulatory environment – less codified, thus leaving more room for discretionary adjudication on the part of the regulator, and based on command-and-control rather than competition principles. In fact, in the few areas where jurisdiction is shared between OFTEL and the ITC their different regulatory approaches remain apparent. For example, whereas according to OFTEL rules EPG operators are bound only by the nondiscriminatory obligations established in Directive 95/47, the ITC code goes a step further by requiring that EPG operators provide "due prominence" to public service broadcasters.

The lobbying campaign led by the BBC, however, turned the transposition of the directive into a major public debate about whether and how to curb Murdoch's growing control of British media. There was considerable pressure to implement the directive through primary legislation to ensure that the regime effectively limited BSkyB's interests in digital TV. Yet, elected officials perceived clear advantages in delegation. For the Major cabinet, handing over the job to OFTEL entailed low shirking risks given OFTEL's regulatory track record. In other words, the administration could obtain tight rules for the operation of CAS and related access services that restrained BSkyB's behavior while at the same time avoiding the political costs of overtly imposing losses on Murdoch. While sympathetic to the BBC's arguments, and despite pressure from several party backbenchers who favored direct legislation, New Labour leaders also supported delegation. With a comfortable lead in the polls for the upcoming 1997 general elections, party officials were reluctant to jeopardize the Labour's new business-friendly image and its hard-won rapprochement with the Murdoch-controlled press. Ultimately, implementation by OFTEL was as much the result of a deliberate policy choice by the administration as of this blame-shifting strategy.

A second important pattern of the British strategy has been the extensive regime reforms adopted. The introduction of digital TV has been accompanied in the United Kingdom by changes to the legal arrangements for the broadcasting sector to a degree unparalleled in other nations. Whereas in the United States the transition was molded to the existing industry structure, in the United Kingdom it was designed to challenge it. The reform involved manifold changes in the underlying regulatory principles as well as the instruments used to secure desired firm behavior. Instead of licensing DTT operators within the established configuration of analog TV, the government introduced a new framework that differed significantly in terms of licensing structure (notably in the separation of multiplex operators and programmers) and selection criteria. British authorities have also taken broadcast regulation several steps closer to telecom regulation. The goal has been to create a unified regime consisting of platform-neutral rules aimed at addressing problems of access to network facilities and other key resources in a consistent manner. These changes bear the imprint of European policies aimed at advancing reforms that reflect the shifting boundaries between telecom and broadcasting as well as the changing location of bottlenecks in the communications sector (EC, 1997). The extension of rules for the regulation of CAS to other types of access services with the creation of the

access control class license represented an important step in this direction. For the first time, broadcast and telecom network operators would
compete under the same legal parameters.

The remapping of jurisdiction between ITC and OFTEL represented
another key reform that accompanied the British transition. It resulted
in a novel division of labor between the agencies based on the separation between content and transmission services rather than on the
peculiarities of the underlying networks. With this reshuffling, a more
juridical approach was extended to the broadcasting sector, involving
detailed licenses and policy guidelines that left little room for flexible interpretation, thus undermining regulatory discretion. The guidelines for
the pricing of digital TV access services and the recovery of set-top box
subsidies exemplify this juridical approach championed by OFTEL. The
creation of OFCOM (Office of Communications), the mega regulator
proposed by the Blair administration, has been hailed as the final step in
this process of institutional redesign (DTI, 2000). OFCOM would exercise the functions previously dispersed across several regulators, among
them OFTEL, the ITC, the Radio Authority, and the Radiocommuni-
cations Agency. In reality, administrative rearrangement has been less
important than the actual adaptation of the applicable regimes in consonance with industry convergence. In the United States, where the FCC
already brings under one roof the regulatory functions proposed for
OFCOM, major legal obstacles exist to the marriage of broadcast and
telecom regulation (notably, the prohibition to regulate cable services
under common carriage legislation). Even within an alphabet soup of
regulators, the United Kingdom has already gone much further in this
direction.

A third pattern of the British strategy has been the confrontational
manner in which the government has pursued its digital TV agenda. Nurturing competition and enacting reforms often involved challenging established interests, particularly as reforms imposed losses on incumbents
or undermined existing arrangements. In contrast to the U.S. experience,
British authorities were generally able to overcome industry resistance
and push forward such reforms. Where the government compromised,
it did so only at the margins. The examples abound. The dual licensing
scheme for the introduction of DTT was fervently resisted by all incumbent broadcasters as well as the ITC. It was attacked as an unnecessary
change to the established industry practices that threatened the success of
digital TV. Potential market entrants, which were poised to benefit from
the new licensing scheme, lacked the organization to counterbalance

this opposition. The Major administration nonetheless pushed the plan through Parliament without major changes. The increase in the guaranteed capacity awarded to existing operators reflected the administration's concern about engaging incumbents in the transition process rather than its vulnerability to industry pressure. In practice, incumbents lacked the political means to block the plan. Likewise, BSkyB lobbied heavily against the government's implementation of Directive 95/47 and the reshuffling of regulatory authority in favor of OFTEL. True, in this case the satellite operator faced a strong coalition of forces led by the BBC that supported the government's plan. However, the fact that the outcome ultimately favored the BBC-led coalition cannot be interpreted as a sign of capitulation to pressure by the public broadcaster. As a matter of fact, the BBC lost several other battles, notably the rejection of the DLF proposed by the Davies Committee. If policymakers were often receptive to the BBC's pleas, this was more a reflection of shared convictions about the need to sustain a mixed broadcasting system than of government weakness.

The adversarial approach to strategy implementation did not preclude the government from offering interested parties opportunities for participation in the policymaking process. The numerous consultation papers issued by the DTI and the DCMS functioned as advanced notices aimed at building consensus and collecting input from a variety of stakeholders. In some sense, these consultations represented proxies for the formalized procedure of interest intermediation that exists in other nations like the United States. The key difference, however, is that these consultations were not part of a legalized procedure of debate and appeal. Ultimately, the government held control over the pace and the agenda of the decision-making process. This partly explains the remarkable speed with which the United Kingdom has introduced DTT. The Major administration was persuaded that DTT needed to be introduced before the launch of BSkyB's digital satellite service. In August 1995 the administration released its DTT proposals. In less than two years, the Parliament had passed the proposals with only minor alterations, and the ITC had awarded the new licenses. Without the concerns raised by European competition authorities about the participation of BSkyB in the winning consortium, the process might have been finalized before the May 1997 general elections as originally planned. Given the scale of the reforms introduced and the range of interests involved, such speed represented an extraordinary policy achievement.

A final pattern worth noting is the privileged role occupied by the BBC in the British transition plan. From the outset, policymakers sought to ensure that the new legislative framework did not impair the corporation. The BBC was the only incumbent to be awarded the operation of an entire DTT multiplex, and the one with the largest geographical coverage. Its efforts to seek tight regulatory controls on BSkyB's practices paid off with the transposition of Directive 95/47 into detailed access rights for independent programmers. The 1996 act guaranteed carriage for public service broadcasters on digital cable systems. After the "financial diet" imposed during the Thatcher administration, the BBC enjoyed a significant expansion of its revenue base through a combination of several years of above-inflation licensee fee increases and the enlargement of its commercial activities, raising the ire of BSkyB and other private competitors. The corporation was also allowed to keep the proceeds from the sale of its transmission network in early 1997, with funds specifically allocated for the development of new digital channels. The Major and the Blair administrations agreed that this expansion was necessary to help the BBC meet the costs associated with the transition and offer attractive programming that would promote take-up. Some have even suggested that the government's entire transition strategy represented a veiled effort to defend the BBC in the context of an increasingly competitive marketplace in which the public service broadcaster would otherwise collapse (e.g., Elstein, 2002). The argument ignores the fact that the government has also utilized the BBC to pursue its own goals. Cooperation with the public broadcaster proved critical to ensure the availability of high-value programming in the launching phase of the transition. Moreover, when ITV Digital collapsed, the BBC quickly stepped up to the plate and offered to rescue the ailing service. If on the one side the BBC received preferential regulatory treatment, on the other the government subtly exercised its control over the corporation's funding and services to solve coordination problems and advance its transition plan. As we shall see in the next section, this is precisely the kind of government-industry partnership that has been notably absent in the American case.

THE AMERICAN WAY: INSTITUTIONALIZED INERTIA

What first transpires from the examination of the American transition is the extraordinary inertia of the existing industry arrangements. In contrast to the British case, the key policy pattern has been one of reinforcement rather than discontinuity. A seamless, smooth migration built on the existing regulatory edifice and led by market incumbents has been the leitmotiv of American digital TV policies. Interestingly, numerous

other studies have identified a similar pattern over a range of policy issues, from telecom tariff rebalancing (Cherry and Bauer, 2002) to health
care reform (Wilsford, 1994). Faced with complex regulatory problems
and a broad spectrum of conflicting interests, American policymakers
have generally favored piecemeal over substantial reform. The strategy
for the introduction of DTT represented an attempt to reinvent spectrum
scarcity when the new technology in fact challenged it, and thus extend
the current quid pro quo between legislators and local broadcasters into
the digital TV era (Hazlett and Spitzer, 2000). This pattern is intrinsically tied to the origins of the American transition as a rent-seeking
maneuver by local broadcasters to thwart the reallocation of broadcast
spectrum to land mobile operators. As discussed in Chapter 4, industry representatives persuaded regulators that such reallocation would
obstruct the upgrade of existing services to HDTV. Awarding each analog licensee a second frequency channel made perfect sense within the
framework of HDTV as a technical improvement to local terrestrial TV.
What is remarkable is how this plan survived after it became clear that
the transition could in fact do much more – among other things, alleviate
the spectrum bottlenecks that had long characterized the industry and
democratize access to the airwaves.

Established bureaucratic routines and normative paradigms favored a
transition based on the mold of the FCC Sixth Report of 1952, which, as
discussed, codified analog broadcasting as a system of local oligopolies.
As Horwitz (1989) and others have argued, from the license freeze of the
1940s to the sabotage of UHF in the 1950s, of cable TV in the 1970s,
and of low-power broadcasting during the 1980s and 1990s, the defense
of local terrestrial oligopolies has been a staple of American broadcasting policies since the beginning. However, regime inertia did not just
naturally happen. For the most part, it required the active engagement
of Congress and the FCC to mobilize, respectively, political resources
and technical expertise to defend the existing industry arrangements.
The commission, particularly during the Sikes years (1989–1993), was
instrumental in this regard. The controversial second-channel plan, formulated jointly by ACATS and the FCC in the early 1990s, became the
blueprint for the American transition. Sikes actively defended the plan
as the only viable way to introduce DTT despite evidence that local
broadcasters were less interested in upgrading facilities to digital than
in protecting their incumbent rents. Regime inertia also permeated the
implementation of the plan. The DTT network was engineered to resemble as closely as possible analog TV. When the FCC allocated a second

frequency channel to the 1,600-plus local incumbents, replication of analog coverage was used as the guiding principle, effectively protecting the technical advantage of the larger VHF stations over their UHF rivals. Likewise, when a broad coalition of reformists attempted to impose enhanced programming obligations for digital broadcasters, including free airtime for political candidates, the commission dragged its feet and eventually acknowledged that the constitutional basis for such obligations was tenuous at best. As a result, the public interest standard in digital broadcasting has remained as vague, and thus unenforceable, as in the analog era (Sunstein, 2000).

Congress has also partaken to preserve the established industry arrangements. Given the significance of the transition exercise, the dearth of primary legislation addressing digital TV is remarkable. Nevertheless, this should not obscure the critical role played by Congress at several key junctures in the transition process. We observed in Chapter 5 that after incumbents reneged on their promise to pursue HDTV, the transition plan became the target of severe criticism. Without HDTV simulcasting, loaning a second channel to every local incumbent was perceived not only as bad public policy but also as being in possible contradiction with the broadcast licensing procedures established by the Supreme Court in *Ashbacker*. As the plan came under increased attack, Congress stepped in to salvage it. The Telecom Act of 1996 codified the second-channel plan by directing the commission to restrict initial eligibility for DTT licenses to existing broadcasters. Hazlett and Spitzer (2000) correctly note that the act did not directly award the DTT licenses to local incumbents.[2] Therefore, in theory, the commission could have withheld the licenses. The authors have interpreted this as an attempt by Congress to shift the blame of a major spectrum windfall to incumbents and, at the same time, avoid the costs in case the transition failed. Ironically, this was done within a bill supposedly intended to prevent rent seeking by relaxing government control of the communications industry and thus reducing policymakers' ability to arbitrate resources between market agents. Delegating the ultimate decision to the FCC served to conceal the spectrum windfall from the public's eye.

This interpretation of the facts has several problems. To begin with, delegation theory would in fact predict the opposite: because benefits are concentrated (local broadcasters) but costs (from poor spectrum utilization) are largely diffused, legislators would prefer not to delegate

---

[2] 47 U.S.C. § 336(a).

in order to claim credit with the incumbents. Second, it was a matter of public record that the commission was far along in the process of awarding the DTT licenses to local broadcasters. As a matter of fact, this is why Congress was called in to endorse a plan that many regarded as unconstitutional. If Congress wanted to avoid the political costs of such governmental largesse, it could have simply waited for the FCC proceeding to follow its course, acting only in case the outcome differed from the congressional majority's preference (e.g., if the FCC changed course – which was not likely – or because judicial challenges bogged down the plan). In any case, if the goal was to conceal the spectrum giveaway, Congress could have acted ex post rather than ex ante. True, by overtly blessing the plan legislators could claim some credit with local broadcasters, but given that the FCC ultimately responds to Congress, the benefits of making the bargain explicit are unclear. The reality is that the second-channel plan, without the blessing of Congress, would not have withstood judicial review. Notwithstanding its final language, the act was unanimously interpreted by the press as well as industry observers as a major congressional dispensation to local broadcasters (e.g., Krattenmaker, 1996; Safire, 1996). In practice, few noticed that the commission could have, according to the letter of the 1996 act, backed away from the plan.

In most other instances, congressional control over FCC implementation of digital TV did not require direct legislation. Legislators have a variety of instruments at their disposal to secure agency compliance (Weingast and Moran, 1983; McCubbins and Schwartz, 1984). Reed Hundt's tenure as FCC chairman was particularly challenging in this respect. Hundt rather openly opposed the transition plan inherited from the Sikes Commission that the congressional majority supported. He actively enlisted the help of the press establishment and the computer industry against the plan. At the very least, he was committed to bargaining with local incumbents anew to extract measurable public interest obligations in return for the digital licenses and to accelerate the return of the analog channels, a plan that the Clinton administration fully endorsed. At first glance, the dearth of primary legislation could have allowed the FCC chairman considerable discretion to deviate from the existing plan and pursue the agenda favored by the White House. The problem for Congress was the prominence of the issue. In general terms, the more important a policy area is to legislators, the less discretion the implementing agency will have (Calvert, McCubbins, and Weingast, 1989). Because legislators had considerable interests in protecting their compact with local broadcasters, significant resources were spent on close oversight of the FCC digital TV proceedings.

Congress managed to minimize FCC noncompliance through a variety of mechanisms. Broadcast trade organizations played a key role in alerting legislators to proposed rules that jeopardized the established regime, thus mitigating informational asymmetries between the commission and congressional staff – the so-called fire-alarm oversight. Blocking the various DTT license auction proposals was a major accomplishment for the broadcast lobby. After all, many forces converged during the 1995–1997 period in favor of broadcast spectrum auctions: a cross-party crusade to combat public deficit, the billions of dollars raised by the PCS license auctions held in early 1995, an ever growing demand for spectrum, and the support of key congressional leaders as well as FCC staff. It is interesting to note that the extraordinary lobbying campaign orchestrated by the NAB was aimed not only at swaying legislators against the auction proposals but also at warning them about FCC maneuvering in favor of auctions.

The dozens of hearings held over the years by different Senate and House committees on a wide range of transition-related topics – from HDTV standards in the late 1980s to broadcast spectrum allocation in the mid-1990s to content protection technology in the early 2000s – is another indicator of the interest with which legislators followed the process. When Hundt dragged its feet on the award of DTT licenses, congressional leaders wrote to urge the commission to proceed "as expeditiously as possible" with the assignment of licenses following the 1996 act. When Kennard refused to address the outstanding standards issues, the Senate Budget Committee, concerned about delays in the recovery of analog TV frequencies, called the chairman to testify. Given such close congressional patrolling, the looming threat of legislation, and the fire alarms set off by broadcast trade organizations, there was generally little room for FCC bureaucrats to deviate from the plan favored by the legislative majority. In this sense, delegation has worked: without explicitly codifying the transition strategy into law (as the British Parliament did), Congress managed to protect a convenient arrangement with local broadcasters from a wave of market reforms and technological innovations that directly challenged the justification for such arrangement.

A second important pattern of the American transition has been the lack of mechanisms for effective coordination of policy action. Enduring resolutions to regulatory battles have been notably absent, thus discouraging long-term investments. Agreements about technical standards between market agents have been equally elusive. Policy coordination faced several obstacles. In some cases, complex issues involving multiple stakeholders were resolved in one policy arena only to resurface later in another. Shortly after the FCC endorsed the ATSC standard in December 1996, a group of broadcasters reopened the debate by petitioning the commission to revise the modulation technology selected. When the commission rejected the petition, these broadcasters took their case to Congress. While few believed that Congress would unilaterally revise the ATSC standard, the fact that the House Telecommunications Subcommittee agreed to hold hearings to examine the issue cast a shadow of doubt over the ATSC system. In other cases, previously neglected stakeholders managed to enter the game at the eleventh-hour, which required the search for a new equilibrium that satisfied all parties. The belated entry of the computer industry in the ACATS derailed for months the adoption of the ATSC system. As the transition progressed, powerful parties such as cable operators and copyright holders joined the conversation and demanded that their interests be accommodated. The entry of each new player fractured the existing compromises and required a new distribution of payoffs.

Why has the U.S. transition, unlike the British, been plagued by prolonged standards battles? In order to address this question, we briefly need to examine alternative standards regimes. Generally speaking, the governance of standards can take three forms (Bar, Borrus, and Steinberg, 1995). Governments can let markets set standards, as has typically been the case in the computer industry. Alternatively, policymakers can mandate standards, which has the benefit of creating immediate coordination among market agents; however, the perils of such an approach, particularly when applied to high-tech markets, are widely documented both theoretically (e.g., David, 1986; Arthur, 1989) and empirically (recall the debacle of the MAC initiative in Europe discussed in Chapter 7). Finally, governments can sponsor and ratify standards developed by private industry consortia, an approach whose importance has grown in parallel to the liberalization of telecommunications and broadcasting markets in the United States and Western Europe. Among its numerous benefits are timelier standards development following market needs, focus of tasks, compliance from participating firms, and flexibility for incorporating competing technologies (David and Shurmer, 1996). Private industry consortia are, however, prone to a number of potential failures. Because standards are critical for firms' commercial strategies, agreement among parties may often fail to materialize, particularly if the range of interests is broad and the threat of government intervention low (Farrell and Shapiro, 1992; Hawkins, 1999).

Since the early 1990s, policymakers have generally relied on either industry consortia or private agreements to produce standards for digital TV. Overall, this approach has worked better in Europe than in the United States. Notwithstanding occasional failures (notably the case of CAS), the work of European consortia such as the DVB and nation-specific groups such as the UK Digital TV Group has minimized uncertainties and allowed for significant coordination of investments and R&D. This created favorable conditions for the introduction and adoption of services, as the case of Britain revealed. The near abandonment of HDTV in Europe certainly created a less complex situation than in the United States because replacement of analog TV sets became less critical, thus favoring the rapid deployment of relatively inexpensive set-top box converters (which, as noted, consumers received at heavily subsidized prices). It also relegated equipment manufacturers to a secondary role, and with fewer parties on the table standards agreements became easier. In the United States, by contrast, the governance of standards through private agreements has been much less effective. A key problem has been the reluctance of regulators to intervene in protracted disputes, thereby reducing the threat of mandated standards. Throughout the transition, the FCC was unwilling to endorse standards without support from all major industry stakeholders. In the absence of credible regulatory threats, these stakeholders often delayed agreements or walked out of previous bargains knowing that retaliation was unlikely to go beyond regulatory jawboning on the part of the commission and a few congressmen. The cable compatibility issue, for example, became the subject of iterative bargaining between cable operators and equipment manufacturers. Despite several years of fruitless negotiations and growing pressure from Congress to expedite the transition, the FCC failed to intervene beyond a very narrow ruling on the labeling for cable-ready sets. As this and other critical pieces of the digital TV puzzle remained unresolved, the transition stalled.

Enlisting the cooperation and securing regulatory compliance from the industry also proved challenging for U.S. regulators. At first glance, the American strategy has been more government-driven than in the United Kingdom and other nations, essentially because the FCC established a detailed timetable for the construction of facilities, the introduction of services, and the shutdown of analog TV. Nonetheless, the relative weakness of the sanction instruments available to the commission, the lack of corporatist links between government and industry, the fragmentation of industry representation into several trade associations, and the existence of multiple policy arenas often led market actors to privilege confrontation over cooperation. Because the strategy relied heavily on cooperation from incumbent broadcasters, equipment manufacturers, and content originators, and the FCC lacked both the formal and informal mechanisms to secure desired behavior from these market agents, the U.S. transition began faltering. The aggressive timetable negotiated between government and the NAB in return for flexibility in the use of the second channel was never taken seriously by local incumbents. When in May 2002 more than 800 local broadcasters missed the statutory deadline for the start of DTT services, the FCC failed to impose any sanctions and reluctantly but surely granted an extension to most stations.[3] Clearly, notwithstanding its statutory instruments to enforce compliance by licensees, the commission lacked the political muscle to initiate a massive forfeiture of licenses.

Moreover, the FCC was often thwarted by regulatory battles being waged on other fronts. Because multiple mechanisms of appeal existed, stakeholders were unwilling to accept regulatory losses. Judicial litigation – or the threat of it – was often used to block commission proceedings and exact payoffs. To bargain for better terms on the issue of cable compatibility, cable operators took the commission to court on the implementation of provisions in the 1996 act that required the creation of retail market for cable decoders. The NAB effectively used its close association with several congressmen to raise the threat of congressional action. Congressional hearings and draft bills often paralyzed commission action. The result has been repeated regulatory stalemate. A former FCC general counsel explains how the system works:

> An industry displeased by an FCC action or proposal runs to the powerful congressional committee chairmen, who then "yank the commission's chain" and force either delay, revision, or a freeze. It can be argued that some such interventions serve a worthy public interest purpose and are part of a de facto system of checks and balances upon which the US system is based. But all too often they give powerful industries an unwarranted club to blunt or delay

---

[3] See Remedial Steps for Failure to Comply with Digital Television Construction Schedule, MM Docket No. 02-113, Order and Notice of Proposed Rulemaking, FCC 02-150 (2002).

needed responses to emerging technologies or competition. (Geller, 1995: 119)

Because no government department or regulator controlled the necessary instruments to carry out the transition in a coherent manner, implementation occurred in fits and starts. In some cases, personnel changes at the FCC or executive agencies proved critical to accelerate or decelerate progress. When Hundt arrived at the commission in November 1993, he deliberately pulled the brakes on the ongoing proceedings in an attempt to force changes in consonance with the technology agenda of the new administration. Likewise, changes in the composition of key congressional committees also influenced the political visibility of digital TV, translating into more or less pressure on the commission to act. The important point is that no single department or agency was able to manage policy implementation in a coherent fashion. Oftentimes, interest groups struck unexpected wins that required considerable policy adjustments. The switch-off safeguards that local broadcasters managed to work into the Balanced Budget Act of 1997 undermined the aggressive timetable for the introduction of services and the return of analog frequencies imposed by the commission. Similarly, because the ultimate resolution of the digital must-carry issue is likely to demand a Supreme Court revision of *Turner II*, broadcasters and cable operators have been unwilling to negotiate extensive digital carriage deals, thus limiting content availability.

The lack of a centralized policy apparatus has sometimes been characterized as a positive feature rather than a weakness of the American institutional design (e.g., D. Vogel, 1987; McKnight and Neuman, 1995). Lacking the capabilities for implementing industrial policies in comparison with their counterparts in Japan or France, American policymakers have opted for a more-ad hoc, flexible approach that ultimately has promoted innovation and fomented competition. For example, by not mandating an HDTV standard in the late 1980s, American regulators promoted research into new ways of compressing HDTV signals that led to the development of the first digital TV system. By contrast, the ambitious HDTV initiatives endorsed by the Japanese and European governments both resulted in major losses for the governments as well as the national champions involved. Our analysis has nonetheless unearthed the other facet of a decentralized policy apparatus: poor policy coordination has considerably slowed the U.S. transition by fueling uncertainties and aggravating the market coordination problems inherent to a complex technological migration. Having developed the world's first digital TV system is a rather Pyrrhic victory for a nation without substantial interests in TV set manufacturing and that has been largely unable to capitalize on such technological leadership.[4]

Regime inertia has ultimately resulted in a perverse structure of incentives whereby those supposed to lead the transition (incumbent local broadcasters) have the most to lose from adopting a technology that challenges the established political-economic arrangements in the sector. In addition, the FCC was, from the start, ill-equipped to manage this complex undertaking. "This is not the sort of transition that lends itself to central and industrial planning. There are too many industries involved. There are too many market variables involved," acknowledged William Kennard (West, 1998). And, yet, this is precisely what he was expected to do as FCC chairman. Such is the crux of the U.S. digital TV dilemma: for more than a decade, the commission has been asked to direct a major overhaul of the broadcasting industry without the policy instruments (and, in many cases, the inclination) for doing so.

---

[4] Interestingly, this has also been the case in the VCR market. While the technology was developed and originally patented by an American firm (Ampex), VCRs were ultimately popularized and marketed by Japanese manufacturers (see D'Andrea Tyson, 1992).

THIRTEEN

Explaining National Variations in Digital TV Policies

Let us retrace the steps taken so far. Part I addressed the paradox of government activism in digital TV and identified the factors that encouraged the formulation of national transition strategies (our first research question). Parts II and III discussed the evolution of digital TV in the United States and Britain, and the first chapter of Part IV identified the main differences between the transition policies adopted in each nation (our second research question). We now turn to our third research question: why have these nations made considerably different choices in the regulation and promotion of digital TV? This task invites us to reflect more abstractly about the determinants of policy action in the communication sector. Contrasting policy outcomes across nationals is a long-standing concern of comparative politics (Eckstein and Apter, 1963; Lijphart, 1971).[1] At the most basic level, it requires a theoretical framework that links policy outcomes to politics (Gourevitch, 1986). In other words, we need to lay out a framework that offers a conception of the state, which is ultimately where public policies are formed and implemented, a conception of the actors and organizations involved in the policy arena, and a theory that links these actors, the state, and policy outputs – that is, a theory of how the preferences and orientations of the different stakeholders are transformed into actual rules and initiatives.

Interest-group approaches stress the most visible aspect of regulatory politics – the battle between social actors advocating different policies. Because policy outcomes typically affect the distribution of resources among market agents, it is logical that these agents attempt to influence outcomes in a variety of ways. As Olson (1971) and others have shown, the higher and more concentrated the stakes, the more a group will seek

---

[1] For a more recent overview, see Katznelson (1997).

EXPLAINING NATIONAL VARIATIONS

to organize and participate in the policy process to promote its cause. In the United States, trade associations such as the NAB, MSTV, NCTA, and the CEA have invested significant resources lobbying congressmen, FCC commissioners, and in some cases even the general public in attempts to influence digital TV policies in favor of their constituencies. The same can be said of the BBC, BT, BSkyB, the ITVA, and several other stakeholders that have worked the corridors of Westminster, 10 Downing Street, and British regulatory agencies in pursuit of favorable policies. According to this approach, domestic policies are explained by the organization and the resources available to these interest groups and social coalitions. As the configuration and the distribution of resources among these groups vary from nation to nation, so do the relevant policy outcomes.

By looking at the interplay between competing stakeholders, we have gained important insights about the direction of digital TV policies in the United States and Britain. Nevertheless, this approach lacks an elaborate conception of the state – or, rather, interest-group theories tend to reduce the state to a neutral arena in which stakeholders struggle for legislation that advances their relative position over others (March and Olsen, 1984; Hall, 1997). Consequently, elected officials and bureaucrats are reduced to either arbiters or advocates for the competing interests, and policy outcomes are conceived as a function of the distribution of political resources (i.e., power) among stakeholders. To illustrate this point, let us attempt to apply this approach to the U.S. case. There is ample evidence that American policymakers have been vulnerable to rent-seeking maneuvering by incumbent local broadcasters. Yet the policies adopted did not perfectly reflect the preferences of this powerful group. Although local broadcasters managed to avert DTT license auctions and obtained flexibility in the use of the second frequency channel, the timetable for the introduction of services and the shutdown of analog transmissions was far more aggressive than what the NAB had hoped. This timetable emerged as a compromise between the preferences of the NAB and those of the Clinton administration and the congressional majority in terms of spectrum recovery and budgetary goals. The British case similarly reveals that digital TV policies cannot simply be explained as the product of interest-group pressures. The framework for the launch of DTT services codified in the Broadcasting Act of 1996 largely reflected the Major administration's goal to create competition in the pay-TV market, rather than the interests of particular firms or trade organizations. In fact, we noted that the dual licensing scheme lacked the support of any relevant stakeholder in Britain. In both cases the evidence reveals that

249

NEW TELEVISION, OLD POLITICS

government officials were not simply serving powerful constituencies or arbitrating between competing interests. They have often pushed the envelope in the transition further than most relevant stakeholders would find acceptable.

It is important to underscore that even when policies provided unambiguous benefits to certain groups, this cannot be immediately associated with the ability of these groups to influence government policy. Let us again consider the U.S. case. There is little doubt that incumbent broadcasters have benefited considerably from transition policies molded within the existing analog TV regime. Yet, by pursuing these policies, legislators were also defending their convenient quid pro quo with local broadcasters, which, as discussed in Chapter 5, typically favors incumbent reelection. In rejecting DTT license auctions, the congressional majority was not only favoring incumbent broadcasters but also acting self-interestedly. Similarly, the BBC advocated strongly for the imposition of detailed access obligations on BSkyB and other CAS operators based on EU Directive 95/47. While these obligations were ultimately imposed, this cannot be interpreted as an indication of the BBC's ability to manipulate the government. As discussed, the Major administration had considerable stakes of its own in imposing losses on BSkyB. Besides, implementation was largely delegated to OFTEL officials, who did not particularly favor the BBC. In a nutshell, identifying winners and losers is not enough to make causal assertions about the determinants of policies. Although scholars sometimes equate favorable outcomes with interest-group power, the links through which preferences are translated into policies are often missing.

The analytical problem of interest-group theories stems from the fact that power is not an inherent property of the different political actors, but rather a relational variable – a function of certain institutional arrangements that make policymakers more receptive to certain demands and ideas than others. For example, measured by their level of organization and the resources available for political action, wireless telecommunications operators and the computer industry in the U.S. can hardly be considered less "powerful" than local broadcasters. The fact that American digital TV policies have consistently benefited the broadcasters, sometimes at the expense of these other well-organized and well-financed interest groups (notably with respect to spectrum management), reflects not only the "power" of the NAB and other trade organizations (however that power is measured) but more critically the organization of the American electoral system, which makes congressmen highly receptive to local broadcasters' demands. The configuration of the state thus molds political interactions: it gives a certain shape to interest-group battles by mediating between their demands and policy outputs, and ultimately stacks the deck in favor of certain groups at the expense of others (Zysman, 1994; Cowhey and McCubbins, 1995).

Two points emerge from this discussion. First, elected officials and bureaucrats have preferences that are not reducible to those of interest groups or other policy actors. Members of Congress, cabinet officials, DTI bureaucrats, and FCC commissioners have interpreted the challenges of the transition through their own lenses and embraced distinct policy objectives for digital TV. Of course, their ability to advance an agenda and resist pressure varies considerably. British ministers can typically count on policy capabilities of which American policymakers can only dream. Still, it remains important to consider the motivations of government actors – however constrained they might be – separately from the preferences of other stakeholders. Second, the state does not simply represent a neutral arena in which interest-group conflict takes place. Rather, the organization of the state and the rule-making procedures of its operating agencies induce particular courses of action, thus yielding predictable policy outcomes. Because these arrangements vary only in the long term, we can expect routine patterns of government responses to policy demands (Krasner, 1989; North, 1990).

These are the starting points for the theoretical framework that informs our comparative analysis of digital TV policies in the United States and Britain. The framework is based on the "new institutionalism" literature, a label that refers to a broad range of studies bound together by their emphasis on institutional factors to explain political behavior and economic outcomes within and across nations. This approach underscores how both formal and informal institutional arrangements shape political interactions and influence the outcome of government actions. Government actors make choices within a structure that defines the informational resources available, the policy instruments at hand, and the costs and benefits associated with alternative courses of actions. This structure not only determines the capabilities and constraints of those who make policy but also of those who try to influence policy, for it also defines the opportunities for interest-group pressure (Ikenberry, 1986). The constitutional framework, the electoral system, the bureaucratic procedures, and other formal state arrangements, as well as accepted norms of political behavior and government action, form the structure in which policymaking takes place. Because these institutions vary between the United States and the United Kingdom, so has the structure of incentives within which American and British policymakers have approached digital TV. Institutions alone did not induce the transition. Rather, they mediated between the forces that promoted government activism in digital TV and the actual strategies adopted (recall Figure 1.1). In the next sections we explore the implications of the differences between American and British institutions for digital TV policymaking. We focus on three variables: the organization of the state, the normative models that informed broadcasting policies, and the legacy of the analog TV regime.

THE ORGANIZATION OF THE STATE

In examining the British case, we found a remarkable degree of state autonomy to promote competition and enact significant reforms to the broadcast regime within a very short time frame. This pattern is not exclusive to the case of digital TV. Radical innovations and policy experiments in the regulation of communication industries have been commonplace: Britain was the first European country to introduce commercial television alongside its public broadcaster, the first to license a satellite TV service, and the first to privatize its telecommunications operator and open the market to new operators, to mention just a few examples. In all these cases, the government implemented reforms despite considerable resistance from market incumbents (BT in the telecom case, the BBC in television) as well as from many other political and social actors. The organization of the state explains this pattern of radical reforms and rapid transposition of new policy agendas into legislation. Scholars have long identified the British political system as the quintessential party government model (Cox, 1987). To begin with, there is no independence between the executive and the legislature. The British system concentrates unparalleled powers on the prime minister and the cabinet, whose authority derives from a party majority in Parliament. After the drastic curtailment of the role of the House of Lords in the early twentieth century, legislative power became effectively concentrated in a single parliamentary chamber – the House of Commons. As head of the Parliament, cabinet chief, and majority party leader, the prime minister faces few institutional checks to pass legislation and to direct policymaking tasks. Of the typical mechanisms found in other democracies to restrain government authority (i.e., separation of powers, two equal

legislatures, minority representation in parliament, and a federal structure of government), none is effectively present in the United Kingdom
(Spiller and Vogelsang, 1996).

In addition to this structural concentration of power in the cabinet, the British electoral system tends to produce single-party majorities
and strong party discipline, thereby facilitating policymaking control.
The electoral system is rather simple: in each of 650-plus constituencies
(the exact number varies each election depending on district boundary
redrawing) a first-past-the-post election is held. The candidate who re-
ceives the most votes is elected. The system favors clear-cut majorities
by exaggerating the winning party's lead, thus reducing the need for
coalition governments typical of other European nations (Weaver and
Rockman, 1993). Between 1945 and 1997, no party received more than
50% of the votes, and yet the majority party typically held well over half
of the parliamentary seats (Jeffery, 1998).[2] Furthermore, because of rigid
limits to campaign donations and spending, the lack of a separate executive elected by popular vote, and the relative inability of MPs to serve
particularistic interests, individual politicians face formidable barriers
to cultivating a personal vote within their districts (Cain, Ferejohn, and
Fiorina, 1984). With their political careers largely tied to the electoral fate
of the party and their impression on national party leaders, MPs tend to
vote along party lines. As a result, the bargaining costs involved in policymaking decrease substantially (Cox and McCubbins, 2001). Voting
discipline and control of the legislative process ensure that the majority party's agenda is likely to find its way, rather smoothly, into actual
legislation.

The combination of a parliamentary regime and electoral rules that
skew results in favor of a single legislative majority and discourage free-
lance politicians produces a system in which authority is highly concentrated. As a critic of the system argues, "the British people are invited
every four or five years to choose one of two small committees of mostly
professional politicians to run the government as they see fit, constrained
only by what they think is politically possible, with almost no legal or
institutional checks on what they do."[3] Rapid policy changes and the implementation of controversial reforms thus become possible under a system that provides limited access points for interest-group representation

[2] In 1997, for example, Labour won 43.3 percent of the total vote, but secured
65.2 percent of the seats in Parliament.
[3] *Economist*, October 14, 1995, p. 26.

at the level of primary legislation. We noted how the Major cabinet, despite a slim parliamentary majority, was able to secure swift passage of the controversial Broadcasting Act of 1996, overcoming considerable opposition from industry incumbents and even some internal party dissent (in an exemplary illustration of the dynamics of party politics in the United Kingdom, two Conservative MPs who joined Labour in an attempt to block the bill were forced to resign as ministerial aides). The adversarial manner in which the Major administration implemented its digital TV agenda was facilitated by the lack of veto points in the policymaking process, which sharply reduced the ability of interest groups to block or force changes. Neither BSkyB nor the terrestrial incumbents were able to avert the licensing of new competitors or the introduction of reforms that ended decades of privileged access to spectrum.

Interestingly, one of the few restraints that the architects of the British transition have confronted has been bad press. Because of Murdoch's extensive newspaper holdings, both parties preferred, when possible, to avoid being blamed for regulations that imposed direct losses on BSkyB. This is noteworthy as the nation debates how to reform its cross-ownership rules and the consolidation of regulatory functions under OFCOM. Delegation to independent regulators – notably OFTEL – served this purpose rather well, but the role of European authorities was also critical. By shifting the blame to Brussels, British authorities were able to avoid a more direct confrontation with Murdoch in the licensing of DTT multiplexes (recall that EU competition authorities forced BSkyB out of BDB) and the promotion of competition in digital TV services (i.e., the transposition of Directive 95/47). As the United States currently debates how to reform its own media ownership rules, including a ban on the common ownership of a daily newspaper and a broadcast station in the same market, it should also take note of the constraints to media policymaking that such reforms might entail.

As Cox and McCubbins (2001) and others have pointed out, the trade-off in a system that concentrates policymaking capabilities is commitment – in other words, how can Britain restrain discretion and ensure that today's rules will endure a change of parliamentary majority in the next elections? Spiller and Vogelsang (1996) note that a series of institutional mechanisms exist in the United Kingdom to reduce the threat of policy reversals. Delegation to independent regulators is the most obvious. The plethora of agencies with jurisdiction over different facets of the communications industry reflects the process of historical accretion through which media regulation has developed in Britain. Simply put, new regulators were created to oversee and promote new technologies or to address particular political concerns (Hills and Michalis, 1997). The result has been a complex scheme of overlapping regulators. We noted how the Major administration seized this fragmentation to retain control over digital TV policymaking. Although these agencies are generally not required to provide a basis for decisions, judicial review of regulatory acts is nonetheless uncommon in Britain (Prosser, 1997). Litigation is thus not as central a part of the regulatory process, and the courts do not represent a check against discretion as in the United States. However, the British judiciary has a long tradition of protecting private contracts, and hence rules embedded in long-term licenses are relatively safe from discretionary changes. This explains why the new broadcast regime has been cemented in long-term licenses for DTT multiplexes and CAS providers, as well as extended funding commitments for the BBC. Amending these licenses or the BBC charter is certainly not impossible, but proposed changes must overcome a series of veto points (the ITC or OFTEL, the DTI, and in some cases the Competition Commission) that do no exist in legislative rule making.

The organization of the state in the United States stands in sharp contrast to that of Britain. In a few words, it militates against regime change and policy innovations. The system is devised to curb discretionary government behavior through structural division of power and formalized checks. There is strict separation of authority between the executive, two equally important legislative bodies, and the judiciary. Such fragmentation offers organized interests a myriad of access points into policymaking, and each of them represents a potential veto (Krasner, 1978). Fragmentation of policy authority favors fragmentation of interest representation. Firms often prefer to lobby legislators and regulators directly, or rather to organize around narrow interests rather than in large, industry-wide organizations (Hart, 1992). Because any policy initiative with distributional effects must overcome several veto gates, the system is biased in favor of the status quo and against large-scale reforms (Weaver and Rockman, 1993; Haggard and McCubbins, 2001). As Cowhey and McCubbins explain, "each veto point provides prospective opponents of a policy change an arena in which to make their case. And because of the different modes of election to the various veto offices, the probability of consensus among the veto players is quite low" (1995: 13). Gridlock and poor coordination are thus commonplace in American regulatory politics. This does not rule out the possibility

255

of regime change, but such change is likely to be slow and politically contentious.[4]

Another result of the system is weak party discipline. The American electoral system, based on single-member districts elected in most cases by plurality of votes, creates strong incentives for congressmen to develop a personal vote within their districts (Cain, Ferejohn, and Fiorina, 1984). The fortunes of individual politicians are tied less to the party's national performance than to their ability to raise campaign funds and deliver particularistic benefits to constituencies in return for votes or campaign contributions. The more personal the vote, the more independent participants in the legislative bargaining process, and thus the more difficult it will be to strike compromises and fashion policies targeting collective (as opposed to particularistic) benefits. The system thus tends to produce narrowly targeted policies in favor of well-organized groups capable of controlling any such veto gate (Noll, 1986; Cox and McCubbins, 2001).

Cultivating friendly relations with local broadcasters is crucial for nurturing a personal vote. As former FCC chairman Hundt explains,

> Most members of Congress are afraid of local broadcasters. At first glance, the fear seems groundless. Local television does not run editorials for or against candidates the way local newspapers do. Television networks do not go after a President the way the major newspapers do. No sharp-edged editorial writer sets anchor on the nightly news. The broadcasters do not give huge piles of money to campaigns, like tobacco or health care companies do when they want to stop legislation. But the typical member of Congress is afraid the television station will not put him on the local news. They can make him a non-person. Then he would be no better off than the unknown challenger. (Hundt, 2000: 171)

In all democracies, access to the media represents a key political resource.[5] The United States is nonetheless unique among developed nations for its lax rules on political advertising and the lack of mandatory free airtime for political candidates (Norris, 2000). There are various rules that govern the terms under which candidates can buy TV advertising, notably the "equal time" rule (candidates have the right to buy airtime on the same terms as their opponents), the "reasonable access rule" (candidates

---

[4] For example, Noll and Rosenbluth (1995) have documented the slow but steady process of telecommunications liberalization in the United States.
[5] There are countless studies that support this point. For a recent overview, see Bennett and Entman (2001).

can buy at least some airtime and specify the format and placement of ads), and the "lowest unit charge" rule (limiting the rates charged by broadcasters).[6] However, these rules do not require stations to provide free airtime, and thus candidates are forced to raise and spend considerably on local TV during election periods. Because incumbents are typically better funded than challengers, the practical effect of the system is to favor reelection as well as to make these free-lance politicians highly susceptible to the demands of incumbent broadcasters within their electoral districts (Krasnow and Longley, 1978). In Britain, by contrast, a ban on political advertising on TV and strict rules on editorializing and reporting result in less opportunities for bargains between broadcasters and elected officials, because there is less at stake to begin with.

American digital TV policies reflect the configuration of its political institutions in several ways. The availability of multiple policy arenas and the uncertainty about the outcome of regulatory battles in each of them explain the difficulties in striking durable compromises between policy actors about technical standards, cost bearing, product introduction, and other critical elements of the transition. Moreover, within a system designed to thwart reforms, we should not be surprised that the transition has reinforced the existing industry structure. Local broadcasters effectively responded to threats by mobilizing congressional support and blocking FCC proceedings. It is worth stressing that this pattern does not attest to the superior organization or wealth of broadcast trade organizations vis-à-vis other organized interests (e.g., cable operators, equipment manufacturers, wireless operators). Rather, it reflects a political system that militates against change and makes congressmen dependent on favorable access to local airtime for career advancement.

Fragmentation of authority also militated against what Cox and McCubbins (2001) have called *decisiveness*, namely, the ability to make policy decisions. This was most evident in the inability of the FCC to expedite the transition by arbitrating between competing demands, for example, in the case of technical standards, digital must-carry, and copyright protection. J. Wilson's analogy of American policymaking as a barroom brawl where "anybody can join in, the combatants fight all comers and sometimes change sides, no referee is in charge, and the fight lasts not for a fixed number of rounds but indefinitely" (1989: 299) is an appropriate characterization of the politics of digital TV. Paralyzed by its limited authority, the threat of litigation or congressional overturn

---

[6] 47 U.S.C. § 312, 315.

of its decisions, and the iterative character of the policymaking process, the FCC was unable to establish credible rules for the transition. The contrast with the British case is remarkable: even though the FCC was delegated more power than the ITC or OFTEL to administer the transition, it ultimately lacked the instruments to implement the plan in a coherent fashion. As Moe explains, such contrast between the efficacy of American and British bureaucrats is a function of the different arrangements within which they act:

> The American separation of powers system fragments power and makes new laws exceedingly hard to enact. Anything that is formalized tends to endure – which prompts all actors to rely heavily on formal structure in protecting their interests and solving their commitment problems. The result is a bureaucracy that is vastly overformalized and disabled by its own organization. In a Westminster parliamentary system, this does not happen. Power is concentrated, passing and overturning laws is relatively easy, and formal structure therefore has little strategic value as a protector of interests or solution to commitment problems. This yields a bureaucracy that is not buried in excessive formalism and far better suited to effective performance. (1997: 472)

Overformalization has another important implication for our analysis. The Administrative Procedures Act of 1946 established a complex procedure for rule making and the adjudication of disputes that the FCC and other agencies must follow, including advance notification, public hearings, and written justification of rules adopted, all of which minimize bureaucratic discretion (Noll, 1986). Elaborate procedures with strict evidentiary burdens tend to benefit stakeholders with significant informational and organizational resources. This is particularly important when new technologies are at stake. In their study of three technological innovations in broadcasting (the development of FM radio, the opening of UHF frequencies to television, and the growth of citizens band radio), Krasnow and Longley found that "throughout its history the FCC has lacked sufficient skilled personnel and funds to weigh the merits of new technology and has been forced to rely on outside advice and technical opinion. When faced with complex technical questions, the commission has often taken the easy road of finding in favor of the 'haves' over the 'have-nots'" (1978: 21).

This pattern has held true for digital TV. Since the beginning of the transition, the commission had few alternatives but to rely on the expertise provided by incumbent broadcasters as a basis for decisions. ACATS was largely staffed with broadcast representatives. The commission often used technical tests conducted by broadcast organizations to decide between competing standards, allocate frequency channels, and determine interference protection safeguards. While formal procedures have allowed more participation by consumer advocates and media activist groups representing diffused interests than in Britain, their scarce resources for information gathering and lobbying has limited their effective impact. Even when backed by the Clinton administration, media activists were unable to attach measurable public interest obligations (including free airtime for political candidates) to DTT licenses. The numerous opportunities for seeking judicial review of administrative acts make the commission inherently cautious about changing rules in the absence of conclusive evidence. The problem for reform advocates is that it is generally more difficult to demonstrate the potential benefits of new regulations than to prove the harm caused to the beneficiaries of existing ones. For example, even if authorized by Congress, the commission would have faced a lengthy judicial battle to demonstrate that the benefits of competitive bidding in the allocation of DTT licenses outweigh the direct harm caused to existing licensees. Formalization thus militated against regime change and stacked the deck in favor of local broadcasters, not because this group "captured" its regulator but because decisions require complex procedures and depend on credible information (in a judicial sense), which in many cases can only be supplied the incumbents.

THE IDEOLOGICAL ORIENTATION
OF BROADCASTING POLICIES

In broad perspective, American and British policymakers share a liberal political tradition that favors arm's-length government and discourages industrial policies (Krasner, 1978). This normative orientation is rooted in a culture of individual entrepreneurship and was reinforced by the modest role played by the state in the industrialization of both nations. There is general consensus that neither the United States nor the United Kingdom ever developed the sophisticated apparatus for government management of the economy that exists in France or Japan (D. Vogel, 1987; Weir, 1992). Picking winners and losers in the market is often deemed inappropriate and politically suspicious. Even after the Great Depression, when the role of government grew dramatically, these nations never created institutional mechanisms to assemble broad social coalitions between industry and labor groups (Gourevitch, 1986). In a sense, the regulatory reforms of the last decades have been a return to these basic tenets of minimal government in Anglo-Saxon political culture. This broad normative orientation shaped the way in which policymakers interpreted market signals and weighed policy alternatives throughout the transition. The paradox of government activism in digital TV is even more startling in this context. We noted that the diffusion of the information revolution agenda was critical for legitimizing the adoption of transition policies. However, policymakers in the United States and Britain often resisted pressure to take on a larger role.

Despite their support for the transition, American policymakers refused to commit public funds to expedite the process. In the late 1980s the George Bush administration refused to sponsor a plan to salvage what was left of the American consumer electronics industry based on R&D and promotion of HDTV (it is worth remembering that, at the time, Japan and several European nations were funneling considerable public money toward HDTV). Likewise, the Clinton administration's NII plan involved little public spending or direct industry sponsoring (Kahin, 1997). Congress was willing to lend spectrum to broadcasters but ruled out any direct assistance to cover broadcast station's migration costs (in fact, it only reluctantly allocated about $100 million to help public stations convert to digital). American policymakers also hesitated about dictating technical standards, despite the failure of alternative mechanisms to produce credible agreements on digital TV standards. The claim by former FCC chairman Kennard that "a little bit of chaos is not a bad thing when you're rolling out a new technology, and multiple industries are developing business plans to market it" (West, 1998) expresses well this deep-seated inclination against government micromanaging. What continental European or Japanese policymakers would have interpreted as a problematic lack of coordination among market agents that warranted government action was perceived by Kennard as a perfectly natural stage in a complex process of industrial reorganization.

A similar orientation against micromanaging the transition permeated British policies, though, as discussed, the state did offer some financial assistance, particularly to the BBC. In the early 1990s the Major administration dealt the last blow to the MAC project by vetoing a rescue package, even when the ill-fated European HDTV initiative would have benefited several British electronic manufacturers such as Thorn-EMI

(Hart, 1992). The Blair administration likewise refused to go beyond a mediating role in the contract dispute between ITV Digital and the Football League that catalyzed the bankruptcy of the DTT operator. When pressed about the government's position about the collapse of ITV Digital, DCMS Secretary Tessa Jowell acknowledged that the failure represented "a bump in the transition road" but rapidly added: "ITV Digital was a commercial venture that went wrong. There is no case for government intervention" (Cozens, 2002). In other words, the government promoted the introduction of DTT services but disengaged itself from the outcome of market competition.

The appeal of the information revolution agenda to high-ranking bureaucrats and the debate about convergence was also central to the direction of digital TV policies in the United States and the United Kingdom. In Britain, OFTEL provided key intellectual support for the government's transition strategy. Since its creation in 1984, the telecom regulator cultivated a doctrine of aggressive promotion of competition throughout the communications sector. As S. Vogel (1996) notes, OFTEL deliberately used its powers to favor BT's competitors. With convergence, the same principles applied to broadcasting (OFTEL, 1995). In the eyes of OFTEL officials, BSkyB was the BT of television. It controlled the network and key applications and could leverage this position into new markets. If the transition to digital TV were to succeed, strict rules would be needed to contain the satellite operator and favor its rivals in the markets for the acquisition, packaging, and delivery of video programming. OFTEL's thinking clearly influenced senior DTI officials (see, e.g., DTI, 1996). Government bureaucrats often interpreted regulatory issues in digital TV as identical to those in telecommunications, thus compelling the use of similar instruments and a common oversight authority:

Digital technology is rapidly being adopted for the reproduction, storage, and transmissions of information in all media. This means that any form of content (still or moving pictures, sound, text, data) can be made available via any transmission medium, eroding the traditional distinctions between telecommunications and broadcasting. . . . Our system of regulation faces new challenges as delivery systems adopt a common technology and assume common capabilities. Some new services fall within the remit of more than one regulator, creating a risk of excessive and/or inconsistent regulation. Where an identical service is transmitted over different delivery systems, it may be subject to different regulatory regimes. The development of new services, and their wide availability, must not be jeopardized by such regulatory overlaps and anomalies. (DTI, 1998: 2)

Senior DTI officials became early converts to the information revolution and began preaching the need to overhaul the existing broadcast regime to facilitate digital convergence. Over the years, DTI released several reports praising the strategic value of communications industries to the British economy and the social benefits associated with new information technologies (DTI, 1994; 1998). These documents were instrumental in preparing the terrain for the reforms to the regulatory apparatus that accompanied the transition. The relative stability of top civil servants in Britain helped nourish the new paradigm despite the changes in Parliament. Jumping on the bandwagon of the Bangemann Report, the DTI assumed a leadership role in several new technology initiatives. From the start, DTT was a pet project. The reshuffling of regulatory jurisdiction undertaken by the Major administration also benefited the DTI, because it was charged with drafting and issuing the licenses for CAS and related services. This gave DTI bureaucrats a critical opportunity to pursue their vision of a gradual unification of the telecom and media regimes as the transition progressed.

The U.S. practice of recruiting "inners and outers" provided a fertile ground for the assimilation of the information revolution agenda among key FCC officials.[7] This became particularly noticeable during the Hundt chairmanship. Riding on a wave of support from the White House and the new public prominence of the agency, Hundt welcomed new ways of thinking about digital TV and broadcast regulation in general. Senior officials at the Office of Plans and Policy (OPP) began praising convergence and the need for reforming the outdated legal apparatus of the industry (Pepper and Levy, 1999). In contrast to Britain, however, these bureaucrats could not translate this orientation into actual policies. As discussed, the congressional majority, particularly after Republicans regained control of Congress in 1994, promptly reacted against Hundt's reformist agenda and, with the help of the NAB and other trade organizations, closely monitored the commission's digital TV proceedings. In the end, the orientation favored by senior FCC bureaucrats, much of the academic community, and several White House officials (i.e., the need

---

[7] For a discussion of the system, see Heclo (1988) and Weir (1992).

for major reforms including broadcast spectrum auctions, enforceable public interest obligations for digital broadcasters, and gradual unification of the telecom and media regimes) never materialized because of the lack of a political coalition capable of overcoming the numerous veto points for reform. In fact, the digital TV case contradicts the argument that, because of its fragmented character and the weak allegiance to party ideologies, the American political system is highly permeable to new ideas, which ultimately yields regulatory reforms (e.g., Derthick and Quirk, 1985). If reforms were possible in other sectors because legislators failed to act against reform-oriented bureaucrats (e.g., telecommunications since the early 1970s), in the case of digital TV Congress actively engaged to stop them.

Whereas we find much coincidence between the United States and Britain in their broad regulatory orientations favoring arm's-length government, the differences are apparent in the normative models that have historically guided media policies. A strong tradition of public service permeates British broadcasting. As a result, the BBC can typically count on support from both Labour and Conservative governments, though often for different reasons. For many within Labour, the corporation represents a unique antidote against the commercialization of broadcasting. If television is to preserve its role as a platform for political dialogue and a vehicle for minority-taste programming, a strong public broadcaster is essential. For the Tories, the BBC embodies the soul of British cultural traditions and represents a necessary counterbalance to the low-brow programming that dominates commercial TV. As Mulgan explains:

> Each polity shaped public service broadcasting according to its own traditions. In the UK the tradition was that of Matthew Arnold as redefined by Reith . . . and others, committed to responsibility, impartiality, education and active citizenship. The role of public service was to educate and inform as well as to entertain. It straddled Left and Right in its opposition to the ravages of industrial civilization and its paradoxical faith that technology could serve enlightenment. (1991: 254)

Across the political spectrum, there is broad support for the combination of public service and commercial broadcasting that has characterized British television since 1954. It is true that the BBC has often been the target of criticism and reform initiatives. Yet, even during times of sweeping reforms to the "old Britain" under Prime Minister Thatcher, the corporation managed to escape major changes (as discussed in Chapter 8, Thatcher failed to convince her own party and the public at large of the need to introduce advertising to the BBC). The defense of the Reithian tradition remains an important goal for British policymakers, even when such defense involves active government involvement. As a member of the Blair cabinet explained:

> There is an eternal battle in government to get the balance right between regulation and laissez faire. We know the damage that interference in industry can do, the stifling effect of red tape. The dangers of the nanny state. But we also know that markets don't always act fairly. That they don't always follow the public interest. And that there is more to life than the bottom line. Some principles – including public service broadcasting – should be preserved by regulation if needs be.[8]

This ideological orientation is important in understanding why the BBC typically received favorable treatment in British transition policies. It is worth recalling that the government did not immediately cater to the corporation's demands. BBC officials often had to work hard for such special treatment within a strategy generally intended to favor competition without regard for the nature of the competing firms or the outcome of market battles. The awarding of an entire digital multiplex, the broad access obligations imposed on BSkyB in the transposition of Directive 95/47, an end to the "financial diet" imposed by the Thatcher administration – these gains did not come about easily. They required extensive political maneuvering in Parliament, lengthy submissions to consultations by the DTI, the ITC, and OFTEL, and even a public relations campaign aimed at rallying public support for the BBC's new digital channels. The public broadcasting tradition certainly created a fertile ground for the BBC's demands among legislators and ITC officials, but in other cases (notably OFTEL) its pleas proved a hard sell. The extensive network of personal connections between senior government bureaucrats and BBC officials also facilitated the corporation's lobbying efforts, particularly given the lack of formal channels for interest intermediation. Gavyn Davies, a prominent economist with close ties to the Blair cabinet who chaired the government's review of the BBC license fee in 1999, soon after became the corporation's chairman.

---

[8] Address by Secretary of State for Culture, Media and Sports Tessa Jowell to the Oxford Media Convention, February 15, 2003.

Conversely, Patricia Hodgson, a veteran of the BBC who was instrumental in the reforms implemented by Director General John Birt during the 1990s, became chief executive of the ITC in June 2000. This network of personal ties between cabinet members, senior BBC officials, and industry regulators, all of whom shared a distinct set of attitudes in favor of public broadcasting, proved critical to advance the BBC's case.

In the United States, by contrast, the dominant regulatory orientation has traditionally favored local commercial stations. As discussed in Chapter 3, localism has been, from the beginning, one of the central organizing principles of American television. This principle has endured despite the repeal of rules that codified localism into law during the wave of deregulation in the 1980s and 1990s (Horwitz, 1989).[9] The need to preserve free local TV was often invoked by U.S. policymakers to support the controversial second-channel plan for the introduction of DTT. In the commission's own words, one of the main goals of the transition to digital TV was to "preserve and promote free, universally available, local broadcast television in a digital world."[10] Several observers have argued that localism was simply a rhetorical device used to obscure a plan catering to incumbents and that, given the falling ratings of the terrestrial channels, the consolidation of ownership in the industry following the 1996 act, and the extensive penetration of cable and satellite (more than 85 percent in 2001), the concept has effectively become a fallacy (e.g., Geller, 1998). Such interpretation nonetheless ignores how localism served to interpret the facts and guide policy action throughout the transition. The reality is that no alternative ideological framework emerged to shape digital TV policies in the way localism could.

As Derthick and Quirk (1985) argue, major regulatory reforms require a solid ideological foundation that combines analytical prescription (so that reforms can be defended in the courts) with broad public appeal (so that it can be used by elected officials to rally support for reforms). Policies that are "rational" in terms of the accepted cognitive

[9] Among these were the Prime Time Access Rule (PTAR), which prevented local stations affiliated with the big three networks in the top fifty markets from broadcasting more than three hours of network programming during the four hours of prime time (7–11 P.M.). The rule was repealed in 1995.
[10] Advanced Television Systems and Their Impact on the Existing Television Broadcast Service, MM Docket No. 87-268, Memorandum Opinion and Order on Reconsideration of the Fifth Report and Order, 13 FCC Rcd 6860 (1998).

framework tend to be favored over risky but potentially high-gain policies that demand a new set of evaluation criteria (Krasnow and Longley, 1978). Although many new ideas were promoted by spectrum reformists, taxpayer activists, and media advocates during the 1995–1997 period, none consolidated into a new organizing principle for digital TV. The heterodox coalition that rejected the second-channel licensing plan was internally divided about potential alternatives. Some wanted digital TV to strengthen public and community broadcasters. Others wanted to sell off the airwaves to the highest bidder. All blamed broadcasters for the lack of news reporting that left the transition outside the public agenda (Hickey, 1996). In the end, the naive Jeffersonian view of television as a local service carried the day not only because of its ability to rally political support from the incumbents and the legislative majority but also because a compelling vision that would legitimize alternative proposals failed to emerge.

PATH-DEPENDENCY EFFECTS

We discussed how the transition to digital TV presented complex coordination problems for policymakers and market agents. In the absence of agreements about technical standards, synchronization in the introduction of complementary products, and clear transition rules, the migration slowed to a halt. Generally speaking, the larger the number of stakeholders involved in the transition, and the less organized they were, the more difficult it became to address such coordination problems and find rules acceptable to all. The degree of industry fragmentation is thus an important variable to compare the U.S. and British cases.

In the United Kingdom, coordination problems were minimized by past policy choices favoring industry consolidation, national (as opposed to local) stations, and vertical integration in the pay-TV market. The British analog TV industry developed as a centralized system of London-based operators. The laudable goal of the Television Act of 1954 to combat the "Londonization" of television by setting up ITV as a series of regional franchises soon confronted the realities of network arrangements and dominance by the large operators. The relaxation of ownership rules during the Conservative years furthered consolidation in the commercial TV sector. By 1995, when the transition was formally launched, terrestrial TV was controlled by a handful of companies: the BBC, Carlton, Granada, Channel Four, and later Channel Five. These policy actors essentially represented the entire terrestrial sector. Moreover, because these operators generally produced their programming in-house, a separate content production industry was slow to emerge (in fact, the 1990 act introduced a 25 percent minimum quota for independent productions on terrestrial channels to promote the independent sector). Likewise, pay-TV in Britain was highly concentrated, a result of weak enforcement of antitrust rules at the European level until the 1990s and the unwillingness of the Thatcher administration to challenge BSkyB's growing dominance of the sector (Levy, 1997; Kaitatzi-Whitlock, 1997).

Industry concentration and vertically integrated operators facilitated the resolution of coordination problems because market agents found it easier to achieve voluntary agreements and policymakers faced a more unified industry constituency than in the U.S. case. This explains the rapid resolution of most standards issues within the context of private industry consortia such as the DVB and the DTG. The small number of relevant market actors also allowed the government to orchestrate policies more effectively and respond to market signals. On the other hand, the legacy of a more concentrated industry also constrained policy choices and required the government to adapt its transition strategy. The Major administration's plan to split the award of commercial DTT licenses into a host of new market entrants soon met the realities of an industry where a handful of players controlled the key resources (e.g., programming rights) and expertise, as well as financial markets unwilling to take heavy bets on newcomers. If the ITC acted too conservatively in awarding all commercial DTT licenses to two analog incumbents (Carlton and Granada), it was largely because the regulator was well aware of the uphill battle that the new DTT operator would face against a satellite operator with interests across the pay-TV supply chain, from programming to set-top box technology.

The high degree of vertical integration in the pay-TV sector also constrained choices in the transposition of Directive 95/47. To begin with, the existing business model of pay-TV – based on subsidizing proprietary decoders – created strong opposition from incumbent pay-TV operators to an EU-wide interoperability mandate for digital TV decoders. Directive 95/47 emerged as a compromise solution between the demands of public service broadcasters for access safeguards and the refusal of vertically integrated pay-TV operators to accept interoperability. As discussed, the vague wording of the access safeguards included in the directive left much to be decided at the member state level. In many cases, national regulators – confronted with powerful incumbents in the pay-TV market – failed to translate the directive into meaningful access obligations for digital pay-TV operators (EC, 1999). In Britain, nonetheless, OFTEL successfully integrated these obligations into a comprehensive access regime for digital network operators. This again reveals how British authorities were able to introduce reforms in the broadcast regime that deviated significantly from inherited policies, despite the political and economic costs involved in such reforms. In other words, the preexisting broadcast regime was no less of a constraint to British policymakers than to their American or European counterparts. The difference in the outcome (large reform in Britain, little reform in the others) stems from the instruments available to British authorities to mobilize political resources in favor of change.

Institutional inertia often results from legal arrangements that alter their environment in ways that make them more enduring. For example, the FCC Sixth Report of 1952 that lifted the freeze of new television licenses fragmented the industry into small local markets so that stations would exist in as many congressional districts as possible. This cemented the compact between Congress and local incumbents, from which emerged powerful broadcast industry organizations. MSTV, the trade association that in 1987 rallied the industry behind the FCC petition to initiate an inquiry into HDTV, was founded in 1956 to serve as the industry's self-declared spectrum watchdog. Over the decades, as both sides adapted to the logic of mediated politics, the compact grew stronger. But the Sixth Report also had an unintended consequence: it decentralized the industry to a scale that would present formidable coordination challenges to the transition almost half a century later. Despite a wave of consolidation following the relaxation of ownership restrictions and network arrangement rules during the 1980s and 1990s, the American television industry remains fragmented to a degree unparalleled in other nations. When the FCC awarded the DTT licenses in April 1997, there were almost 1,700 television stations (including public stations) owned by more than 400 separate entities competing in 210 local markets.[11]

Industry fragmentation was also promoted in the analog regime by rules restricting the vertical integration of broadcasters into content

---

[11] See Comments of Consumer Federation of America, In the matter of 2002 Biennial Regulatory Review – Review of the Commission's Broadcast Ownership Rules and Other Rules Adopted Pursuant to Section 202 of the Telecommunications Act of 1996, MB Docket No. 02-277, January 2, 2003.

production (the "fin-syn" rules) as well as by rules limiting the entry of cable operators into cable programming. "Fin-syn" rules prohibited the networks from acquiring financial interest in television programs produced by third parties, limited in-house production, and prevented participation by the networks in the syndication market. In the case of cable, the Cable Act of 1992 directed the commission "to prescribe rules and regulations establishing reasonable limits on the number of channels on a cable system that can be occupied by a video programmer in which a cable operator has an attributable interest."[12] The goal of these rules was to protect the existence of a separate sector of unaffiliated content providers, in effect dominated by the major Hollywood studios and represented by the powerful Motion Picture Association of America (MPAA). Although since the repeal of the "fin-syn" rules in 1995 significant consolidation has taken place between broadcasters and programmers, the Hollywood majors still acted as a separate constituency group, most notably in the context of the debates about digital copyright protection, which often pitted rights holders and content producers against all other stakeholders.

The fragmentation of the American broadcast sector translated into a broad range of interests vis-à-vis digital TV. To begin with, the opportunities and challenges that the transition presented to a large network affiliate in New York (the largest local market) differed considerably from those facing a small station in Glendive, Montana (the smallest local market serving less than 2,000 households), not to mention the noncommercial sector. Industry observers often warned that digital upgrade costs could exceed the actual market value of many small-market licensees. Whereas for some the transition represented a unique opportunity to reinvent terrestrial TV, for others it was, from the outset, a losing proposition. Aggregating such diverse interests also proved problematic. Several trade associations represented broadcasters during the transition proceedings, including the NAB, MSTV, the Association of Public Television Stations (APTS), and the now-defunct Association for Local Television Stations (ALTV, which represented independent stations). In addition, the national networks and several station groups frequently lobbied the commission and Congress directly (recall the petition by the Sinclair Broadcast Group to modify the ATSC standard, or the efforts by Paxson Communications to gain approval of band-clearing

[12] 47 U.S.C. § 533(f)(1)(b).

arrangements with wireless operators, both discussed in Chapter 6). Although these organizations often coordinated their positions and lobbying efforts, they also found themselves deeply divided over issues such as HDTV requirements in the 1996 act, digital must-carry, and spectrum recovery.

The need to accommodate a much more diverse range of interests than in the United Kingdom and the fragmentation of their intermediating associations presented American policymakers with formidable challenges. Former FCC chairman Kennard contrasted the situation with the arrangements at the time of the transition to color TV:

> The economic and technological barriers to rolling out digital TV are so numerous that the market has had a tough time crafting a solution. There are so many industries involved, each with their competing architectures and incentives, that finding common ground has been extremely difficult. This situation contrasts dramatically with the way color TV rolled out in the early 1950s. Things were a lot simpler then. At that time, one firm, RCA, was involved in every aspect of the system, from start to finish. RCA manufactured TVs and transmitters, and it owned a leading TV network, NBC. It had the incentive and the ability to lead the conversion to color, and whether measured by color TV sets sold or color programming transmitted, RCA led the way. In the case of digital TV it is much more complicated.[13]

Multiple players, competing incentives, and fragmented intermediation bred policy gridlock. Unlike the situation in Britain, it proved difficult to gather all relevant stakeholders around a single bargaining table and produce durable agreements. ATSC was initially expected to play this role, but despite the participation of representatives from the cable, equipment manufacturing, and the computer industry, the control exercised by broadcasters prevented the committee from consolidating as a legitimate bargaining forum. After the FCC adopted the Grand Alliance standard in December 1996, ATSC became largely irrelevant. Industry fragmentation also discouraged government officials from attempting to manage the transition process. Because of the heterogeneity of interests at stake and the decentralization of industry representation, the FCC often eschewed intervention. If, as noted earlier, the commission

---

[13] Address by FCC Chairman William Kennard to the Consumer Electronics Show, January 7, 2000.

lacked the policy instruments to manage the transition in any meaningful way, it was also discouraged from doing so by the scope of interests involved and their disaggregation. The legacy of a regime aimed at protecting localism and the separation between broadcasters and programmers would thus exacerbate, almost fifty years later, the difficult task of crafting agreements that could get the American transition on a better track.

FOURTEEN

Conclusion: The Regulation of Digital Communications and the Resilience of National Regimes

Questions about who gets what have always been at the center of political analysis. In the communications sector, these questions have implications that go beyond the mere allocation of economic rents, because the distribution of control over a nation's communication resources affects the patterns of knowledge production and dissemination as well as the character of its political life. This is why telecommunications, broadcasting, and other media have typically been subject to much closer regulatory scrutiny than other economic activities. Even in liberal democracies, the role of the state in the communications sector has typically gone beyond the organization of buying and selling between market actors. Public service broadcasting serves as an example, but so does the American model whereby, according to the statute, commercial licensees are selected on the basis of their capacity to serve as public trustees. In one way or another, every nation has devised a television regime that balances self-regulating markets with administrative control to determine who gets to broadcast what to whom and under what conditions. The reason is apparent: the organization of the communications sector determines who can participate in the market for political loyalties (Price, 2002). Therefore, policymakers have designed mechanisms to manage it. Although these mechanisms have varied in time and across nations, the reality is that the shape of a nation's media sector has rarely been left to markets alone. The variations in the broadcasting system across nations reflect historical differences in such mechanisms. A political logic, rather than an economic one, has traditionally governed the evolution of media industries.

However, many claim that in recent years the twin forces of technological change and globalization have yielded a crisis of state capacity to assert control over the communications sector (e.g., Strange, 1996). The claim is that governments can no longer arbitrate the outcome of media and telecom markets as in the past. They can no longer promote national champions, control market entry or exit, sponsor services through general taxation, or engineer the industry to pursue social and political goals. In a world of internationalized markets and networks that transcend territorial borders, the cost of doing so far outweighs the benefits. States have, in essence, lost their grip on the structure of domestic communications. The market reforms in communications of the past decades have been a response to such de facto loss of state control. As a result, national differences in media and telecom regimes gradually give way to common rules based on free-market principles – the so-called regulatory convergence process (Berger, 2000). The argument takes many forms but can be summarized in two parts as follows.

First, it is argued that new communication technologies compel industry deregulation. The old communications regime rested on a number of assumptions about natural limitations to market competition. The telecom sector was regarded as a "natural monopoly" and thereby required either tight regulation or direct government operation in order to prevent abuses by the monopolist and to advance important social goals such as universal service and national defense (Horwitz, 1989; Cowhey, 1990). In the case of television, the key assumption was the natural limitation in the radio spectrum necessary for the operation of broadcast stations, which legitimized government rationing of broadcast licenses and programming controls. New technologies have challenged these assumptions. Innovations in customer terminal, transmission, and switching equipment have enabled competition in the provision of telecom services and questioned the legitimacy of rules that protected former monopolists. They have compelled state retreat in telecommunications either because old rules became too costly relative to its benefits, or because firms could effectively bypass regulated networks (Huber, 1997). Digital TV has a comparable effect on the broadcast regime. Digital compression has fundamentally challenged spectrum scarcity, enabling traditional policy goals to be achieved through market competition (Owen, 1999; Hazlett, 2001). Distributed intelligence and interactive applications have challenged the public good character of television services, facilitating individual tailoring of programming and the cost-effective deployment of microtransaction systems. Finally, convergence has wreaked havoc on a regime based on precise demarcations between telecom and media. By questioning the legitimacy and rendering the traditional instruments of broadcast regulation obsolete, the transition compels state retreat.

Second, it is argued that international competition and the global nature of the new electronic networks compel industry deregulation. In a world of closed domestic markets, nation-bound networks, and limited economic integration, state control of communications infrastructure was nearly costless. States could effectively utilize such control to pursue a variety of economic and political goals without compromising international competitiveness. These conditions no longer exist. Today, global markets punish companies without access to efficient telecom services. Moreover, competition at home is a critical springboard for the success of telecom and media firms abroad. Once the United States started deregulating its telecom sector, other nations came under great pressure to follow (Aronson and Cowhey, 1988). National regulation of services has become more difficult to enforce as new technologies make cross-border data flows easier and cheaper. The Internet is the most disrupting of all: "[T]he rise of an electronic medium that disregards geographical boundaries throws the law into disarray by creating entirely new phenomena that need to become the subject of clear legal rules but that cannot be governed, satisfactorily, by any current territorially based sovereign" (Johnson and Post, 1996: 1375). Global networks prompt many firms to relocate (or threaten to) in nations that offer favorable regulatory treatment, unleashing a regulatory "race to the bottom" (Froomkin, 1997).

The dynamics of international competition for investments and the inadequacy of territory-based rules force governments to relax regulation of communication infrastructure and services, including arrangements to protect national champions and control media flows. In the end, it matters little what policy agenda elected officials bring to bear because globalization has tied the hands of those who once used the state's powers to engineer telecom and media markets. Hirst and Thompson explain:

> Just as nuclear weapons have transformed the conditions of war, weakening the central rationale for the state in the process, so too the new communications and information technologies have loosened the state's exclusiveness of control of its territory, reducing its capacities for cultural control and homogenization. It is a commonplace that digitized communications, satellites, fax machines, and computer networks have rendered the licensing and control of information media by the state all but impossible, not merely undermining ideological dictatorships but also subverting all attempts to preserve cultural homogeneity by state force. (1999: 266)

Whereas much agreement exists about the origins of such national sovereignty crises, scholars have interpreted them differently. For the optimists, new technologies have undermined inefficient and often authoritative state institutions. Control is increasingly in the hands of users as well as new market entrants, who can now participate in the innovation cycle and the self-regulation of open networks (Neuman et al., 1997). Unrestricted data flows across borders have enhanced global democracy by opening up channels of political information and participation that challenge oppressive states (Pool, 1983; Froomkin, 1997). For the pessimists, on the other hand, control has migrated not to citizens or small entrepreneurs but to big multinational corporations that are increasingly forcing the dismantling of democratic media and telecom arrangements based on the mobility of capital and their access to credit. Deregulation in the communications sector has led to unprecedented industry concentration, leaving media and telecom markets worldwide in the hands of a few corporations unaccountable to the public at large (Sassen, 1998; McChesney, 2003). Ironically, the result has been less competition, less diversity in terms of editorial perspectives and the national origin of media products, and a greater gap between the commercial imperatives of market players and the democratic needs of the public (Mosco and Schiller, 2001).

In this conclusion, I seek to contrast these arguments with the findings of our examination of the digital TV transition in the United States and the United Kingdom. I generally find that globalization critics and detractors have equally exaggerated the degree to which states have lost their capacity to structure the communications sector. Faced with common macroeconomic challenges and a technology that challenged the fundamental parameters of the analog TV regime, nations forged distinct policy responses that in many ways strengthened their preexisting differences in the organization of broadcasting. The United States set out to preserve free local TV and the quid pro quo between legislators and incumbent commercial operators based on zero-priced spectrum rights. The United Kingdom, by contrast, embarked on a path of procompetitive reforms, albeit preserving the dual character (public and commercial) of its system. Neither was compelled to respond to digital TV in a deregulatory way. If transition policies were sometimes accompanied by the relaxation of ownership restrictions, they also involved new government powers to define the terms of access to broadcast network facilities and the technical configuration of customer terminals. What we observed, rather than deregulation, is a reconfiguration of government mechanisms to administer the broadcast sector in consonance with the new industry parameters (increased spectrum availability, convergence of networks and services, distributed intelligence, etc.). There is thus little evidence about the gradual convergence of media regimes in the United States and Britain. Such resilience of national media systems should not be surprising. In a sense, our modernist fascination with technology often obscures the fact that, while technological innovations are universal and rather easily transferable across borders, the economic and political arrangements that define how these innovations are deployed are not.

REINTERPRETING MEDIA DEREGULATION

Governments have assembled a wide array of instruments to control the communications industry. Moreover, when old instruments seem obsolete, new ones can be forged. Most analyses of the regulatory reforms of the past decades have concentrated on a specific family of instruments associated with ownership of media and telecom firms. A common argument is that the privatization of public operators and the relaxation of ownership restrictions have deprived policymakers of key instruments to manage the evolution of media and telecom markets and accomplish social goals such as universal service and editorial diversity. The empirical evidence seems overwhelming. In the United States, the Telecom Act of 1996 repealed the prohibition on the common ownership of cable and telephone systems, eliminated the national and relaxed the local restrictions on radio holdings, eased the prohibition on the dual network ownership rule for television, and directed the FCC to eliminate the cap on the number of television stations any one company may own and to increase from twenty-five to thirty-five the maximum percentage of American households a single broadcaster may reach.[1] Likewise, the British Broadcasting Act of 1996 abolished numerical limits on the holding of television licenses (replacing it with a 15 percent cap of the total TV audience any one company may control) and directed the privatization of the BBC's transmission network. In both nations, further easing of media ownership rules – including the controversial ban on foreign ownership of broadcast stations – is on the agenda.

On both sides of the Atlantic, these changes incited passionate debates. Critics interpreted them as a fundamental assault on the state's ability

---

[1] For a discussion, see 2002 Biennial Regulatory Review – Review of the Commission's Broadcast Ownership Rules and Other Rules Adopted Pursuant to Section 202 of the Telecommunications Act of 1996, MB Docket No. 02-277, 17 FCC Rcd 18503 (2002).

to regulate communications; on the other side, advocates declared them necessary steps to unfetter the industry from onerous and outdated rules. Interestingly, these reforms were adopted as the United States and Britain prepared for the introduction of digital TV. Unfortunately, ownership debates often trumped debate about the licensing of DTT, the switch-off of analog stations, and other policies that arguably have been of much greater consequence to the structure of the communications sector than ownership rules. Moreover, I suggest that if we shift attention to digital TV policies we hardly find any evidence of state retreat in the communications sector. Our examination of the American and British cases revealed that, for the most part, policymakers have not let market agents determine when or how to implement digital TV. Instead, governments used a combination of resource allocation, tax incentives, statutory deadlines, and informal cooperation – in a sense, a combination of carrots and sticks – to shape the transition in consonance with different policy agendas for the media and telecom sectors. Such is what I have called the paradox of digital TV. In the late 1980s, the modernization of the broadcast sector was deemed critical for the international competitiveness of consumer electronic manufacturers. In the early 1990s the issue became successful participation in the information society; and in the late 1990s, spectrum recovery and fiscal stability. Through the years, a theme persisted: the transition is just too important (and complex) to leave it up to chance.

The most obvious manifestation of government management of the transition has been the allocation of frequencies for DTT. The British Broadcasting Act of 1996 specified in detail who would get which frequencies to launch digital services and established exhaustive guidelines for the ITC in the selection of the new commercial entrants. The U.S. Telecom Act of 1996 went even further: it essentially directed the FCC to restrict allocation of DTT licenses to existing broadcasters. Under different circumstances, both governments rather explicitly rejected the more "deregulatory" solution: to structure a price-based mechanism (e.g., license auctions) through which market agents would compete for these property rights. In the United States, auction proposals were repeatedly defeated in Congress, despite pressure from a coalition of academics, media access advocates, mobile telephony operators, key legislators, and the implicit acquiescence of the Clinton administration. In Britain, the Major government rejected calls to introduce a cash bid component in the selection of DTT multiplex operators, despite general support among Tories and New Labour leaders for pricing spectrum use. Likewise, governments by and large set the pace of the migration process (or at least attempted to do so). In America, the FCC established a detailed timetable for the building of DTT facilities, the introduction of services, and the shutdown of analog channels. Although British authorities have so far declined to set a precise date for the switch-off of analog TV, the Blair administration established a series of rather arbitrary tests to determine the start of the switchover process.

Government involvement has also been widespread in the creation of digital TV standards, often requiring the threat of direct legislation to force agreements and secure compliance. If cooperation between private industry consortia and the government sometimes failed – notably in the United States – it is because those threats lacked credibility. The governance of arrangements between digital TV network operators, programmers, and equipment manufacturers has been another area of much regulatory activity. Choices about digital TV terminal specifications, security interfaces, the pricing of CAS and related services, the design of EPGs, and the recovery of terminal subsidies, to mention a few examples, have not been left to market actors. Rather, government rules set the terms and conditions under which these choices have been made. In essence, we find that state actors have been central in the reorganization of the industry triggered by the transition. Disengagement in traditional areas of government control has been offset by involvement in new ones. While ownership restrictions were being loosened, governments were tightening their grip over the allocation of broadcast licenses, partnering with private consortia in the establishment of technical standards, bringing new rules to bear upon digital TV terminals, renewing their commitment to specific programmers (the BBC in Britain, terrestrial incumbents in the United States), and taking a fresh look at the application of antitrust policies to the sector. This study has generally stressed the differences between the transition strategies of the United States and Britain. Yet, in this respect they share a common goal: to renew the government's powers to shape the architecture and control outputs in the broadcast industry. Transition policies have provided a convenient vehicle for such renewal.

This study thus raises fundamental questions about broadcast deregulation. Should digital TV policies be interpreted as an exception, a small setback to the deregulation of communications in the past decades? Hardly so. There is much evidence that, amid the manifold regulatory challenges created by the revolution in information and communication technologies, states have come back with a vengeance. They have not accepted regulatory losses passively but rather attempted to adapt existing regimes to new technologies as they emerged. Reforms in telecommunications have unfolded differently both among industrialized and developing nations, powerfully shaped by domestic policy concerns (S. Vogel, 1996; Levy and Spiller, 1996). Media reforms have followed the same route (Waisbord and Morris, 2001). Even the Internet has been, if not brought under control, at least domesticated by national authorities (Marsden, 2000). Of course, this is not to deny that multiple changes have taken place in the nature of communications regulation over the past decades. That change has been pervasive is self-evident. What I suggest is that the deregulation narrative only partially explains the nature of such change.

For an alternative interpretation, let us start from a taxonomy developed by Mulgan (1991). This author identifies three types of state control over communications. The first is a sponsoring type of control. Governments have often used their powers to promote the development of communications infrastructure and support specific services. Sponsorship has been most common in the initial phase of new technology development. The BBC, BT, ITV Digital, and other companies that spearheaded new technologies in the United Kingdom have in one way or another benefited from direct government support in the form of licensee fee revenues, protection from market entry, privileged access to public resources, and low-cost credits. The same can be said of AT&T, RCA, the members of the HDTV Grand Alliance, and several other companies that, through the years, benefited from U.S. government sponsorship of their efforts to introduce innovations in the communications sector. Even BSkyB, often referred to as the prime example of nonsponsored market entrant, benefited from the Thatcher administration's zeal to develop competition to challenge the BBC. To say that the Internet would not have developed without critical sponsorship from the U.S. government is now commonplace (Kahin, 1997). The early period in the history of digital TV, most closely associated with the development of different HDTV systems in the United States, Europe, and Japan in the late 1980s, bears the mark of widespread state sponsoring.

The second type of state control is restrictive. As new technologies mature, governments start to develop mechanisms to restrain the behavior of dominant market players and impose obligations in order to secure the realization of social and political goals. Once fledging companies sponsored by the state are now seen as overpowerful creatures that need to be contained to prevent abuses of market power. Rate regulation and common-carrier obligations were deemed necessary to prevent AT&T and BT from abusing their "natural monopoly" position. As television became central to modern social and political life, controls over programming, editorializing, ownership, and advertising were imposed to prevent the handful of broadcast licensees from manipulating public opinion and abusing their control of the "naturally" scarce radio frequencies. These and other command-and-control regulations formed the core of the old communications regime, a regime that emerged as a way to restrain the behavior of the few government-blessed firms that, in each national market, dominated communications through much of the twentieth century.

The third type of government control is arbitration. In this case, instead of imposing constraints on a few dominant companies, the state seeks to manage competition between multiple market actors and address social goals through targeted efforts. This type of control has evolved in consonance with the growing complexity of communication networks and the technological challenge to the established cartel of government-sanctioned operators (Noam, 2001). The key to this type of control lies in the understanding that many of the traditional goals of communications policy can be achieved by embracing complexity and network openness. In this case, the state oversees network interconnection, promotes standardization, and manages the terms of access to essential physical and intangible resources (from digital TV terminals to premium content rights) in order to nourish competition and protect openness. While arbitration often requires relaxation of the rules associated with restrictive control, it does not necessarily imply state retreat. In fact, as Mulgan explains, "this type of control can be every bit as interventionist as the two others. What distinguishes it is the idea that the state's role is to manage the parameters of an open ecology of communication, rather than directly to plan it" (1991: 142).

In broad terms, each type of control can be more closely associated with a specific historical period in the evolution of modern communications. Sponsorship prevailed in the early twentieth century, when the goal of state policy was to promote research and large-scale deployment of innovations in communications technologies. Restrictions began to emerge in the interwar period as concerns about competitive abuses by dominant telecommunications operators and the dissemination of political propaganda by broadcasters gained strength. Arbitration surfaced in the 1970s as a response to the growing complexity of communication networks and the emergence of new market players ready to challenge the restrictions that favored the former telecom and media incumbents. Nonetheless, it is important to note that the regimes that govern communications have evolved through a process of historical accretion rather than substitution. In other words, new types of control have not thoroughly replaced old ones. Rather, they became part of what is now a complex mix of sponsoring, restrictions, and arbitration.

In this perspective, deregulation is a misnomer for a fundamental transformation in the way governments regulate communications, associated with the gradual phasing out of restrictive controls and the phasing in of arbitration. Digital TV has been closely related to this progression. In the context of the transition, governments began dismantling controls designed for a broadcast industry characterized by spectrum shortages, dumb analog terminals, and clear market demarcations, replacing them with controls better suited to address problems associated with digital convergence, access bottlenecks, and global networks. The migration from restriction to arbitration has been most noticeable in Britain, where the government has taken significant steps to adapt the broadcast regime to the growing industry complexity associated with digital TV and broadband digital networks in general. However, regime adaptation has not implied the abandonment of fundamental principles. Arbitration controls have been introduced precisely to renew the government's capacity to preserve the unique combination of commercial and public services that characterizes British broadcasting. The problem in the United States has been that the phasing out of ownership limitations and other restrictive controls has not been accompanied by reforms favoring structural decentralization of control in the broadcast sector or the phasing in of new instruments for state arbitration of access (Benkler, 1998). As a result, the American debate about broadcast reforms is often a zero-sum game between those who advocate dismantling the old regime of restrictions and those who want to preserve at least some of it, when the real debate should be about the fundamental goals of media regulation and how to enable – rather than disable – the state to achieve them in a post-transition context.

DIGITAL MEDIA AND THE NATION-STATE

Globalization scholars often identify the communications sector as a core example of state sovereignty loss. In telecommunications, new technologies and pressure from large users have undermined national regimes based on closed domestic markets, gradually bringing the industry under the umbrella of multilateral free-trade rules (Cowhey, 1990; Drake, 2000). Computer networks spanning the globe have wreaked havoc with domestic regulation and taxation of information services (OECD, 1997b). Satellite TV footprints that disrespect national boundaries have undercut the power of governments to license and impose obligations on broadcasters (Collins, 1994). These and other examples suggest a fundamental decline in the ability of national governments to engineer markets and manage trade in the communications sector. Control has shifted into the hands of multinational corporations and multilateral organizations in which national regulators are one among many voices. As globalization links markets worldwide, protecting national media and telecom champions becomes increasingly costly. Governments that attempt to manipulate this process to favor local firms or reinforce political control do so at the peril of economic backwardness and political isolation. As Mulgan puts it:

> Public service in communication has traditionally been associated with the nation state. In the past, the rules of provision were also the rules of limitation. With exceptions in radio such as the BBC, Radios Luxembourg, Cairo, Moscow or Free Europe, signals respected the jurisdiction of states and rarely transgressed national boundaries. Because of the propagation characteristics of VHF and UHF, television signals only marginally spilled over into neighbouring countries while telephone systems were unambiguously under the control of national authorities. What the State licensed or directly provided was the beginning and end of electronic communications. Nowadays, however, signals spill much more easily, making it harder to define the public by means of political boundaries.... Low-powered satellites broadcast signals to cable headends and medium- or high-powered satellites broadcast signals directly to antennae attached to homes. Pirate radio or television stations can broadcast from the sea. Thriving markets for video bypass censorship and quotas aimed at cinema. In telecommunications private networks have expanded ahead of the law.... In all of these areas public service under the national State has become, de facto, just one element in the organization of communications rather than its guiding principle. There is no real prospect of a return to simplicity, to the situation where a State could easily control what its citizens see or hear or who they speak to. (1991: 258–259)

Berger correctly points out that the argument is also about fundamental losses in the political legitimacy of state action:

> Globalization undermines the national state, these observers claim, not only by shrinking the resources under national control for shaping economic and social outcomes, but also by reducing government's legitimacy and authority in the eyes of the public. Across virtually all advanced industrial countries over the past two decades, there has been an erosion of public confidence in central governments. Even when analysts mention the role of specific national causes in this loss of trust, still they tend to emphasize the universality of the shifts – how everywhere globalization destroys national control of information flows, hence weakens a government's ability to influence its public. The effects of the internationalization of the media, the marketing and export of American popular culture, and the deregulation of information all combine to weaken national values and traditions, and in so doing, they dry up the springs of support for national action. (2000: 45)

Let us contrast our findings with these arguments. A good starting point is the question of whether states have lost their ability to manipulate media and telecom markets to sponsor local firms. In Chapter 2, we noted that concerns about the competitiveness of domestic players in the consumer electronics and related high-tech markets were critical to jump-start the digital TV transition. It was NHK's attempt to gain global adoption of its HDTV system in the late 1980s that brought the transition to the attention of European and American leaders. Local electronics firms effectively capitalized on these concerns to assemble support for policies favoring local technology development and the forced modernization of broadcast TV facilities. For the most part, these government-led initiatives to develop local HDTV standards proved unsuccessful. Nonetheless, such failures did not discourage policymakers from attempting to favor local players through other means. Governments could still dictate the technical standards for television broadcasting within their territories and had often done so in the past to advance domestic interests. In the 1960s the main industrialized nations supported their national champions in efforts to export their competing color TV systems (NTSC, PAL, and SECAM) worldwide (Crane, 1979).[2] In the 1970s and 1980s these

---

[2] Unlike the case of telecom, intergovernmental bargaining within the ITU was never able to produce durable agreements on broadcast TV standards (Krasner, 1991).

nations entered into iterative negotiations to manage trade in VCRs and consumer electronic components (D'Andrea Tyson, 1992).

Much had changed by the time the transition to digital TV began in the late 1990s. Notably, nations were bound by free-trade commitments under the World Trade Organization (WTO) and regional or bilateral trade agreements that limited the available instruments for such policies. Moreover, the national allegiances of the competing digital TV systems were much less well defined than, for example, in the case of color TV. The ATSC system was developed in the United States by the members of the HDTV Grand Alliance, but included two large European manufacturers (Thomson and Philips) and Zenith, which in 1999 became a wholly owned subsidiary of the South Korean electronics giant LGE. The DVB system was developed by the European DVB consortium, to which many American and Japanese firms were members (ISDB, developed by a consortium of Japanese electronic manufacturers after NHK abandoned Hi-Vision MUSE, was the only system with a clear-cut national origin). Nevertheless, national governments continued to engage in efforts to favor "their" systems, notably by mandating use within local markets (regional in the case of the EU) and by aiding companies in diplomatic efforts to gain adoption in other nations (Hart and Prakash, 1997). Interestingly, after the failure of the HDTV initiatives in the late 1980s, governments showed little interest in reaching agreement on a worldwide digital TV standard that would facilitate global trade in programming and equipment. To the contrary, there has been no letdown of strategic maneuvering among the leading industrialized nations (sometimes pooled together as in the case of Europe) to procure competitive advantages through international diplomacy. The role states play in shaping competition in the broadcast technology market, if less hostile than in the analog world, has hardly subsided.

Our findings further suggest that international forces have not compelled policymakers in the United States and Britain to implement digital TV in any particular way. In other words, governments have had considerable autonomy to shape the transition in consonance with domestic policy agendas and protect established arrangements in the communications sector. While the international forces discussed in Chapter 2 compelled governments to formulate a response to digital TV, our examination of the American and British cases revealed the variety of responses adopted. Interestingly, the evidence from other nations points in the same direction: in each country, the transition has unfolded uniquely, driven by domestic factors rather than international forces.

For example, French officials have taken a very cautious approach to the transition, delaying significantly both the licensing of DTT and the implementation of Directive 95/47. The Audiovisual Law of 2000 finally established the framework for the introduction of DTT services, combining the dual licensing system adopted in Britain with traditional French concerns about local content origination. In France, unlike in the United States and Britain, concerns about spectrum recovery from analog TV have been secondary to the maintenance of a balance between public and commercial services as well as between national and local ones (Boyon, 2002). In Japan, by contrast, the transition has been engineered to maximize spectrum recovery in order to promote the development of 3G mobile telephony and other wireless services. After the abandonment of its analog HDTV initiative, the Japanese government began planning a market-by-market roll-out of DTT based on full simulcasting by incumbent operators. Authorities strongly encouraged local development of a digital TV standard, which resulted in the ISDB system. Unlike in most other nations, the government has suggested it is prepared to spend about U.S.$1.5 billion from its own coffers to finance the transition. The target switchover date has been set for 2011. Germany offers yet another contrasting case. The German Constitution stipulates that the sole responsibility for broadcasting rests with the states (*Länder*). Therefore, despite federal guidelines and significant interstate coordination attempts, the implementation of digital TV has varied considerably from region to region (Holznagel and Grünwald, 2000).

It is thus apparent that neither stronger economic and political ties between nations nor new communication technologies have precluded distinct policy choices in the reorganization of the broadcast industry and the adaptation of domestic regimes to digital TV. Each nation has taken a distinct course of action, driven by different domestic concerns and regime legacies. Different national arrangements relating to spectrum management, the funding of public service broadcasters, and free local services have not been dismantled. In fact, the transition has reinforced them. Moreover, there is little evidence of a regulatory "race to the bottom" to attract or retain investments. To the contrary, our findings draw attention to a common strengthening of governments' powers to arbitrate access to essential industry facilities and the increasing use of instruments of telecom regulation and antitrust law to achieve traditional media policy goals. As noted, these new instruments tend to complement rather than replace old ones. Whereas many globalization scholars would predict a gradual vanishing of historical differences in the organization of media systems across nations – what the more alarmist of them would associate with an irreversible trend toward worldwide cultural homogenization – we find that the transition to digital TV has been a vehicle for cementing those differences.

These findings invite revision of common assumptions about how globalization affects domestic policymaking capabilities in the communications and information technology sectors. Does the transition to digital TV represent an outlier case of state sovereignty or does it raise more fundamental questions about the national sovereignty loss hypothesis? Many recent studies suggest that globalization advocates and critics alike have been too quick in sounding the death knell for the state. The evidence from studies in areas as diverse as telecommunications (S. Vogel, 1996; Thatcher, 1999), environmental protection (D. Vogel, 1986), health care (Wilsford, 1994), and macroeconomic policy (Gilpin, 2000) suggests that nations (particularly large industrialized ones) have retained considerable policymaking autonomy despite being increasingly interlinked economically, politically, and culturally. This study corroborates these findings. However, the peculiarities of the media industry should also be carefully considered when drawing theoretical inferences from this study. Broadcasting is, in many ways, a peculiar political creature from which governments refuse to disengage. Television plays a key role in the market for political loyalties and social identification (Garnham, 1990; Price, 2002). As a result, elected officials and regulators tend to attempt to retain control over market structure and outputs.

In addition, broadcast services are not easily tradable. While over the past decades media ownership has become increasingly internationalized, competition in the production and distribution of television programming continues to take place in fairly fragmented national markets, separated by deep-seated linguistic and cultural barriers (Sinclair, 1996). As Levy writes, "while the technical possibility of engaging in trans-frontier broadcasting has been available for more than a decade, the reality is that most broadcasting – even via satellite – is still targeted at specific countries or linguistic regions" (1999: 156). This is why the combination of increasingly open media markets and global communications networks that to some degree escape national regulation has not translated into a blanket Americanization of television worldwide (Straubhaar, 1997). The resounding failure of policies aimed at creating a single European audiovisual market attests to the enduring differences in the preferences and behavior of national audiences (Schlesinger, 1997). Moreover, unlike telecommunications, broadcasting has not come under the umbrella of the international trade regime even as this regime has gradually expanded into services. Despite considerable pressure from the United States, concerns about cultural and political sovereignty raised by France and other nations led to limited opening of audiovisual trade under the General Agreement of Trade in Services (GATS) (Cahn and Schimmel, 1997). Overall, there have been only limited steps toward a more multilateral system of media governance (Galperin, 1999). This combination of natural and legal barriers to trade and asset mobility lowers the potential costs of imposing local controls and manipulating the evolution of domestic media. In other words, because television markets remain fragmented, governments have more leeway to organize them in peculiar ways.

Averting national sovereignty losses has also been an important consideration in digital TV policies. This explains why even in nations where cable and satellite are approaching universal penetration (e.g., the United States and Germany) governments have made DTT a central consideration. Unlike satellite TV, terrestrial broadcasting tends to overlap with national borders and offers less opportunities for regulatory arbitrage, making them more amenable to domestic controls. Of course, government policies specifically designed to domesticate the impact of globalization and renew state powers are not unique to the media sector. Evans (1997) and others show how public institutions continue to shape the impact of globalization on domestic markets, from labor to banking. The transition to digital TV reveals that policymakers have not passively accepted losses in their ability to organize the media sector. In some cases, intergovernmental bargaining has led to harmonization of rules (notably in the EU). In others, the institutional design and the instruments of broadcast regulation were adjusted to technological and political-economic changes. Different national media regimes have therefore proved compatible with digital communications on a global scale and the strengthening of political and economic links between nations. This should be good news for those engaged in efforts to democratize media access or protect arrangements aimed at securing the supply of public goods that media markets may undersupply (e.g., minority-oriented programming, political speech), for the future of television seems less wedded to the evolution of technology or global market forces than to politics, as usual.

References

Aaron, Harris J. 2000. I Want My MTV: The Debate over Digital Must-Carry. *Boston University Law Review* 80: 885–906.

Advisory Committee on Public Interest Obligations of Digital Television Broadcasters. 1998. *Final Report*. Washington, DC: author.

Albiniak, Page. 2001. Stations "Waiver" on DTV. *Broadcasting & Cable*, August 20.

Andrews, Edmund L. 1995. Telecom Bill: Another Day, Another Rift. *New York Times*, December 29.

Annan Committee. 1977. *The Future of Broadcasting*. London: HMSO.

Aronson, Jonathan D., and Peter F. Cowhey. 1988. *When Countries Talk: International Trade in Telecommunications Service*. Cambridge, MA: Ballinger.

Arthur D. Little. 1994. *Conditional Access Systems: Ensuring Growth and Competition in Digital Broadcasting*. London: author.

Arthur, Brian. 1989. Competing Technologies, Increasing Returns, and Lock-In by Historical Events. *Economic Journal* 99: 116–131.

Banks, Jeffrey S., Linda R. Cohen, and Roger G. Noll. 1991. The Politics of Commercial R&D Programs. In Linda R. Cohen and Roger G. Noll, eds., *The Technology Pork Barrel*. Washington, DC: Brookings Institution, pp. 53–76.

Bar, François, Michael Borrus, and Richard Steinberg. 1995. Interoperability and the NII: Mapping the Debate. *Information Infrastructure and Policy* 4(4): 235–254.

Baran, Paul. 1995. *Is the UHF Frequency Shortage a Self Made Problem?* Marconi Centennial Symposium, Bologna, Italy, June 23.

Barendt, Eric. 1995. *Broadcasting Law: A Comparative Study*. Oxford: Clarendon Press.

Barnett, Steven. 1997. A Brave New World: A Brave New Decision? *Guardian*, April 14.

Barnouw, Erik. 1968. *A History of Broadcasting in the United States*. New York: Oxford University Press.

Bazelon, Coleman. 1999. *Completing the Transition to Digital Television*. Washington, DC: Congressional Budget Office.

Beltz, Cynthia A. 1991. *High-Tech Maneuvers: Industrial Policy Lessons of HDTV*. Washington, DC: AEI Press.

Benkler, Yochai. 1998. Communications Infrastructure Regulation and the Distribution of Control over Content. *Telecommunications Policy* 22(3): 183–196.

REFERENCES

Bennett, Lance, and Robert M. Entman, eds. 2001. *Mediated Politics: Communication in the Future of Democracy.* Cambridge: Cambridge University Press.
Berger, Suzanne. 2000. Globalization and Politics. *Annual Review of Political Science* 3: 43–62.
Besen, Stanley M., and Leland L. Johnson. 1986. *Compatibility Standards, Competition, and Innovation in the Broadcasting Industry.* Santa Monica, CA: Rand.
BIPE. 2002. *Digital Switchover in Broadcasting: A BIPE Consulting Study for the European Commission.* <http://europa.eu.int/information_society/index_en.htm>.
Blackman, Colin R. 1998. Convergence between Telecommunications and Other Media: How Should Regulation Adapt? *Telecommunications Policy* 22(3): 163–170.
Bottomley, Virginia. 2000. Maintaining the Gold Standard. In Steven Barnett et al., *E-Britannia: The Communications Revolution.* Luton: University of Luton Press, pp. 116–122.
Boyon, Michel. 2002. *La télévision numérique terrestre: Rapport établi à la demande du premier ministre.* <www.ddm.gouv.fr>.
Briggs, Asa. 1961. *The History of Broadcasting in the United Kingdom.* New York: Oxford University Press.
    1985. *The BBC: The First Fifty Years.* New York: Oxford University Press.
Brinkley, Joel. 1997. *Defining Vision: The Battle for the Future of Television.* New York: Harcourt Brace.
    1996. Congress Asks the FCC to Begin Lending Channels for Digital TV Broadcasts. *New York Times,* June 24.
British Broadcasting Corporation. 1992. *Extending Choice: The BBC's Role in the New Broadcasting Age.* London: BBC Publications.
    1995. *Britain's Digital Opportunity: The BBC's Response to the Government's Proposals for Digital Terrestrial Broadcasting.* London: BBC Publications.
    1996. *Extending Choice in the Digital Era.* London: BBC Publications.
    1999. *BBC Evidence to the Licence Fee Review Panel.* London: author.
Brock, Gerald W. 1994. *Telecommunication Policy for the Information Age: From Monopoly to Competition.* Cambridge, MA: Harvard University Press.
Butler, David, and Dennis Kavanagh. 1997. *The British General Election of 1997.* New York: St. Martin's Press.
Butler, Joy R. 1992. HDTV Demystified: History, Regulatory Options, and the Role of Telephone Companies. *Harvard Journal of Law and Technology* 6: 155–182.
Cahn, Sandrine, and Daniel Schimmel. 1997. The Cultural Exception: Does It Exist in GATT and GATS Frameworks? How Does It Affect or Is It Affected by the Agreement on TRIPS? *Cardozo Arts & Entertainment Law Journal* 15: 281–314.
Cain, Bruce E., John A. Ferejohn, and Morris P. Fiorina. 1984. The Constituency Service Basis of the Personal Vote for U.S. Representatives and British Members of Parliament. *American Political Science Review* 78(1): 110–125.
Calvert, Randall L., Mathew D. McCubbins, and Barry R. Weingast. 1989. A Theory of Political Control and Agency Discretion. *American Journal of Political Science* 33(3): 588–611.
Cave, Martin. 1997. Regulating Digital TV in a Convergent World. *Telecommunications Policy* 21(7): 575–596.
    2002. *Review of Radio Spectrum Management: An Independent Review for Department of Trade and Industry and HM Treasury.* London: HMSO.

Cave, Martin, and Peter Williamson. 1995. The Reregulation of British Broadcasting. In Matthew Bishop, John Kay, and Colin Mayer, eds., *The Regulatory Challenge.* New York: Oxford University Press, pp. 160–190.

Cawson, Alan, Kevin Morgan, Douglas Webber, Peter Holmes, and Anne Stevens. 1990. *Hostile Brothers: Competition and Closure in the European Electronics Industry.* Oxford: Clarendon Press.

Cherry, Barbara A., and Johannes M. Bauer. 2002. Institutional Arrangements and Price Rebalancing: Empirical Evidence from the United States and Europe. *Information Economics and Policy* 14: 495–517.

Coase, Roland H. 1959. The Federal Communications Commission. *Journal of Economics* 2: 1–40.

Cohen, Robert, and Kenneth Donow. 1989. *Telecommunications Policy, High Definition Television, and U.S. Competitiveness.* Washington, DC: Economic Policy Institute.

Collins, Richard. 1994. *Broadcasting and Audiovisual Policy in the European Single Market.* Luton: John Libbey.

1995. Reflections across the Atlantic: Contrasts and Complementarities in Broadcasting Policy in Canada and the European Community in the 1990s. *Canadian Journal of Communication* 20: 483–504.

1997. Digital Television and Convergence in the United Kingdom. *Telecommunications Policy* 22(4–5): 383–396.

Collins, Richard, and Cristina Murroni. 1996. *New Media, New Policies: Media and Communications for the Future.* London: Polity Press.

Congressional Budget Office. 1997. *Where Do We Go from Here? The FCC Auctions and the Future of Radio Spectrum Management.* Washington, DC: author.

Consumer Electronics Association. 2001. *Digital America.* Arlington, VA: CEA.

Council of Economic Advisors. 2000. The Economic Impact of Third-Generation Wireless Technology. Washington, DC: author.

Cowhey, Peter F. 1990. The International Telecommunications Regime: The Political Roots of Regimes for High Technology. *International Organization* 44(2): 169–199.

Cowhey, Peter F., and Matthew D. McCubbins, eds. 1995. *Structure and Policy in Japan and the United States.* Cambridge: Cambridge University Press.

Cowie, Campbell, and Chris T. Marsden. 1999. Convergence: Navigating Bottlenecks in Digital Pay-TV. *Info* 1(1): 53–67.

Cox, Gary W. 1987. The Efficient Secret: *The Cabinet and the Development of Political Parties in Victorian England.* Cambridge: Cambridge University Press.

Cox, Gary W., and Mathew D. McCubbins. 2001. The Institutional Determinants of Economic Policy Outcomes. In Stephan Haggard and Mathew D. McCubbins, eds., *Presidents, Parliaments, and Policy.* Cambridge: Cambridge University Press, pp. 21–63.

Cozens, Claire. 2002. Jowell Stands Firm on Switch-Off Date. *Guardian,* March 28.

Crandall, Robert W., and Harold Furchtgott-Roth. 1996. *Cable TV: Regulation or Competition?* Washington, DC: Brookings Institution.

Crane, Rhonda J. 1979. *The Politics of International Standards: France and the Color TV War.* Norwood, NJ: Ablex.

Creigh-Tyte, Stephen. 2000. *The Impact of a Digital License Fee on Digital TV Adoption: An Assessment.* London: DCMS.

Crisell, Andrew. 1997. *An Introductory History of British Broadcasting.* New York: Routledge.

Culf, Andrew. 1997. The Television Revolution: Coup Jump-Starts Digital. *Guardian*, February 1.

Culture, Media, and Sport Committee. 1999. *The Funding of the BBC: Third Report.* London: HMSO.

——— 2002. *Communications: Fourth Report.* London: HMSO.

D'Andrea Tyson, Laura. 1992. *Who's Bashing Whom: Trade Conflicts in High-Technology Industries.* Washington, DC: Institute for International Economics.

David, Paul A. 1986. *Narrow Windows, Blind Giants, and Angry Orphans: The Dynamics of Systems Rivalries and Dilemmas of Technology Policy.* CEPR Working Paper 10. Stanford, CA: CEPR.

David, Paul A., and Mark Shurmer. 1996. Formal Standards-Setting for Global Telecommunications and Information Services: Towards an Institutional Regime Transformation? *Telecommunications Policy* 20(10): 789–815.

de Cockborne, Jean-Eric, Bernard Clements, and Adam Watson-Brown. 1999. *EU Policy on Multimedia Regulation.* World Digital Television Summit, Montreux, Switzerland, June.

De Witt, Karen. 1995. Foe of Public Broadcasting Aid Backs Auction Financing Plan. *New York Times*, September 14.

Department for Culture, Media, and Sport. 1999. *The Future Funding of the BBC: Report of the Independent Review Panel.* London: HMSO.

——— 2000. *The Future Funding of the BBC: Government Response to the Third Report from the Culture, Media and Sport Committee.* London: DCMS.

Department of National Heritage. 1992. *The Future of the BBC: A Consultation Document.* London: HMSO.

——— 1994. *The Future of the BBC: Serving the Nation, Competing Worldwide.* London: HMSO.

——— 1995a. *Digital Terrestrial Broadcasting: The Government's Proposals.* London: HMSO.

——— 1995b. *Media Ownership: The Government's Proposals.* London: HMSO.

——— 1996. *Digital Terrestrial Broadcasting: An Explanatory Guide to the Provisions Introduced by the Broadcasting Act 1996.* London: HMSO.

Department of Trade and Industry. 1994. *Creating the Superhighways of the Future: Developing Broadband Communications in the UK.* London: HMSO.

——— 1996. *The Regulation of Conditional Access Services for Digital Television.* London: DTI.

——— 1998. *Regulating Communications: Approaching Convergence in the Information Age.* London: HMSO.

——— 2000. *A New Future for Communications.* London: HMSO.

——— 2002. *Digital Television: The Principles for Spectrum Planning.* London: DTI.

Derthick, Martha, and Paul J. Quirk. 1985. *The Politics of Deregulation.* Washington, DC: Brookings Institution.

Digital Television Group. 2000. *A Study on the Technical Impediments to Analogue Switchover.* London: author.

Drake, William J., ed. 1995. *The New Information Infrastructure: Strategies for U.S. Policy.* New York: Twentieth Century Fund Press.

——— 2000. The Rise and Decline of the International Telecommunications Regime. In Chris T. Marsden, ed., *Regulating the Global Information Society.* New York: Routledge, pp. 124–177.

Dupagne, Michel. 1998. *High Definition Television: A Global Perspective.* Ames: Iowa State University Press.

Dutton, William H., and Jay G. Blumler. 1988. The Faltering Development of Cable Television in Britain. *International Political Science Review* 9(4): 279–303.

Dutton, William H., and Thierry Vedel. 1992. Dynamics of Cable Television in the U.S., Britain, and France. In Jay G. Blumler, Jack M. McLeod, and Karl E. Rosengren, eds., *Comparatively Speaking: Communication and Culture across Space and Time.* Newbury Park, CA: Sage, pp. 70–93.

Eckstein, Harry, and David E. Apter, eds. 1963. *Comparative Politics: A Reader.* New York: Free Press.

Economides, Nicholas. 1996. The Economics of Networks. *International Journal of Industrial Organization* 14(6): 673–699.

Elstein, David. 2001. *Digital Terrestrial Television (DTT): An Economic Assessment.* Unpublished manuscript.

———. 2002. The Politics of Digital TV in the UK. *Opendemocracy.net*, July 17.

European Commission. 1991. *The European Electronics and Information Technology Industry: State of Play, Issues at Stake and Proposals for Action.* SEC(91) 565.

———. 1993. *White Paper on Growth, Competitiveness, and Employment: The Challenges and Ways Forward into the 21st Century.* COM(93) 700 final.

———. 1994. *Europe and the Global Information Society: Recommendations to the European Council.* Report from the High Level Group on the Information Society ("Bangemann Report"), May.

———. 1997. *Green Paper on the Convergence of the Telecommunications, Media and Information Technology Sectors, and the Implications for Regulation.* COM(97) 623.

———. 1998a. *Summary of the Results of the Public Consultation on the Green Paper on the Convergence of the Telecommunications, Media, and Information Technology Sectors.* SEC(98) 1284.

———. 1998b. *Notice on the Application of the Competition Rules to Access Agreements in the Telecommunications Sector: Framework, Relevant Markets and Principles* ("Access Notice"). Luxembourg: Official Journal of the European Communities C 265.

———. 1999. *The Development of the Market for Digital Television in the European Union.* COM(99) 540.

———. 2001. *The Introduction of Third Generation Mobile Communications in the European Union: State of Play and the Way Forward.* COM(2001) 141 final.

Evans, Peter. 1997. The Eclipse of the State? Reflections on Stateness in an Era of Globalization. *World Politics* 50(1): 62–87.

Farrell, Joseph, and Carl Shapiro. 1992. Standard Setting in High-Definition Television. *Brookings Papers: Microeconomics* 1992: 1–77.

Frean, Alexandra. 1995. Broadcasters Clash on Plans for Digital TV. *Times*, September 16.

Froomkin, Michael A. 1997. The Internet as a Source of Regulatory Arbitrage. In Brian Kahin and Charles Nesson, eds., *Borders in Cyberspace: Information Policy and the Global Information Infrastructure.* Cambridge, MA: MIT Press, pp. 129–163.

Galperin, Hernan. 1999. Cultural Industries Policy in Regional Trade Agreements: The Case of NAFTA, the European Union and MERCOSUR. *Media, Culture, & Society* 21: 627–648.

Galperin, Hernan, and François Bar. 2002. The Regulation of Interactive TV in the US and the European Union. *Federal Communications Law Journal* 55(1): 61–84.

Garnham, Nicholas. 1990. *Capitalism and Communication: Global Culture and the Economics of Information.* London: Sage.

Geller, Henry. 1995. Reforming the U.S. Telecommunications Policymaking Process. In William J. Drake, ed., *The New Information Infrastructure: Strategies for U.S. Policy.* New York: Twentieth Century Fund Press, pp. 115–135.

1998. Public Interest Regulation in the Digital TV Era. *Cardozo Arts & Entertainment Law Journal* 16(2–3): 341–368.

General Accounting Office. 2002. *Many Broadcasters Will Not Meet May 2002 Digital Television Deadline.* Washington, DC: author.

Gibbons, Thomas. 1998. *Regulating the Media.* London: Sweet & Maxwell.

Gilpin, Robert. 2000. *The Challenge of Global Capitalism: The World Economy in the 21st Century.* Princeton: Princeton University Press.

Goodman, Ellen P. 1997. Digital Television and the Allure of Auctions: The Birth and Stillbirth of DTV Legislation. *Federal Communication Law Journal* 49(3): 517–549.

Goodwin, Peter. 1998. *Television under the Tories: Broadcasting Policy 1979–1997.* London: BFI.

Gourevitch, Peter. 1986. *Politics in Hard Times: Comparative Responses to International Economic Crises.* Ithaca, NY: Cornell University Press.

Graham, Andrew. 1997. *Public Policy and Electronic Programme Guides: A Response to OFTEL and the Independent Television Commission.* Unpublished manuscript.

Graham, Andrew, and Gavyn Davies. 1997. *Broadcasting, Society and Policy in the Multimedia Age.* Luton: John Libbey.

Guerrieri, Paolo, and Carlo Milana. 1991. *Technological and Trade Competition in High-Tech Products.* BRIE Working Paper 54, October.

Haggard, Stephan, and Mathew D. McCubbins. 2001. Introduction: Political Institutions and the Determinants of Public Policy. In Stephan Haggard and Mathew D. McCubbins, eds., *Presidents, Parliaments, and Policy.* Cambridge: Cambridge University Press, pp. 1–17.

Hall, Peter A. 1986. *Governing the Economy: The Politics of State Intervention in Britain and France.* New York: Oxford University Press.

1997. The Role of Interests, Institutions, and Ideas in the Comparative Political Economy of the Industrialized Nations. In Mark I. Lichbach and Alan S. Zuckerman, eds., *Comparative Politics: Rationality, Culture, and Structure.* Cambridge: Cambridge University Press, pp. 174–207.

Hart, Jeffrey A. 1992. *Rival Capitalists: International Competitiveness in the United States, Japan, and Western Europe.* Ithaca, NY: Cornell University Press.

Hart, Jeffrey A., and Aseem Prakash. 1997. Strategic Trade and Investment Policies: Implications for the Study of International Political Economy. *World Economy* 20(4): 457–476.

Hart, Jeffrey A., and John C. Thomas. 1995. European Policies toward HDTV. *Communication & Strategies* 20: 23–61.

Hart, Jeffrey A., and Laura D'Andrea Tyson. 1989. Responding to the Challenge of HDTV. *California Management Review* 31(4): 132–145.

Hawkins, Richard. 1999. The Rise of Consortia in the Information and Communication Technology Industries: Emerging Implications for Policy. *Telecommunications Policy* 23(2): 159–173.

Hazlett, Thomas W. 1998. Assigning Property Rights to Radio Spectrum Users: Why Did FCC License Auctions Take 67 Years? *Journal of Law and Economics* 41(2): 529–575.

———. 2001. The Wireless Craze, the Unlimited Bandwidth Myth, the Spectrum Auction Faux Pas, and the Punchline to Ronald Coase's "Big Joke." *Harvard Journal of Law and Technology* 14(2): 335–469.

Hazlett, Thomas W., and Matthew L. Spitzer. 2000. Digital Television and the Quid Pro Quo. *Business and Politics* 2(2): 115–159.

Heclo, Hugh. 1988. The In-and-Outer System: A Critical Assessment. *Political Science Quarterly* 103(1): 37–56.

Hickey, Neil. 1996. What's at Stake in the Spectrum War? Only Billions of Dollars and the Future of Television. *Columbia Journalism Review* 35(2): 39–44.

Hills, Jill, and Maria Michalis. 1997. Digital Television and Regulatory Issues: The British Case. *Communication & Strategies* 27: 75–101.

Hirst, Paul, and Grahame Thompson. 1999. *Globalization in Question: The International Economy and the Possibilities of Governance.* London: Blackwell.

Hoffmann-Riem, Wolfgang. 1996. *Regulating Media: The Licensing and Supervision of Broadcasting in Six Countries.* New York: Guilford.

Holznagel, Bernd, and Andreas Grünwald. 2000. The Introduction of Digital Television in Germany. *International Journal of Communications Law and Policy* 4. <www.ijclp.org>.

Horwitz, Robert B. 1989. *The Irony of Regulatory Reform: The Deregulation of American Telecommunications.* New York: Oxford University Press.

Huber, Peter. 1997. *Law and Disorder in Cyberspace: Abolish the FCC and Let Common Law Rule the Telecosm.* New York: Oxford University Press.

Hulsink, Willem. 1999. *Privatisation and Liberalisation in European Telecommunications: Comparing Britain, the Netherlands and France.* New York: Routledge.

Hundt, Reed E. 2000. *You Say You Want a Revolution: A Story of Information Age Politics.* New Haven: Yale University Press.

Ikenberry, John G. 1986. The Irony of State Strength: Comparative Responses to the Oil Shocks in the 1970s. *International Organization* 40(1): 105–137.

Independent Television Association. 1995. *Response to the Government's Proposals for the Introduction of Digital Terrestrial Television.* London: author.

Independent Television Commission. 1993. *Discussion Document on Digital Television.* London: ITC.

———. 1995. *Digital Terrestrial Broadcasting: ITC Response to the Government's Proposals.* London: ITC.

———. 1996. *Invitation to Apply for Multiplex Service Licenses.* London: ITC.

———. 2000. *The Genesis Project: Final Report.* London: ITC.

Information Infrastructure Task Force. 1993. *The National Information Infrastructure: Agenda for Action.* Washington, DC: author.

———. 1995. *Advanced Digital Video and the National Information Infrastructure.* Washington, DC: author.

Information Technology Advisory Panel. 1982. *Cable Systems.* London: HMSO.

Institut de l'Audiovisual et des Telecommunications en Europe. 2000. *Development of Digital Television in the European Union*. Montpellier: author.

Jeffery, Charlie. 1998. Electoral Reform: Learning from Germany. *Political Quarterly* 69(3): 241–252.

Johnson, David R., and David Post. 1996. Law and Borders – The Rise of Law in Cyberspace. *Stanford Law Review* 48: 1367–1402.

Kahin, Brian. 1997. The U.S. National Information Infrastructure Initiative: The Market, the Web, and the Virtual Project. In Brian Kahin and Ernest J. Wilson IV, eds., *National Information Infrastructure Initiatives: Vision and Policy Design*. Cambridge, MA: MIT Press, pp. 150–189.

Kaitatzi-Whitlock, Sophia. 1997. The Privatization of Conditional Access in the European Union. *Communications & Strategies* 25: 91–122.

Katznelson, Ira. 1997. Structure and Configuration in Comparative Politics. In Mark I. Lichbach and Alan S. Zuckerman, eds., *Comparative Politics: Rationality, Culture, and Structure*. Cambridge: Cambridge University Press, pp. 81–112.

Krasner, Stephen D. 1978. United States Commercial and Monetary Policy: Unraveling the Paradox of External Strength and Internal Weakness. In Peter J. Katzenstein, ed., *Between Power and Plenty: Foreign Economic Policies of Advanced Industrial States*. Madison: University of Wisconsin Press, pp. 51–87.

   1989. Sovereignty: An Institutional Perspective. In James A. Caporaso, ed., *The Elusive State: International and Comparative Perspectives*. New York: Sage, pp. 69–96.

   1991. Global Communications and National Power: Life on the Pareto Frontier. *World Politics* 43(3): 336–366.

Krasnow, Erwin G., and Lawrence D. Longley. 1978. *The Politics of Broadcast Regulation*. New York: St. Martin's Press.

Krattenmaker, Thomas G. 1996. The Telecommunications Act of 1996. *Federal Communications Law Journal* 49(6): 1–49.

Krugman, Paul R. 1990. *Rethinking International Trade*. Cambridge, MA: MIT Press.

Labaton, Stephen. 2001. A Turf Fight for the Airwaves. *New York Times*, March 28.

Larouche, Pierre. 1998. EC Competition Law and the Convergence of the Telecommunications and Broadcasting Sectors. *Telecommunications Policy* 22(3): 219–242.

Levy, David A. 1997. The Regulation of Digital Conditional Access Systems: A Case Study in European Policy Making. *Telecommunications Policy* 21(7): 661–676.

   1999. *Europe's Digital Revolution: Broadcasting Regulation, the EU and the Nation State*. New York: Routledge.

Levy, Brian, and Pablo T. Spiller. 1996. *Regulations, Institutions, and Commitment: Comparative Studies of Telecommunications*. Cambridge: Cambridge University Press.

Lijphart, Arend. 1971. Comparative Politics and the Comparative Method. *American Political Science Review* 65(3): 682–693.

London Economics. 1999. *Assessing the Potential Impact of a Digital License Fee on the Take-up of Digital Television*. London: author.

Mansell, Robin. 1999. New Media Competition and Access. *New Media & Society* 1(2): 155–182.

March, James G., and Johan P. Olsen. 1984. The New Institutionalism: Organizational Factors in Political Life. *American Political Science Review* 78: 734–749.

Marsden, Chris T. 2000. Introduction: Information and Communications Technologies, Globalisation, and Regulation. In Chris T. Marsden, ed., *Regulating the Global Information Society*. New York: Routledge, pp. 1–40.

Marsden, Chris T., and Stefaan Verhulst. 1999. Convergence: A Framework for Discussion. In Chris T. Marsden and Stefaan Verhulst, eds., *Convergence in European Digital TV Regulation*. London: Blackstone Press, pp. 1–20.

McCallum, Lisa. 1999. EC Competition Law and Digital Pay TV. *Competition Policy Newsletter* 1: 4–16.

McChesney, Robert W. 1993. *Telecommunications, Mass Media, and Democracy: The Battle for the Control of U.S. Broadcasting, 1928–1935*. New York: Oxford University Press.

2003. Theses on Media Deregulation. *Media, Culture, & Society* 25(1): 125–133.

McConnell, Bill. 2002. The Long Fight to Settle Must-Carry. *Broadcasting & Cable*, October 21.

McCubbins, Mathew D. 1985. The Legislative Design of Regulatory Structure. *American Journal of Political Science* 29(4): 721–748.

McCubbins, Mathew D., and Thomas Schwartz. 1984. Congressional Oversight Overlooked: Police Patrols versus Fire Alarms. *American Journal of Political Science* 28(1): 165–179.

McKnight, Lee W., and Russell Neuman. 1995. Technology Policy and the National Information Infrastructure. In William J. Drake, ed., *The New Information Infrastructure: Strategies for U.S. Policy*. New York: Twentieth Century Fund Press, pp. 137–154.

Melody, William. 1996. Toward a Framework for Designing Information Society Policies. *Telecommunications Policy* 20(4): 243–259.

Mintz, John, and Paul Farhi. 1997. TV Broadcast Spectrum Plan Is Called Giveaway. *Washington Post*, July 20.

MIT Commission on Industrial Productivity. 1989. *The Decline of US Consumer Electronics Manufacturing: History, Hypotheses, and Remedies*. Cambridge, MA: MIT Press.

Moe, Terry M. 1997. The Positive Theory of Public Bureaucracy. In Dennis C. Mueller, ed., *Perspectives on Public Choice: A Handbook*. Cambridge: Cambridge University Press, pp. 455–480.

Mosco, Vincent, and Dan Schiller, eds. 2001. *Continental Order? Integrating North America for Cybercapitalism*. New York: Rowman & Littelfield.

Mulgan, Geoff J. 1991. *Communication and Control: Networks and the New Economies of Communication*. New York: Guilford.

Negrine, Ralph. 1989. *Politics and the Mass Media in Britain*. New York: Routledge.

1998. *Television and the Press since 1945*. Manchester: Manchester University Press.

NERA. 1999. *The Impact of a Digital License Fee on the Take-up of Digital Television*. London: author.

NERA/Smith. 1998. *A Study to Estimate the Economic Impact of Government Policies towards Digital Television*. London: author.

Neuman, Russell, Lee W. McKnight, and Richard J. Solomon. 1997. *The Gordian Knot: Political Gridlock in the Information Highway*. Cambridge, MA: MIT Press.

Nihoul, Paul. 1998. Competition or Regulation for Multimedia? *Telecommunications Policy* 22(3): 207–218.

Noam, Eli M. 1991. *Television in Europe*. New York: Oxford University Press.

1997. Beyond Spectrum Auctions: Taking the Next Step to Open Spectrum Access. *Telecommunications Policy* 21(5): 461–475.

2001. *Interconnecting the Network of Networks*. Cambridge, MA: MIT Press.

Noll, Roger G. 1986. The Political and Institutional Context of Communication Policy. In Marcellus S. Snow, ed., *Marketplace for Telecommunications: Regulation and Deregulation in Industrialized Democracies*. New York: Longman, pp. 42–65.

Noll, Roger G., and Frances M. Rosenbluth. 1995. Telecommunications Policy: Structure, Process, Outcomes. In Peter F. Cowhey and Mathew M. McCubbins, eds., *Structure and Policy in Japan and the United States*. Cambridge: Cambridge University Press, pp. 119–175.

Noll, Roger G., Merton J. Peck, and John J. McGowan. 1973. *Economic Aspects of Television Regulation*. Washington, DC: Brookings Institution.

Nora, Simon, and Alain Minc. 1980. *The Computerization of Society*. Cambridge, MA: MIT Press.

Norris, Pippa. 1997. *Electoral Change in Britain since 1945*. Cambridge, MA: Blackwell.

2000. *A Virtuous Circle: Political Communications in Postindustrial Societies*. Cambridge: Cambridge University Press.

North, Douglass C. 1990. *Institutions, Institutional Change, and Economic Performance*. Cambridge: Cambridge University Press.

1993. Toward a Theory of Institutional Change. In William Barnett, Melvin Hinich, and Norman Schofield, eds., *Political Economy: Institutions, Competition, and Representation*. Cambridge: Cambridge University Press, pp. 61–69.

NTL. 1991. *Frequency Planning for SPECTRE*. London: author.

Office of Fair Trading. 1996. *The Director General's Review of BSkyB's Position in the Wholesale Pay TV Market*. London: OFT.

Office of Technology Assessment. 1990. *The Big Picture: HDTV and High-Resolution Systems*. Washington, DC: U.S. Government Printing Office.

1995. *Wireless Technologies and the National Information Infrastructure*. Washington, DC: U.S. Government Printing Office.

Office of Telecommunications. 1995. *Beyond the Telephone, the Television, and the PC*. London: OFTEL.

1996. *Conditional Access: Consultative Document on Draft OFTEL Guidelines*. London: OFTEL.

1997. *Submission to the ITC on Competition Issues Arising from the Award of Digital Terrestrial Television Multiplex Licenses*. London: OFTEL.

1998. *Conditional Access Charges for Digital Television: Statement*. London: OFTEL.

Olson, Mancur. 1971. *The Logic of Collective Action: Public Goods and the Theory of Groups*. Cambridge, MA: Harvard University Press.

Organization for Economic Cooperation and Development. 1997a. *Global Information Infrastructure – Global Information Society: Policy Requirements*. Paris: OECD.

1997b. *Webcasting and Convergence: Policy Implications*. Paris: OECD.

Owen, Bruce M. 1999. *The Internet Challenge to Television*. Cambridge, MA: Harvard University Press.

Paulu, Burton. 1981. *Television and Radio in the United Kingdom*. Minneapolis: University of Minnesota Press.

Peacock Committee. 1986. *Report of the Committee on the Financing of the BBC*. London: HMSO.

Pepper, Robert, and Jonathan Levy. 1999. Convergence: Public Benefits and Policy Challenges. In Chris T. Marsden and Stefaan Verhulst, eds., *Convergence in European Digital TV Regulation*. London: Blackstone Press, pp. 21–36.

Polanyi, Karl. 1944. *The Great Transformation*. Boston: Beacon Press.

Pool, Ithiel de Sola. 1983. *Technologies of Freedom*. Cambridge, MA: Harvard University Press.

Powe, Lucas A., Jr. 1987. *American Broadcasting and the First Amendment*. Berkeley: University of California Press.

Price, Monroe E. 2002. *Media and Sovereignty: The Global Information Revolution and Its Challenge to State Power*. Cambridge, MA: MIT Press.

Prosser, Tony. 1997. *Law and the Regulators*. Oxford: Clarendon Press.

Robinson, Glen O. 1978. The Federal Communications Commission: An Essay on Regulatory Watchdogs. *Virginia Law Review* 69(2): 169–262.

———. 1998. Spectrum Property Law 101. *Journal of Law and Economics* 41(2): 609–625.

Rogers, Peter. 1995. Who Should Regulate Digital Television? *Consumer Policy Review* 5(5): 172–174.

Romer, Paul. 1990. Endogenous Technological Change. *Journal of Political Economy* 98(5): 71–102.

Safire, William. 1996. Stop the Giveaway. *New York Times*, January 4.

Sandholtz, Wayne. 1992. *High-Tech Europe: The Politics of International Cooperation*. Berkeley: University of California Press.

Sassen, Saskia. 1998. *Globalization and Its Discontents: Essays on the Mobility of People and Money*. New York: New Press.

Sauter, Wolf. 1999. Regulation for Convergence: Arguments for a Constitutional Approach. In Chris T. Marsden and Stefaan Verhulst, eds., *Convergence in European Digital TV Regulation*. London: Blackstone Press, pp. 65–98.

Scannell, Paddy, and David Cardiff. 1991. *A Social History of Broadcasting, 1923–1939*. Oxford: Blackwell.

Schlesinger, Philip. 1997. From Cultural Defence to Political Culture: Media, Politics and Collective Identity in the European Union. *Media, Culture, & Society* 19: 369–391.

Seel, Peter B. 1998. The Path from Analog HDTV to DTV in Japan. *Prometheus* 16(2): 209–216.

Servaes, Jan. 1992. "Europe 1992": The Audiovisual Challenge. *Gazette* 49: 75–92.

Shelanski, Howard A., and Peter W. Huber. 1998. Administrative Creation of Property Rights to Radio Spectrum. *Journal of Law and Economics* 41(2): 581–607.

Sinclair, John. 1996. Culture and Trade: Some Theoretical and Practical Considerations. In Emile G. McAnany and Kenton T. Wilkinson, eds., *Mass Media and Free Trade: NAFTA and the Cultural Industries*. Austin: University of Texas Press, pp. 30–60.

Siune, Karen, and Olof Hultén. 1998. What Future for Public Broadcasting? In Denis McQuail and Karen Siune, eds., *Media Policy: Convergence, Concentration, Commerce*. London: Sage, pp. 23–37.

Smith, Paul. 1999. The Politics of UK Television Policy: The Introduction of Digital Television. *International Journal of Communications Law and Policy* 3. <www.ijclp.org>.

Snider, James H. 2001. The Paradox of News Bias: How Local Broadcasters Influence Information Policy. In Roderick P. Hart and Bartholomew H. Sparrow, eds., *Politics, Discourse, and American Society: New Agendas*. New York: Rowman & Littlefield, pp. 111–128.

Snoddy, Raymond. 1995. Broadcasters Attack Plans for Digital TV. *Financial Times,* September 16.

Spiller, Pablo T., and Ingo Vogelsang. 1996. The United Kingdom: A Pacesetter in Regulatory Incentives. In Brian Levy and Pablo T. Spiller, eds., *Regulations, Institutions, and Commitment: Comparative Studies of Telecommunications.* Cambridge: Cambridge University Press, pp. 79–120.

Strange, Susan. 1996. *The Retreat of the State: The Diffusion of Power in the World Economy.* Cambridge: Cambridge University Press.

Straubhaar, Joseph. 1997. Distinguishing the Global, Regional, and National Levels of World Television. In Annabelle Sreberny-Mohammadi, Dwayne Winseck, Jim McKenna, and Oliver Boyd-Barrett, eds., *Media in a Global Context: A Reader.* New York: Arnold, pp. 284–298.

Sunstein, Cass R. 2000. Television and the Public Interest. *California Law Review* 88: 499–564.

Taylor, Paul, and Norman Ornstein. 2002. *A Broadcast Spectrum Fee for Campaign Finance Reform.* New America Foundation Spectrum Series Working Paper 4, June.

Thatcher, Mark. 1999. *The Politics of Telecommunications: National Institutions, Convergence, and Change in Britain and France.* New York: Oxford University Press.

Ungerer, Herbert. 2000. *Access Issues under EU Regulation and Antitrust Law: The Case of Telecommunications and Internet Markets.* Harvard University Program on Information Resources Policy, July.

Veljanovski, Cento. 1999. *Competitive Regulation of Digital Pay TV.* Unpublished manuscript.

Verhulst, Stefaan. 1998. The United Kingdom. In David Goldberg, Tony Prosser, and Stefaan Verhulst, eds., *Regulating the Changing Media: A Comparative Study.* Oxford: Clarendon Press, pp. 101–143.

Vogel, David. 1986. *National Styles of Regulation: Environmental Policy in Great Britain and the United States.* Ithaca, NY: Cornell University Press.

1987. Government-Industry Relations in the United States: An Overview. In Stephen Wilks and Maurice Wright, eds., *Comparative Government-Industry Relations.* Oxford: Clarendon Press, pp. 91–116.

Vogel, Steven K. 1996. *Freer Markets, More Rules: Regulatory Reform in Advanced Industrial Countries.* Ithaca, NY: Cornell University Press.

Waisbord, Silvio, and Nancy Morris, eds. 2001. *Media and Globalization: Why the State Matters.* New York: Rowman & Littlefield.

Weaver, Kent R., and Bert A. Rockman, eds. 1993. *Do Institutions Matter? Government Capabilities in the United States and Abroad.* Washington, DC: Brookings Institution.

Webre, Philip C. 1989. *The Scope of the High-Definition Television Market and Its Implications for Competitiveness.* Washington, DC: Congressional Budget Office.

Weingast, Barry R., and Mark J. Moran. 1983. Bureaucratic Discretion or Congressional Control? Regulatory Policymaking by the Federal Trade Commission. *Journal of Political Economy* 91(5): 765–800.

Weir, Margaret. 1992. Ideas and the Politics of Bounded Innovation. In Sven Steinmo, Kathleen Thelen, and Frank Longstreth, eds., *Structuring Politics: Historical Institutionalism in Comparative Analysis.* Cambridge: Cambridge University Press, pp. 188–216.

West, Donald. 1998. The Dawn of Digital Television. *Broadcasting & Cable,* November 11.

Wiley, Richard E. 1994. The Challenge of Choice. *Federal Communications Law Journal* 47(2): 401–404.

Williamson, Oliver E. 1985. *The Economic Institutions of Capitalism.* New York: Free Press.

Wilsford, David. 1994. Path Dependency or Why History Makes It Difficult but Not Impossible to Reform Health Systems in a Big Way. *Journal of Public Policy* 14(3): 251–283.

Wilson, Hubert H. 1961. *Pressure Group: The Campaign for Commercial Television.* London: Secker & Warburg.

Wilson, James Q. 1989. *Bureaucracy: What Government Agencies Do and Why They Do It.* New York: Basic Books.

Zysman, John. 1994. How Institutions Create Historically Rooted Trajectories of Growth. *Industrial and Corporate Change* 3: 243–283.

Index

Printed in the United States
80186LV00002B/89